THE RISE AND FALL OF THE HOUSE OF BARNEYS

A FAMILY TALE
OF CHUTZPAH,
GLORY, AND GREED

WILLIAM MORROW AND COMPANY, INC.   NEW YORK

THE
RISE AND
FALL OF THE
HOUSE OF
BARNEYS

JOSHUA LEVINE

Library of Congress Cataloging-in-Publication Data

Levine, Joshua.
    The rise and fall of the house of Barneys : a family tale of
chutzpah, glory, and greed / Joshua Levine. — 1st ed.
        p.   cm.
    Includes index.
    ISBN 0-688-15502-2
    1. Barneys New York—History. 2. Men's clothing industry—New
York (State)—New York—History. I. Title.
HD9940.U6B375 1999
381'.45687'097471—dc21   98–51429
                                                                     CIP

Printed in the United States of America

First Edition

1 2 3 4 5 6 7 8 9 10

BOOK DESIGN BY MICHAEL MENDELSOHN AT MM DESIGN 2000, INC.

www.williammorrow.com

To my mother and to the memory
of my father

ACKNOWLEDGMENTS

I would like to thank Alice Martell from the bottom of my heart. She stuck by me steadfastly through some dicey times, and I will never forget it. I would also like to thank Paul Bresnick, my editor, who believed in this book from the beginning, and the many people at William Morrow who helped bring it into being. One source in particular gave me his crucial help and insight despite the evident pain of doing so. This book would never have come together as it has without him, and I bear him a great debt of gratitude. To Vendela, whose tireless research threw up a stout bulwark of fact, thank you. Laurie Platt Winfrey and Fay Torres-Yap made the frightening task of photo research painless and, indeed, pleasant. Finally, the company of my dear friend Michael Sivy over coffee buoyed me up after many dispiriting nights at the word processor. I pity the writer who undertakes such a task without such a friend.

CONTENTS

THE RISE
AND FALL
OF THE
HOUSE OF
BARNEYS

THE LESSON OF THE CUPS

The escalators were screaming that night in 1993 when the Pressmans unveiled their spectacular new store at 660 Madison Avenue. For three years, the Pressman family, which owned Barneys New York, had spent $267 million to make this the most beautiful store in the world. Now the international haut monde had come to gawk at what someone else's money had bought: real goatskin and platinum leaf on the walls (silver leaf tarnishes); mother-of-pearl shelves and silk dressing-room curtains; exotic woods like bleached bubinga for the perfume counter, English sycamore for hosiery; and in the center of the main floor, an intricate mosaic of Carrara marble that was hand-assembled chip by chip. This floor alone cost $600,000—about $100 a square foot. That's roughly what a modest store might pay for a thorough, floor-to-ceiling overhaul.

But as guests like Edgar Bronfman, Julia Child, Calvin Klein, and a potpourri of drag queens took in all this splendor, they couldn't help hearing the weird shrieks and agonized moans that kept intruding on the festivities. It was the twenty-three brand-new escalators, which were loudly proclaiming, Dorian Gray–like, the rot just underneath the facade. (Newly installed escalators must be run for about two weeks to stretch out their belts and work out the kinks. Barneys never had the chance to do this, because the breathless pace of construction continued until just seconds before the guests walked through the door. The Pressmans had already postponed the opening date as the helter-skelter construction fell further and further behind schedule.)

The opening simply could not be pushed past September 8, and so the Pressmans threw money at the problem in a headlong dash to finish in time: In the final three months before the opening, Barneys spent $75 million on construction, a record for the construction company, Lehrer McGovern Bovis, that will likely stand for a long, long time. Of that, $10 million alone went for overtime labor as three shifts worked round the clock. Two workmen died on the project under mysterious circumstances—one fell down an empty elevator shaft. And even then, a long list of unfinished tasks were simply camouflaged as artfully as possible so the party could proceed.

But there was nothing to be done about the hysterical escalators. As the guests traveled from floor to floor, nibbling $250,000 worth of canapés, the escalators kept up a wordless commentary on Barneys' dire financial condition—a condition that resulted, in some small part, from the Pressmans' insistence on using real goatskin instead of faux goatskin. A repairman at the party scurried from escalator to escalator, trying vainly to suppress the noise.

What would Barney Pressman, who had died two years before at the age of ninety-six, have thought? "At the end of the day, he'd call in for the numbers," opined Barney's youngest granddaughter, Nancy. He would not have been pleased.

It is good for a man to know who he is, and Barney Pressman certainly knew who he was: He was a clothing man—maybe *the* clothing man of his day. The store he founded grew to the point where it sold more clothing than any other store in the world. Clothing, in the clothing business, means, simply, men's sport jackets, suits, and overcoats. Shirts, sweaters, socks, these aren't considered *clothing*—the clothing men pronounced the word all woolly and thick with reverence at the back of the throat, giving it a tone of reverence. "Oh, Shapiro— he's a good clothing man," you would hear one of them say of his colleague, and you would know that no superlatives were needed.

Barneys at its peak sold close to 80,000 suits a year—a number that swelled the pride of all the clothing men who ever worked there. What cattle are to the Masai, suits were to the clothing men. There was a TV commercial for Barneys in the early '60s that featured a cleaning lady dusting the empty Barneys store. Suddenly, she starts counting the suits—15,423, 15,424. She's approaching 30,000 and still counting when the commercial ends. Nothing more needed to be said: To stock that many suits was simply unheard of.

This is the story of the clothing business that Barney built and his grandsons lost.

His family was as much a part of Barney Pressman's dream as was the store. Family and business went hand in hand, as they did for so many of the first-generation entrepreneurs who sprang up in the early part of the century. In Europe, the same vision has made for some very sturdy dynasties. Whatever demons might haunt the sons and grand- sons of oversized patriarchs, the dynasties themselves often live a life apart. They do not corrode simply by existing.

In America, this is rarely true. Peace of mind and self-respect often prove harder to come by within the narrow walls of the family business, and so the sons dare too much, and their sons dare still more—if they even have the heart to continue to run, and not sell, the business, that is. "Although Martin Dressler was a shopkeeper's son," wrote Steven Millhauser a few years ago in his story of a Jewish hotelier much like Barney Pressman, "he too dreamed his dream, and at last he was lucky enough to do what few people even dare to imagine: He satisfied his heart's desire. But this is a perilous privilege, which the gods watch jealously, waiting for the flaw, the little flaw, that brings everything to ruin in the end."

*   *   *

Barneys declared bankruptcy on January 11, 1996, done in by debt and disorder. "In five generations, I don't know if we'll be able to pay for this," Fred Pressman told *Los Angeles* magazine shortly after the Madison Avenue store opened. He got his answer in one. The original Barneys store on Seventh Avenue closed for good on August 17, 1997, and for many people, that meant the real end of Barneys right there. In its final days, the Seventh Avenue store had shrunk back to close to its original size after having expanded upward into the doctor's offices and apartments of the massive building above it and outward into the town houses along Seventeenth Street, all on the back of its suits. Barney's son Fred, born the same year that Barneys opened, honored his father by surpassing him as a clothing man. That was as Barney had hoped when he'd let Fred dismantle the institution he had cobbled together, suit by suit, to create an entirely new kind of store in its place. "It's Fred's store," Barney always used to say, and he really meant it.

Fred Pressman may have been the greatest merchant of his day when that term still meant something. It denoted someone who could put his personal stamp on the merchandise he sold and use it to sketch out a distinct style and a way of living. You visited a real merchant's store not as a depot for the particular brands it carried, or for the price it charged, but because you wanted to wrap yourself in a swatch of the merchant's persona.

Nowadays, the great merchants are pretty much gone from retailing altogether. Computers do much of the buying today, spitting out rigid formulas based on an algorithm of what has sold well in the past season and what hasn't. There's nothing remotely romantic about the process. It leaves little room for the effortless finesse Fred Pressman displayed when he scanned a rack of suits. The great merchants were the raconteurs of retailing. They used worsted and serge to "tell a story"— the phrase is still used in the business to describe how an expert buys a line of clothes. The narrative of one story may revolve around, say, shirts with stripes. The merchant-storyteller will use the different stripe widths to embellish his theme, never introducing a jarring element that could disrupt the flow of the narrative. So when the customer finally looks down a row of shirts in the store, he will see similar-looking stripes, all of which amplify the merchant's tale. Selecting those garments is still called editing, and a computer can do this about as well as it can tell a good dirty joke.

Stanley Marcus, now ninety-three, may legitimately lay claim to Fred Pressman's title of this century's greatest American merchant. Fred Pressman undoubtedly knew more than Marcus about the placement of a buttonhole on a gabardine raincoat, but no one could match Stanley Marcus's instinct for the jaw-dropping gesture when he ran Dallas's Neiman Marcus. It takes a merchant of genius to conclude that his clothing store should sell matching his-and-her elephants because, as Marcus explains, "I decided that women would like to buy panty hose from a store that sells elephants." Of course, competitors quickly installed their own menageries, but the great merchants are inimitable. "A rival of ours advertised boa constrictors, but that's simply tasteless," Marcus says matter-of-factly. "Elephants are funny. Boa constrictors are not funny—people don't like to think about them."

Despite their differences, Fred Pressman and Stanley Marcus hark back to the same vanishing tradition. Marcus tells the story of his own father, Herbert Marcus, who founded Neiman Marcus, to illustrate the great merchant's lustful fixation on his own merchandise. "My father in later years was quite blind, but he still came to the store every day, and it was my job and the job of my brother to keep him entertained," Marcus recalled. " 'I want to see some merchandise,' he would say. So they brought him up some furs from the fur department. He would run his hand over the mink—a real merchant can visualize color through his hands. 'Now that's the kind of mink I like to see,' he would say."

Fred Pressman lived that role. He loved nothing better than to discourse for hours on the intricacies of a raincoat's construction, and often did. Under Fred, Barneys simply chose merchandise more imaginatively than any other store in America, and was duly recognized for it. Not many people knew it, but Fred Pressman was color-blind. Like Herbert Marcus, however, his hands could see better than most people's eyes. He could tell you the weight of a fabric swatch to the fraction of an ounce simply by passing it between his thumb and forefinger. In Fred's time, Barneys—the apostrophe disappeared in 1982—became fashion's Yale and Harvard, as Melville's Ishmael called his whaling ship. In other words, if you didn't know how to dress with style and finesse, a few trips to Barneys could teach you.

Fred Pressman died on July 14, 1996, at age seventy-three, living just long enough to see the company his father had founded seek protection from creditors under Chapter 11 of the bankruptcy code. "*Yud aleph,*" the Jewish clothing men called Chapter 11—ten and one in Hebrew. But well before that, Fred had made way for the grander ambitions of his two sons: Eugene, the eldest, and Robert.

In everything, the pattern was the same as it had been in the years after the war, when Freddie gently, and not so gently, elbowed Barney aside and created a new Barneys in his own more refined image. Twice, Pressman sons pried the store from their father, and twice the Pressman fathers chose to let go without a struggle. Some people close to the family detected a fleeting grimace or a twinge of regret as the fathers yielded, but if the fathers had any lingering doubts about leaving the stage prematurely, the mothers made sure those doubts didn't impede their sons, whom they worshiped unreasonably. In the end, the fathers' family pride overrode their personal pride, or at least suppressed it—a rare thing in the annals of family business. Sadly, it also overrode personal judgment, and that judgment might have proved wiser in the end.

Fred imagined a store with no discounts or sales, which was closed on Sundays, like the high-class uptown stores Saks and Bergdorf Goodman, and filled with only the finer things that he would choose with unerring confidence. Barney always cared more about price than he cared about style, but he let Fred pursue his different dream. Fred's sons, Gene and Bobby, imagined not so much a different Barneys, but a much grander Barneys—a Barneys that stepped out of the gloomy shadows of Chelsea and took its rightful place alongside the fabled names of retailing whose reputations it had in many ways eclipsed. If

Fred took Barneys uptown in spirit, the sons took it there in fact—to Sixtieth Street and Madison Avenue in the heart of the most fashionable shopping district in the world. They took it across America and abroad as well. Fred, like Barney, backed off, despite misgivings that he expressed to only his closest friends.

"In my heart, I don't think that Freddie really cared for this," says Martin Greenfield sadly. Greenfield was very close to both Barney and Fred. It was Greenfield who got Barney Pressman his first custom-made suit from a tailor named Joe Bovacchio on lower Fifth Avenue, because Bovacchio was the best there was. Greenfield himself made Bovacchio's suits by machine in the old 3Gs clothing factory out on Varet Street in Brooklyn, because the great tailors never did have the time to make their own clothes. "I don't even know Freddie wanted too much to go into that partnership with the Japanese," muses Greenfield, "but he said the boys wanted this. The boys are young, and they wanted to maybe go public or something. . . . They had the money. It is unfortunate that things didn't work out." Greenfield shakes his head ruefully.

"Unfortunate." Other people use harsher language, but "unfortunate" comes from a fonder spot—without censure, but with immense sadness for everything that was lost along the way. Nick DeMarco met Gene Pressman in the wild nightclubbing years when the crowds outside Studio 54 would part and the velvet rope would vanish for this prince of retail. Nick DeMarco loves Gene still, but he has a slightly different perspective: "The problem that the Pressmans had was that the store was their God, and in that, you knew there would be tragedy."

The Pressman family has steadfastly refused to cooperate with the writing of this book. They have prohibited their employees from being interviewed, and they have asked their friends and associates to withhold any help or information. That didn't stop many, many people—over one hundred of them—from speaking out. Some spoke out of an abiding respect for Fred Pressman and pride in their own contribution to the unique store he built. Others spoke from regret and anger at the wastefulness that killed it. Most of them asked that their names not be used. The Pressmans have a reputation for vindictiveness and an uncanny knack for bouncing back in a nasty-minded business. Even a dead wasp can still sting.

The Pressmans probably want no part of any eulogies for the business, at least insofar as it was owned and run by Pressmans for three generations. The boys, Gene and Bobby, as everyone calls them, fought hard to keep a fingerhold on the business they no longer own, and even made their own employment a condition of their agreement with any potential buyer. They got both—barely.

More than a few of their creditors questioned that priority. The creditors felt, not unjustifiably, that the family was honor-bound to make as near whole as it could the many people who lost millions by doing business with Barneys. Barney Pressman would not have acted that way, they feel, and most surely, neither would Fred.

The family—it is fair to talk about the Pressmans as the family, since they have always shown to the word a fierce, monolithic loyalty, even as they hissed and spat among themselves—believes it has a future. It is waiting, or the sons are anyway, for another chance to gain back what they squandered should the new owners ever sell the store to the public. If that ever happens, it will be time to review the lesson of the paper cups.

Chester Kessler's father had asked him to run by Barneys on some business. As he stood outside Barney Pressman's office chatting amiably with the receptionist, he spied Barney himself, his head just peeking out over a pile of invoices on his desk. His mood was black, and Chester made to leave, figuring he would return when the storm had passed, but before he could, Barney beckoned him in. "You've got to watch your business, Chester," said Barney emphatically. "Pay attention to what I am going to tell you. You've got to watch your business. Just look at this. Here is an invoice for paper cups—twenty cartons of cups, with twenty boxes of cups in each carton. In each box, there is one hundred cups. Each carton is fifty dollars. So that's a thousand dollars' worth of cups. Now, Chester, stay with me here. There are forty thousand cups! What the fuck am I? Am I in the cup business? No, I am not. I am in the clothing business. If I buy two cartons of cups, I've got four thousand cups. That's enough to last me two weeks. Those two cartons cost me a hundred dollars. I've got nine hundred dollars left. With nine hundred dollars, I can buy ninety pairs of pants. I sell the pants for double, and I've got more money to buy cups. Do not forget this, Chester."

2

CLOTHING MEN

Barney Pressman built the world's biggest men's suit store on pure bluster. When Barney was at the peak of his powers, he would hail a taxicab near his apartment at 650 Park Avenue and tell the cabbie, "Take me to Barneys." In the New York of the 1950s, few cabbies need to ask where that is. They know without asking that it stands near the corner of Seventh Avenue and Seventeenth Street, a furiously bustling shop among the deserted warehouses and tenements of Manhattan's Chelsea neighborhood. In fact, everybody in New York knows where Barneys is. Barney Pressman has seen to that with his pugnacious flair for self-promotion and his store's uncanny ability to fit every dimension of man, no matter how mischievously God has shaped him, with a good suit at a good price. NO BUNK. NO JUNK. NO IMITATIONS. Barney Pressman tacked that shingle outside his storefront when he opened the doors in 1923. Then, so you shouldn't forget it, he had it printed on thousands of matchbook covers, along with the store's out-of-the-way address. And then, so you shouldn't forget to take a matchbook, he hired fine-looking women, told them to take off their clothes, and gave them wooden barrels to wear as they passed out his matchbooks on Seventh Avenue. It wasn't long before Barneys' name and address became very widely known in New York.

So Barney tells the cabdriver, "Take me to Barneys," and this particular cabdriver doesn't know the address, which would happen from time to time. The cabdriver then makes his first and only mistake: He asks the stocky, goggle-eyed passenger in his backseat where that might be. It's almost as if Barney Pressman is waiting for this to happen, and perversely relishes it whenever it does. He responds the same way every time. (Barney Pressman, it should be noted, had a pronounced stutter. He was frequently known to tell a wickedly funny stuttering joke with himself as the butt of it. This was not one of the jokes he told.) "F-F-F-F-F-uck you!" he explodes, a Molotov cocktail in a size 40 cadet portly suit. And with that Barney Pressman, crude, funny, infinitely resourceful, very, very proud, and more than a bit of a lout, bursts out of the taxicab and hails another one.

The origin of Barneys has passed into legend with a might-as-well-be-trueness that freezes further inquiry. Barney saw to that, too, in his spirited telling and retelling of the story. In 1923, the scrappy kid from Elizabeth Street on the Lower East Side, who pressed pants for three cents a pair after school in his father's shop, hocked his wife Bertha's engagement ring for five hundred dollars, which he spent on the lease and fixtures for a store with five hundred square feet of space and twenty feet of frontage on Seventh Avenue. With whatever was left over, he purchased forty suits to sell from his new hole-in-the-wall. Where he got the suits nobody knows, because manufacturers wouldn't touch a nobody like Barney in his nowhere store back then.

The neighborhood where Barney set up shop was first called Chelsea by retired British Army captain Thomas Clarke, who in 1750 bought a farm that encompassed a large part of the district. The neighborhood had its ups and downs. Clement Clarke Moore, a descendant of the captain's who is known chiefly as the author of the yule ditty " 'Twas the Night Before Christmas," donated a site on Ninth Avenue to the General Theological Seminary, where he also taught. Gaiety skipped into the neighborhood from the theater district along Twenty-third Street in the 1860s, and in 1869, the robber barons Jay Gould and Jim Fisk opened the Grand Opera House west of Eighth Avenue on Twenty-third Street. Fisk's funeral was held there in 1872.

The theater flourished until the early twentieth century—many of the performers camped at the grand old Chelsea Hotel on West Twenty-third Street—but commerce was fast crowding both God and the Muses out of Chelsea. Warehousing and freight handling flourished, serving the lumberyards, breweries, factories, railheads, and piers along the Hudson River. Tenements sprang up to house the working class that formed the backbone of the neighborhood's residents. By the time Barneys opened for business, the district's carefree theatricals and Christmas carols were a faint echo. Chelsea had almost no stores, almost no wealth, and only the distant waterfront din to give it the sound of life.

Not unreasonably, clothing manufacturers didn't rush to do business with the neighborhood's only merchant. So Barney bought his suits wherever he could find them. He bought closeouts; he bought at bankruptcy sales; he bought odd lots that manufacturers couldn't get rid of. Selling used clothes was not a new idea. It held a semirespectable place on the underside of the city's clothing business. There were other used clothing stores tucked away in the city's low-rent neighborhoods, particularly in the years when Barneys opened. But selling used clothing was not generally seen as something to boast about. The men who ran these stores preferred to call as little attention as possible to their businesses. Buying a used suit was an admission of second-rateness and defeat, of an American dream that had slipped through your fingers. And, in a way, so was selling it. So the merchants who ran the secondhand suit stores tended to transact their business meekly, because they had much to be meek about.

Several of the fancier New York department stores had flourished briefly just to the east of Barneys' Chelsea neighborhood on a strip of Sixth Avenue known as Ladies' Mile, but the current had carried them farther uptown a long time before. In 1902, Macy's moved from

Fourteenth Street and Sixth Avenue up to Herald Square, on Thirty-fourth Street, which soon became a new hub of New York's retail scene. B. Altman leapfrogged to the new neighborhood in 1906, Best and Company in 1910, and Lord and Taylor in 1914. By the outbreak of the First World War, the Ladies' Mile was just a desolate collection of grand cast-iron buildings.

Many of their occupants ceased to exist altogether, with only their forgotten monograms above the entrance to commemorate New York's Belle Epoque. But the stores that survived and continued to thrive closer to the hub of New York commercial life haunted Barney Pressman's descendants. Almost from the beginning, the word "uptown" had a special meaning for the clan, representing an El Dorado that remained out of reach and inspired the Pressman grandchildren with a mix of envy and hatred. As a young man, not long out of college, Gene Pressman took an apartment on Third Avenue and Sixty-first Street. A block away stood Bloomingdale's, which had moved to that location in 1872 and was then the trendiest store in New York. "I like to think that when I flush my toilet, I'm shitting on Bloomingdale's," Gene told a friend.

Barney himself had no time for envy, nor would he accept the second-class status that geography and lack of funds had saddled him with. To find inventory, he would scan the newspaper for notices of death and divorce among the city's fancy dressers. "If he left her, or if she left him, he would go to the apartment—'Do you want to get rid of his clothing? Maybe I could buy some.' And she would throw it out—'Here, take it. I don't want to see,'" remembers Martin Green-field, pantomiming the shamefaced way Barney's society benefactors would discard their castoffs and the avidity with which Barney would scoop them up.

If the original wearer of the suit was some notorious swell, Barney would trumpet his pedigree in the store window. But Barney was no snob. Not for nothing did he style himself the "cut-rate clothing king." If you wanted to get rid of the suit you were wearing, Barney would buy it off your back, and then he would drag you off the street into his store to buy a replacement.

A well-to-do Park Avenue matron called Barney and offered to sell him a closetful of her husband's old, expensive suits, just so she wouldn't have to look at her husband in them anymore. Of course, Barney bought every last one of them. A few weeks later, in comes a fellow who asks if the store can fit him with a few suits, and Barney says why sure he can and together they try on some of those Park Avenue suits he had bought just the other week. Every suits fits like a glove—not a single stitch needed. The fellow buys them all.

"Well, this is certainly a lucky day for both of us," says Barney. "I told you I could fit you perfectly."

"Of course you could—they're my suits," says the man.

The old Barneys salesman who tells this story swears it's true, and he does that because Barney Pressman swore it was a true story when he told it to him. And that doesn't mean that it isn't true, either.

The early years were perilous, and Barneys came very close to going under. In later years, Barney himself ascribed his survival to one big score, without which his teetering store would have failed. Barney had read in the *Daily News* of the sudden death of one of society's best-dressed gentlemen. He waited about a week, snuck past the doorman of the deceased's apartment building, and rang the doorbell of the man's apartment. A beautiful woman, impeccably dressed, answered the door and looked down at the squat man facing her. Barney, all five feet three of him, asked politely for the deceased and was told through loud sobs that the man was, in fact, deceased. The woman asked if Barney was a friend. No, said Barney, but he, Barney, had heard through a mutual friend of theirs that the late Mr. So-and-so had some suits he wasn't using anymore, and since Barney ran a used clothing store—and, besides that, Barney was also a Navy veteran (more loud sobs)—he had said Barney might purchase them. Barney would then describe a walk-in closet the size of a stateroom, filled with expensive Savile Row suits. Please, said the tearful widow, take everything—he would never have accepted money from you. Luckier still, the man was a size 42 regular—as close to Adam's template as a man's suit can get.

"And somehow the word got out—I'm sure Barney helped the word get out—that he had acquired this wardrobe," remembers Harvey Weinstein, whose father supplied Barneys with tuxedos. " 'I took the chance,' Barney told me. 'I knew I was failing here. I wasn't going to be able to make it. But after the word got out, my business took off.' Now, whether Barney was embroidering, I don't know," says Weinstein, "but my father bought it hook, line, and sinker." In this way, Barney weathered the Depression and the war years, surviving on secondhand clothing and a few trusted suppliers.

Look at America in the early part of the twentieth century and you will see a vast and varied landscape of men dressed in ready-to-wear suits. Americans made them and Americans wore them—to ball games, to restaurants, to church. In Europe, the suit still carried a whiff of the laboring classes. It was made of a single fabric—hence, was less costly—and was tailored more crudely than the flashier frock coats and striped trousers worn in town. If you wanted a suit, you picked out your woolens at a shop and had a local tailor make you one after he had measured you for it. But the science of putting that suit together was none too exact. In England in the early part of the century, the three-piece suit played a sartorial role much like blue jeans today. No gentleman would be caught dead in one, unless he was lounging in tweeds on his country estate. To call a fellow "ill-fitting" impugned both his shabby suit and the shabby person it draped.

America was something else altogether. It prided itself on the leveling instinct to clothe its gentlemen the way it clothed its farm laborers and shopkeepers, as well as on the manufacturing ingenuity to produce this fashion for the whole wide run of humanity at a very high level of quality. If haberdashery goes a long way toward distinguishing the hierarchy of class, then the American suit left an observer from abroad without a social scorecard. You just couldn't tell who was who in America by looking at the way men dressed, since everybody looked pretty much alike—a form of social camouflage that had baffled European visitors since the 1820s.

"If you take a look at a picture of a baseball game in the 1920s and '30s, everybody wore a suit or a vest, and 90 percent had straw hats on," remembers Irwin Grossman, an old clothing man himself. "And this is during a depressed era. At the height of the Depression, Sidney Hellman was president of the union, and he made a deal with the government to buy up surplus suits for the unemployed, so even if you didn't have a job, you still wore a suit." After getting out of law school in the early 1930s, Grossman promptly went into his father's business making suits. "We had one lawyer in the family who wasn't making out, so I was politely informed, 'Forget the law business.'"

The clothing business, as it turned out, wasn't much better. Chester Kessler also went into the family clothing business back then. Kessler's father owned the William B. Kessler Company, which made Hammonton Park suits, Kessler's dad competed with Grossman's dad, whose company, Grossman Clothing Co., made Austin Leeds and Groshire suits, but in the early days, Kessler's dad would sell to Barney and Grossman's dad wouldn't.

"It was very tough for us, and very tough for Barney," says Kessler. "There was a tremendous amount of mistrust. The attitude of the manufacturer was, 'The retailer is going to screw me. He's going to take advantage of me.' The retailer would think, 'This manufacturer is bigger than I am anyway, so he's going to cheat me.'

"I had a customer at a store in Chicago, a terrific guy—he loved to eat, so when he would come to New York, we would go to dinner, but we would go to one restaurant for the appetizer, another one for the main course, and another one for dessert—and he taught me an awful lot about the clothing business. He said to me, 'Chet, look what a nice relationship we have, but did you know that in 1930, I didn't give your father an order because of twenty-five cents?' He said, 'Your dad's price was twenty-two dollars and twenty-five cents, and somebody came in and sold me the suit for twenty-two dollars, and I passed your father up. I didn't give him an order.' He said, 'Isn't that just terrible?' 'But,' he added, 'the truth of the matter is that twenty-five cents was what I had in the bank.' "

Often, Barney didn't even have that. A vendor who came to collect learned to look down at the floor to see if Barney had the cash to pay his bill. The floor is where Barney left the tags he ripped off the suits when he sold them, and the floor was none too tidy. So if the vendor saw the floor littered with tags, he knew that Barney had managed to move some merchandise that week, and there would be some cash around. Except that Barney knew this, too, and when things got especially tight, you could sometimes see him performing this odd little half-shuffle, half-hop as he danced away the tags he hadn't had a chance to sweep up when a vendor surprised him.

Barney survived by his wits, which were very keen, and by his moxie. For decades, the better-quality suit manufacturers like Hickey-Freeman, 3Gs, Oxxford, and Hart, Schaffner and Marx refused to sell to Barneys. It was partly because Barneys drove a hard bargain, but more than that, the suit makers were afraid to rattle the established menswear retailers who lined Seventh Avenue farther uptown. "If one of your salesmen was even caught *near* Barneys, all hell would bust loose for your other retail customers in New York, which was just a tremendous clothing market," recalls Irwin Grossman.

Barney sold at a discount, maybe 8 or 10 percent lower than the competition uptown on new merchandise, but that was a hell of a savings in those days. It was the only way to entice customers down to the slightly menacing streets of Chelsea from the residential neighborhoods much farther uptown. Kolmer Marcus up on Thirty-seventh Street and Broadway didn't like that one bit, and Kolmer Marcus had more muscle than any other menswear store in New York in the 1930s and '40s. It sold about $4 million worth of menswear a year—an astronomical number for the time—mostly 3Gs and Hickey-Freeman.

Irritating Kolmer Marcus was bad business indeed for the manufacturer. "You protected every retailer, so they were afraid of Barney because of his discount, and they were afraid that he was going to always advertise and discount, so it is going to hurt the other people's business," says Martin Greenfield.

The end of World War II brought a marked change in Barney's fortunes. The first thing the GIs needed when they returned home was a good suit, and the first indignity they suffered was that they couldn't get one at any price. The clothing racks were bare. Beating swords into plowshares takes a lot less time than beating them into woolen mills and clothing factories. The single-mindedness of the war effort had militarized much of the economy and when the war ended, decommissioning the troops proved far speedier than decommissioning the factories that kept them fighting. No fabrics were being made, and this was because the cotton wasn't being milled, and when the cotton finally came back on line, and the fabrics duly followed, you still couldn't make a suit, because no one was making rayon for the linings. Production returned in fits and starts. The clothing business was in chaos, and stayed that way for some time.

Chester Kessler came home from the war in 1946, and went immediately into the family business, Hammonton Park, making suits for Barney Pressman, among others. The factory had thirty thousand suits in production, but Barneys couldn't get its hands on a single one of them. No pockets were available. There was simply no pants pocketing to be had. Kessler became a hero in his father's eyes, not to mention Barney Pressman's, when he bumped into an old Army buddy from Georgia whose family ran a cotton mill. The two got to talking, and one thing soon led to another. A phone call from Kessler's buddy to his family factory brought a relief shipment from Georgia: cotton for pants pockets. Hammonton Park found itself back in the suit-making business.

This is the herky-jerky way things went for well over a year as the clothing men retooled to make peacetime uniforms. A chance encounter got you pants pocketing one week; another week, it didn't.

Profiteers flourished, as they always do when shortage, chaos, and greed conspire to disrupt the orderly conventions of buying and selling. Unscrupulous manufacturers would tack an extra ten dollars onto the normal price of a suit, and the retailer had no choice but to pay up if he wanted merchandise to sell. Those who wouldn't pay faced hard times, Barneys no less than any of them. Even reputable manufacturers like Hammonton Park were forced to put their steady customers on allocation. If Barney Pressman got four blue longs one month, he got four brown shorts the next, because that's just how the schedule worked.

The war changed Barneys profoundly: It shook up a generation of American boys and cut them loose from their social moorings. In so doing, it cut their clothes loose, too. Before the war, England had counted men's fashion among its colonies, and it ruled the waistcoat as imperiously as it ruled India. Between the wars, the English upper classes ordained the dress code with a casual arrogance and the ready-to-wears obeyed. In suits, this meant the unchallenged authority of something called the London cut, a silhouette marked by wide shoulders, narrow waists, and ample armholes. A jacket cut this way sports a waist several inches higher than the pant waist and shoulders wide enough to align with the triceps. But to see the real genius of the design, you must look to the armpit. The extra material around the armhole allowed the chest to swell out with a man's breath and sink back in a languid drape—hence the style's other name, the drape cut.

For this the world can thank Frederick Scholte, a Dutch immigrant who apprenticed as a tailor to England's Household Guards, whose manly greatcoats inspired him. Scholte's reimagining of the military greatcoat was a bracing clap on the back to stoop-shouldered, hollow-chested civilians everywhere. Buck up! said Scholte's athletic silhouette. In 1914, Scholte set up his own shop and tailored the rest of the world—by extension, of course, since he was a terrible snob and loathed riffraff. Into this category Scholte even put the impeccable Fred Astaire, whom Scholte declined to fit.

Barney Pressman and the Americans who bought their suits from him never heard of Scholte, of course, but they certainly knew Edward, duke of Windsor, a Scholte customer from 1919 onward. If there was anything remotely regal about Edward, who fortunately abdicated the throne of England to marry the American divorcée Wallis Simpson, it was the way he wore his clothes. Edward invested his outfits with absolute confidence, even while he snubbed the starchy conventions of dress he inherited. He wore his trousers cuffed, to the immense consternation of his father who considered cuffs unseemly. They were also unpatriotic during the war, since they required extra fabric, then in painfully short supply. Edward didn't care. Nor did Edward like buttons on his trousers, so he had them made with the clunky zippers of the working classes. It took a while for this innovation to take hold, since men didn't like zippers and, what's more, they didn't trust them, but the duke carried the day.

"I was in fact produced as a leader of fashion, with the clothiers as my showmen and the world as my audience," he pronounced smugly. But it was true—especially in America, which swooned over the duke's sartorial posturing. The duke could be merciless when it came to fashion, but it only enhanced his authority. Hollywood fell under his spell before the war, and raffish leading men like Gary Cooper and Cary Grant served as a conduit for the duke's notions of style. So much so that the London cut took on a new nationality. By the late 1930s, it had come to be known as the American cut. The rule of thumb over here was, when in doubt, do like the duke.

The war changed all that. By the war's end, men's fashion had become just one more outpost of the British Empire on which the sun had set. This was not nearly so sudden or so dramatic as the empire's political unraveling but it subtly tilted the entire axis of style. In 1946, there were only the first hints of this. The dangerous drape of the zoot suit—oversized jacket with low buttons and low-crotched pants that bagged at the thighs—had emerged as a riotously indiscreet counter-uniform to the restrained drape cut. This was bad-boy fashion, menacing, slightly sinister, and in no way beholden to any duke.

The liberated lines of the zoot suit swept through Europe during the war on the hot wings of jazz. In France, for instance, the Vichy government launched a campaign against a tribe of harmless local hipsters known as zazous, who took their name and their cues in dress indirectly from Cab Calloway and his jitterbug aesthetic. Zazous were rounded up and beaten, while a collaborationist youth group called Jeunesses Populaires Françaises ran around stupidly shouting, "Scalp the zazous!"—a reference to the zazous' decadent and rather ludicrous pompadours. No more need be said here about the zazous, except to point out that the reckless spirit of zazouism everywhere helped strip the duke of Windsor of his only true authority. Fashion authority would no longer filter down exclusively from the aristocracy. In their own silly way, the zazous also had a direct effect on Barneys. Years later, Barneys would be among the first men's stores in the United States to sell European clothing, which retained a peacocky flair from the zazou days.

Barneys thrived in this turbulent postwar environment. Even in the early 1950s, Barneys catered to a somewhat zootier customer. The politicians shopped there. It was where you found suits with shoulders a little squarer and knees a little wider—in other words, a racier kind of suit. You could find a kind of gray flannel suit at Barneys different from the gray flannel you found at Macy's up on Herald Square. At Macy's, where they did more of a business with conventional brands like Hart, Schaffner and Marx, you found gray flannels made with a stain—a slightly bluish tinge to the white threads, giving the flannel a flatter, smoother look—"an uninteresting gray," Kessler snorts. Kessler's gray flannel, which Barneys carried, mixed sharply colored black and white threads, making for a brassier kind of gray.

It was a sharp look, and it appealed to the gritty spirit of the tough ethnic kids who came back from Europe and the Pacific ready to make their mark on New York life—the Poles, the Chinese, the Italians, and, of course, the Jews. Self-effacement, in clothes and in deportment, is a luxury of the privileged. The kids who grew up poorer had a hungrier style. They didn't consider it a lapse of taste to announce by the way they dressed that they were on the make, and they shopped at Barneys to deliver that message.

"The department stores—they were elegant, they were for gentiles. Jewish people didn't go to Macy's and Gimbel's for clothing," says Kessler. At least not for "clothing" the way Kessler says it: "Only dumb people went to Macy's." Barneys always had more of a fashion sense, and that sense would only grow more pronounced after the war. It was an outsider's take on clothes for outsider customers—outsiders who were coming to set the cultural and social agenda for New York City.

That is not to say that Barneys was louche. Leighton's uptown on Broadway and Forty-seventh Street, now that was louche. That's where the showbiz people shopped, and the gamblers and hoodlums, too. "Even the salesmen looked like gangsters with their hair slicked back," remembers Neil O'Brien, who was just starting out selling suits for Oxxford in the early 1950s. "Everyone looked like he came straight out of Damon Runyon's stories."

Barney Pressman was still managing to give his competitors fits—and growing at an estimated 20 percent a year. On Thursday, March 24, Barneys opened an hour early, at eight in the morning, to handle the overflow crowd it was expecting: It had 1,248 worsted gabardine topcoats that it planned to sell for $33.00 apiece instead of the $47.50 they brought elsewhere. Manufacturers tried everything they could to stymie Barney and enforce the standardized prices that Barney gleefully undercut. In 1951, Daroff and Sons, which produced the popular Botany 500 suit, brought a complaint accusing Barneys of selling Botany rejects for $48.75 when the "fair trade" price was $69.75. The court threw out the complaint, primarily because the Botany suits Barneys sold were just the same as everybody else's.

Daroff went after Barneys a month later, once again charging fraud. It demanded that the court bar Barneys from advertising Botany 500 suits if the suits didn't have the Botany 500 labels when Barneys bought them, which, of course, they didn't. The court took a dim view of this gambit, too. "On the facts disclosed, there is no fraud shown or deceptive practice established; defendant appears to be conducting its business honestly."

In 1954, a company called Palm Beach, which made lightweight resort suits, won a round for fair trade. A New York Supreme Court justice named Irving Saypol backed Palm Beach's request for a temporary restraining order, conceding that Barney Pressman had the means and the motivation to do the poor plaintiff "immediate and irreparable harm" by the way he sold Palm Beach's clothes—$45.00 "Sunfrost" suits for $33.45, for instance, or $32.50 "Cooltrim" suits for $23.95. A month later, Judge Saypol made himself clearer: Barney could sell Sunfrost and Cooltrim at any price he wanted, but only if he cut out the Palm Beach labels. So Barney dutifully cut out the labels.

Getting those suits in the first place was a dicey operation. Barney employed a secret agent named Irving Parker, whose thick lips and hooded eyes made him look like a predatory penguin. Parker was a rough customer, a good clothing man, they said, but something of a bruiser when he drove a bargain. In later years, he ran afoul of Fred Pressman, who despised Parker's strong-arm style and didn't much need it anymore, since by then Fred had made Barneys a highly desirable store to sell to. But in the years when the store struggled to get merchandise, it was Parker's job to sniff out hidden sources for all the manufacturers who boycotted Barneys.

Parker wasn't just tough; he was unstoppable. He had his own underground network of pliable retailers around the country that kept him supplied with contraband suits. At first, he bought their excess inventory. "If Parker landed fifteen Hickey-Freeman suits in Rochester, Minnesota, it was a great day," says Harvey Weinstein. "The Rochester merchant didn't want to carry them until the next season, so Parker paid eighty dollars apiece for them, the Rochester store got cash on the barrelhead from Parker, and those Hickey-Freemans ended up at Barneys."

Before long, though, Parker started cutting his own deals, and by the mid-1950s, he was directing his own underground railroad of contraband suits. A store in the South might be a two-hundred-unit

Hickey-Freeman customer. Parker would slyly suggest that the store order five hundred units, and Parker would take three hundred and, moreover, squeeze an extra 8 or 10 percent out of Hickey for the added volume. The suits would arrive at Barneys with the labels sewn under the inside pocket under the Hickey label, and Barneys simply cut them out. But on every sleeve, Barneys would staple a guarantee that here was a genuine Hickey, nationally advertised at $295, available in Barneys for $279. "And that was Barneys way back when," says Alan Katzman, who worked at Barneys in the late 1960s.

Some manufacturers never stopped trying to figure out how their merchandise wound up in Barneys despite their best efforts to outwit Parker. Oxxford Clothing, perhaps the premier American suit maker then and now, would send one of its Midwest salesmen to sniff around the store regularly—an East Coast man might be recognized. He would examine the neatly clipped labels for evidence that would lead Oxxford to the stores that had served as Barneys shadow suppliers. Barneys was simply too clever. "I never did find out," says Neil O'Brien, who started at Oxxford in 1957 and snooped regularly on Barneys. Most manufacturers preferred to look the other way. No one turns down an order for an extra three hundred units. If their steady retailers complained, they would claim they knew nothing of Parker and his shenanigans.

In Barney Pressman's time, the buyers for the store worked a very long day, six days a week. Arriving well before the store opened at nine, they would spend the morning and early afternoon selling suits on the floor. Then, after two o'clock, they could take calls from suit manufacturers and other merchandise vendors. If a vendor attempted to call a buyer before two o'clock, he simply wouldn't get through, because above the switchboard with its tangle of phone plugs were posted signs that read BUYERS WILL NOT TAKE VENDOR CALLS BEFORE TWO, and that was that.

But with the selling done by two, and the buying done by six or seven, it was time to take a break and some honest satisfaction from the day's work. This the buyers did by gathering across the street in

Kap's over a cup of coffee and counting the racks of suits they had sold. Every day, starting at around six in the evening, the suits were rolled out of the store and taken across the street to the tailoring room, where 150 tailors would let out the waists, shorten the sleeves, and hem the pants. On a really good day, a sale day, the buyers would sit in Kap's and watch fifteen racks roll out between six and nine o'clock, each rack with twenty suits hanging from it. Today if a store sells ten or fifteen suits, it's a banner day.

"That's what it was all about. I mean, I could look at a suit and it was better than sex, it was so beautiful—it was the best thing in the world! You would wake up in the morning and you would think about suits," says Alan Katzman. "You would eat lunch and think about suits. When you went to sleep at night, you counted suits."

Barneys was a lot more than a suit smuggler. Most stores at the time worked on a gross margin of around 40 percent, which means they paid $60 for a suit that cost $100 in the store. Today the gross margin runs 55 or 60 percent or higher, but a much higher percentage of a merchant's goods are ultimately sold at a marked-down price. When Barneys was making a name for itself, markdowns were infrequent, so a store's maintained margin—the margin it ended up booking after markdowns were calculated—ended up nearer 36 percent.

Barneys could make money off a gross margin of 30 percent. It could do that because it had a lower rent in Chelsea, but, more to the point, because it bought smarter than the competition. The official buying duties—as distinct from Parker's operations behind enemy lines—fell to a man named Ira Weiser. "Ira Weiser was simply the smartest buyer I ever encountered," says Harvey Weinstein. "Before you shook hands, he would nickel-and-dime you to death, but Ira knew. He knew fabrics. He knew workmanship. He knew enough to go out to the plant and look to see where you could put in labor-saving devices. He knew that the suit you were selling with handmade buttonholes had imitation handmade buttonholes, and he wanted something off the price right away. But once you shook hands with

Ira, you knew you had a deal, and he would never come back to try to nickel-and-dime you afterwards."

Weiser would also bargain for a manufacturer's piece goods after the season, something few buyers were savvy enough to do, and something no one does anymore at all. Basically, it meant Weiser could look at thousands of yards, and compose a full array of clothing from the scraps he saw before him. Piece goods are the pieces of fabric for styles that didn't sell, or the fabric that was left over from the manufacturing process. With the season over in September or October, Weiser would visit the plant and survey a room filled with fabric swatches—maybe ten thousand yards. Then, in his head, he would construct a mammoth order of suits and pants, mentally weaving them out of the thousands of yards of fabric that he saw in front of him, size by size.

Those who saw him work say it was a very impressive feat. By doing this, Weiser saved the manufacturer from dumping the piece goods for pennies on the secondary market, and, at the same time, allowed the manufacturer to keep its plant running later in the season. This had a tremendous value to the manufacturer, and allowed Weiser to cut some extraordinary deals for Barneys. But it only worked because Weiser's handshake was ironclad, and, where needed, he paid cash up front for merchandise Barneys wouldn't sell until the following season. If Barneys was undermining the clubby pricing structure that governed the men's clothing business, as the uptown retailers inveighed ceaselessly, this was how it was doing it. It was a good business run by great clothing men employing what Henry James called "the vocabulary of thrift."

Step into Barneys on a Saturday afternoon in those heady days of bootleg suits and piece goods, say around 1955. The store is still one floor, although it's taken over some of the adjoining space and the basement downstairs. Just inside the entrance is a row of chairs where men in all shapes and sizes wait for a salesmen to assist them. The pictures of salesmen line the walls, so the men who have shopped there already—which means most of the people there—can identify the salesman who helped them before and ask for him again.

Barney's picture hangs on the wall, too, not that you need it to identify the owner of the store. He is visible everywhere. Barney is around, always around, walking the floor with a big cigar in his mouth, kibbitzing with customers, adding his two cents. "Don't take that suit, it doesn't look right—here, try this one. Ah—perfect! What do you mean your wife doesn't like the coat? Who wears the pants around here?" Later on, his son Fred would go numb with chagrin as Barney continued to roll boisterously around the store. And in truth, you could never tell what Barney might say, which gave Fred reasonable pause in a new era of smaller sizes and thinner skins.

When Barney rules, though, his style is positively magisterial. Barney will come up behind a customer being fitted for a jacket, and fondle the merchandise admiringly, maybe pull up the shoulders a bit as he stands behind, because Barney knows that when you pull back on the shoulders, the jacket looks better. It's just one of the tricks the clothing men know, and Barney knows them all. This personal attention from the cigar-chomping boss of Barneys had a bracing effect on customers. "You would be so impressed that the owner of the store, a store that did twenty-eight million dollars' worth of business, mind you, took time with you that, of course, you would buy another suit, and whatever you bought that he didn't like, you canceled. Barney says it is not good, it is not good," says Katzman.

Barney also knew that no one would go out of his way to reach the store without the firm intention to spend some money once there. If a salesman couldn't close a sale, that salesman was doing something horribly wrong, went the thinking. In which case, there was always the button. The button was hidden somewhere on the wall so the customer couldn't see it. If a salesman saw his fish about to slip off the hook, he would sidle up to the button surreptitiously and maybe lean against it, all nonchalant. The button would alert the store manager to this emergency, and the manager would arrange to have the salesman paged. "Phone call for Mr. Cohen! Phone call for Mr. Cohen!" The manager or the assistant manager, all graciousness and solicitation, would approach, Mr. Cohen would excuse himself with profuse apologies to the customer, and the manager would take over to bludgeon the recalcitrant fish into submission. Very few got away.

This is not to suggest that there's anything of the huckster about Barney. Quite the contrary: He's still got an inconveniently located store that requires a steady and loyal clientele to keep it going. Barneys gets no walk-in traffic—absolutely none. Nobody ever strolls the dingy streets around Barneys. So while Barney may flatter and wheedle, sometimes yap, he also knows that his livelihood depends on pleasing his customers to the point where they return repeatedly. The suit has to look good even if there's no one to pull the suit jacket back when the customer gets home.

Barney understood the cardinal rule of tailoring: that a tailor measures in quarter inches. A suit has a line and a balance to it that can be easily thrown out of whack with too much fussing, Martin Greenfield remembers: "If a fitter did some alterations that were huge, he would kick their butt. He wouldn't let them sell anything unless it was the simplest way to alter, not to go in and take garments apart. Because, you know, if you do too many alterations, you spoil a lot of clothing. You don't satisfy the customer. You spend a lot of money, and you don't make a profit. Why sell it in the first place? If you can't sell something simple, do not sell it. You know, a lot of the fitters, they would look for tips on the side for the alterations. Barney knew all those tricks, and he wouldn't let them. Very shrewd . . . very shrewd."

Barney loved to make a sale no doubt, but he never lost sight that he was building something grander that he could one day bequeath to his son Fred. The story goes that Barney once watched one of his pushier salesmen bulldoze a customer into complete submission. The customer bought suit after suit, helpless before the salesman's relentless onslaught. He left with eight, maybe nine, suits of clothes. The salesman, spotting Barney on the floor, walked up to gloat over his triumph. "See that sale?" Barney says, "Yeah." The salesman says, "That was really something, wasn't it?" And Barney says, "That was terrible." The salesman says, "What do you mean it was terrible?" Barney says, "Sure, you sold the man a lot of goods, but you didn't sell him the store. You didn't make him feel that this was the only place he could get that clothing and that you were doing him a favor; that he was getting the kind of service and the kind of selection he couldn't get anyplace else. The truth is," said a red-faced Barney, "you made a sale, but you didn't make a customer."

When aroused, which was frequently, Barney would bury the target of his wrath under a torrent of bombast. Usually, he spent his wrath quickly, and moreover, he could be easily defused. But like so much else about Barney Pressman, his exuberant bluster was legendary among the clothing men. "Barney was engaged in one of his screaming tirades in my office," recalls Harvey Weinstein. " 'I want you to take every fucking tuxedo out of this store, they're a disgrace—you'll never be half the man your father was,' and so on. I said, 'Excuse me just a second, Barney.' And I popped two of the pills I was taking then for back spasms. Barney said, 'What's that, Harvey?' I said, 'My doctor warned me that someday, Barney Pressman is going to walk into your office and start screaming at you, and in that event, I want you to be prepared.' We got along perfectly after that."

Barney was right, though, when he berated his high-pressure salesman. His store was indeed the only place where many men could find clothing to fit figures less than Greek, as Lorenz Hart described the misshapen lover in his song "My Funny Valentine." It is one of the many ironies of the Barneys story that a store whose salesmen would regularly assassinate an ungainly customer with a sneer in its later days started life by welcoming nature's irregulars. Barney himself was a cadet portly, a regrettable size for men built low and wide, and he prided himself on stocking a bulging assortment of suits for people that kinder stores called "hard to fit." Barney was a straight talker, so those men trooped to what his store candidly called its "odd-size room."

In Barney Pressman's office in the back was a standing pole with five or six blackboards swinging from it. The blackboards displayed the inventory of Barneys' odd-size suits. When the store sold out of size 56 or size 58, Barney would change blackboards to indicate just how many he had left, never wanting to get caught short when one of his ampler customers came into the store. "Look at that," said Barney to Chester Kessler one day, pointing at his blackboards filled with scribbled numbers in the high fifties. Kessler's family business, William B. Kessler Company, made Hammonton Park suits, a mainstay of Barneys' business. "At our rate of sale, that should last us three years," Barney said, beaming proudly.

Of course, it didn't. "Two months later, Barney would call me up—it didn't matter where I was, he would manage to find me," remembers Kessler. "Chester, I need twenty suits each in sizes fifty-six, fifty-eight, and sixty. How did I know all these big schmucks would get together at a meeting and come in to buy me out?" Normally, an order like that would take Kessler eight or ten weeks to manufacture, but Kessler would get them to the store in ten days. And that's how Kessler would compensate Barney for the huge volume of suits he bought, instead of by giving Barneys a discount.

Many of these big men had been shopping at Barneys for years, starting with their first humiliating excursion to Barneys Boys Town, in the store's basement. Downstairs was the domain of Barney's wife, Bertha—Bertha Gewirtz Pressman. Taking a Pressman for a husband has always meant working alongside that Pressman, for otherwise, there would be little opportunity and even less reason to have a marriage in the first place. That was certainly true of Bertha Pressman, whose suggestion that Barney hock her engagement ring for seed money was a kind of marriage ceremony of its own. It was the sincerest "I do" a Pressman wife could utter and her dutiful presence in the store constituted a daily renewal of that vow.

In a history of repeated patterns, this one is repeated most faithfully. Gene Pressman's wife, Bonnie, a former Ford model who ran the store's women's fashion department, was interviewed shortly after her wedding in 1982. She reported some surprise that, on first meeting her husband's family, conversation around the dinner table rarely strayed from the store. At the time, she assumed that the family would soon exhaust the topic and that subsequent dinners would reveal other dimensions of shared family life: tenacious winters, world politics, the leak in the bathroom faucet, the petunias in their Westchester garden. They never did. Eventually, Bonnie Pressman confessed, she realized there was only one conversation at the table and resigned herself to family life in one obsessive dimension.

Bertha was the model for her daughter and granddaughters-in-law. It was she who started the Barneys boys department. Under her stern gaze, several generations of city kids squirmed awkwardly into their first suits. It was a ritual few ever forgot. That was where you found the overfed offspring of New York's food-proud Jewish and Italian mothers on the eve of their bar mitzvahs and first communions: in Barneys Husky section—a term that denoted large sizes in a way that was meant to soften the fat child's shame. Of course, it never did. You could see the mortification on his plump face all too plainly as he wrestled with a reluctant waist button, his mother looking on, glowing.

No one beamed more proudly than Barney himself. "I would stop in at the store and Barney would be downstairs, and I'd say, Barney, let me drive you home, but I've got to leave in twenty minutes," says Chester Kessler. "And Barney would say, just wait, just wait. See that kid there. Look at that rear end. I love it. I love it. Another little kid would walk by with his mother. Look at that little *schmendrik*, Barney would say. Such love that mother has. She doesn't know I own that kid, because no one could fit that big fat ass but me."

It was Barneys Boys Town that finally got Irwin Grossman to sell him Austin Leeds and Groshire suits. Mrs. Grossman had the idea to dress her two little boys in matching blazers, but the woman who ran the small boys department at the store out on Long Island where the Grossmans lived told her there was only one store where she could find what she was looking for—that, of course, being Barneys. "So she dragged me by the ear and we had to go in. And we're standing down-stairs, and I was standing in the front of the stairway, and there's Bar-ney. He says, 'Aha, Grossman! I see you came to buy your kids' clothes here. What, you're too fancy to have your salesman call on me?' So I said, 'No, Barney, he must have just neglected it.' So we took another man from the sales staff outside New York and we sent him in. And that's when we started doing business with Barneys."

From the start, Barney Pressman realized the value of his natural showmanship to the store. Running a great store often lies halfway between business and theater, since people shop as much to be amused as they do to be provisioned. "It's not what you say, it's the way that you say it," Barney used to intone portentously, banging his fist on the table between each word for unnecessary emphasis. Barney hardly invented hype in the retail business, but he stood out from virtually all of his competitors in his riotous application of it, particularly given his store's humble roots.

It was one thing for a Stanley Marcus to tickle the well-to-do of Dallas with elephants. Neiman Marcus, from its founding in 1907, had conspicuously set out to dazzle the local elite with the most luxurious store ever seen in those parts. It was quite another thing for Barney Pressman to drape naked women in wooden barrels and send them out to give away matchbooks—matchbooks—to lure customers to a used clothing store near lower Manhattan's ramshackle waterfront. This took true chutzpah, which Barney possessed in large drafts.

Among Barney's closest friends in the store's early days was a man named Emil Mogul, a former radio salesman who started his own advertising agency. In the early years, local newspapers refused to sell Barneys space for advertising, since the powerful retail stores around town—big advertising spenders all—pressured them not to. That didn't faze Barney. Emil Mogul and Barney Pressman forged a formidable alliance, relying on the new and unruly medium of radio to put the store on the map. It was something of a first for retail advertising. "I want to buy that thing—that thing you blow into," Barney announced. He meant a microphone.

Barney caught on quick. In 1932, Charles Lindbergh's two-year-old son, Charles junior, was kidnapped from the Lindbergh home in Hopewell, New Jersey, and murdered. Bruno Richard Hauptmann was convicted of the crime, and in 1936, he was electrocuted. Hauptmann's trial mesmerized America. It was the biggest media event of its time, and the medium that captured it most grippingly was the radio. Reporters were barred from broadcasting from the courtroom itself, but the radio men set up their transmitters just outside to give listeners a blow-by-blow account of the proceedings.

The trial was brought to you, in part, by Barneys—"No bunk, no junk, and no imitations!"—which sponsored broadcast coverage of the Hauptmann trial in one of Barney Pressman's more grisly suit-selling brainstorms. Think of a small local haberdasher you had never heard of using the murder trial of Timothy McVeigh to hawk cheap suits, and you get an idea of the exhilarating tastelessness of the whole thing.

Mogul had also formed a friendship with Milton Biow, who had written one of the catchiest advertising slogans of its day—"Call for Philip Morris!" Barney Pressman wanted something like that, a catch-all phrase that fell easily on the ear and lodged in the brain so you would never forget it. Biow thought for a moment and suggested that Barneys might adapt the police radio dispatcher's alert: calling all cars. Except instead of calling all cars, why not make it calling all men. Calling all men to Barneys. It is difficult to underestimate the impact of that hokey phrase. To this day, people who have only a hazy recollection of shopping at the store will spout it when the store's name is mentioned. Barney knew he had his slogan as soon as Biow suggested it, and the phrase served as the store's calling card for many years thereafter. It still pops up as a nostalgic reminder in Barneys advertising from time to time, sure to awaken memories of better times and cheaper suits. It is even printed on a banner that hangs outside Barneys flagship store on Madison Avenue.

Barney never lost his knack for grabbing the public's attention, one way or another. He sponsored Irish jig music on Irish radio stations. He staged rodeos for children in the parking lot across the street from the store, with pony rides and Indian war dances, to promote Barneys Boys Town.

In the 1950s, Barney finally broke down the barrier at *The New York Times*. Barney and his advertising man, Milton Guttenplan, approached *The New York Times* and proposed running an ad that avoided any mention of price. The store was still known chiefly for lower prices that undercut the fancy uptown stores and drove them bananas. How can you object, Barney asked the *Times*, if we don't advertise any price at all? It was a formula that Bill Bernbach, the greatest ad practitioner of that day and a close friend of Emil Mogul, had pioneered for a store called Ohrbachs.

The *Times* relented, although it continued to treat Barneys with a certain *froideur*, always anxious to avoid offending its better-established advertisers. By the early sixties, Barneys was beginning to pull in a more respectable clientele—an uptown kind of crowd. That is what it wanted to show in its new ads in the *Times*. So, reasoned Barney, "why don't we just show a hearse outside of the store?" By this, he meant a Rolls-Royce. It was one of Barneys' first print ads in *The New York Times*—a Rolls-Royce parked majestically at the curb outside the store at Seventh Avenue and Seventeenth Street while the chauffeur opens the car door for the kind of person Barney and his son Fred wanted the world to see shopping there.

But it was not all smooth sailing with *The New York Times*. Barneys was still a second-class citizen relegated to the buried pages of the paper. Thursday was the biggest day of the week for retail advertising, falling as it did just before payday and two days before Saturday shopping outings. So Barneys chose to advertise on Mondays, which, although it fell on a day of the week when people thought much more about making their salary than spending it, had the same kind of cockeyed advantage as the store's location: There was no one else around. But like the store's location, it also meant that Barney had to compensate for his overlooked ad placement with his customary guile and chutzpah. Which he did.

One famous ad from that time played off an exhibit at the Brooklyn Museum of Art on the life of George Washington, which Barneys was sponsoring. The Monday *Times* ran a double-page spread for Barneys with a painting from the exhibit of the young George Washington in a skirtlike thing that young children, boys as well as girls, wore during that period. "When George Washington was a boy, he dressed like his mother," ran the headline, while the ad went on to show the kinds of outfits George could have bought at Barneys Boys Town.

As much of a showman as he was, Barney Pressman didn't survive on razzle-dazzle alone. Barney forged a reputation for unusual integrity in a shifty business, and that reputation saw him through the hard early years. Early on, with the wolf at the door of so many Jewish clothing men—many of whom were devoured—he had had the good sense to realize that he could always fall back on his character should his wit fail to pull him through.

The same people who loved to tell off-color Barney stories would often contrast his prickly husk with his sturdy core. God knows, they would tell you, Barney helped them all out of innumerable jams. "You just liked the guy," says Irwin Grossman. "The degree of refinement was questionable, but the degree of sincerity and raw meaning was exceptional in that business. What's going on with Barneys today would make him turn over in his grave, because if a manufacturer needed money back then, he'd call Barney up and he'd get a check the next morning. The unique thing about him was not the fact that he was a good businessman or a good salesman, but he was a very decent guy."

Barney and William Kessler, Chester Kessler's dad and the manufacturer of Hammonton Park clothing, had a particularly close relationship and often propped each other up during the tough Depression years. If Barney would need a few thousand, Kessler would float him. If Kessler couldn't meet his payroll and needed the few thousand back and then some before the Barneys bill came due, Barney Pressman would dig deep to carry him.

Back when times were good, after the war when Chester had taken over Hammonton Park from his father, he needed a great deal of cash. Manufacturers built their autumn inventories in May, June, and July to ship in August. With payment terms running sixty days, that meant Hammonton Park didn't get a check until October. Kessler needed $250,000 cash one September and didn't want to draw down his bank credit for the five or so days until he could cover the loan.

"So I called Barney on the phone, and I said, Barney, I've got a problem. I need two hundred fifty thousand dollars. He said come down to the store. I said, well I can't come down to the store, because I am in Hammonton Park, New Jersey. He says, send your secretary down. I said, well, Barney, don't you want to get something in writing from me—I'll give the money back to you Tuesday, Wednesday. He said, did I ask you? I got Barney's check and paid my taxes, and I got into my car to go back to New York. I drove about five or six miles, and I thought to myself, you know, nobody knows about this, and so I turned around and went back to the factory, and I called the controller and I asked him to come back to the factory and make me out a promissory note. I put the note in the mail and I wrote a little letter saying, dear Barney, thanks very much, I'll see you Tuesday, but because nobody knows about this, I want the loan to be a matter of record. As soon as Barney got the mail, he picks up the phone: You s-s-s-son of a bitch. You think I don't t-t-trust you? Don't you ever do a thing like that again!"

For Harvey Weinstein, the tuxedo man, it was a godsend that this kind of story got around. "When some of my other accounts would call me to complain that my tuxedo cost fifteen dollars less at Barneys than they were selling it for, and threatened to cut me off unless I stopped doing business with Barneys, I would simply fall back on the same bullshit story every time. I said, well, there was a time when my dad couldn't make payroll, so Barney loaned him the money to keep his payroll and hold on to his business without going under. There's no way I can cut Barneys out, you know." Weinstein lets out a gravelly laugh at the memory. "It was all bullshit. But it worked because Barney was known by everybody to do exactly that, because you were one of his people and he loved you and he trusted you."

In 1973, William B. Kessler Company finally gave up the ghost. It had hung on longer than most of the local clothing makers around New York, but finally, it too succumbed to competition from cheaper factories overseas and changing tastes. Over the course of the fifty-odd years the Kesslers and the Pressmans did business together, various discrepancies had crept into the books. Kessler always charged for the hangers their suits came on; Barneys made it a practice never to pay for hangers. Barneys would send back a suit because the seam was manufactured improperly, and charge the suit back to Kessler; Kessler wouldn't accept the charge and would fix the seam and send the suit back to Barneys, but Kessler never rebilled the store, so Barneys kept the credit for the suit on its books.

These were just the stray threads from a lifetime of doing business together. When Chester Kessler closed his books for good, he simply wanted to tie them up so this chapter of his life could be finished neatly. He presented Barneys with a bill for close to forty thousand dollars, although, he admitted, he no longer had any idea how to verify each individual transaction, or indeed whether the mistakes were Barneys' or his own. Barneys' accountants spent many months hunting through its records. Almost a year later, Barneys mailed Kessler a check for $26,809.18. "Now, that's what I call integrity," says Kessler, shaking his head ruefully. "That is why I say, I am very surprised—very surprised—at what has happened."

3

"HOW DO YOU HANDLE YOUR DAD?"

When World War II broke out, Barney's son, Fred, was studying history at Rutgers University in New Jersey, and entertaining vague notions of going on to law school. In 1943, he enlisted in the Army. When Fred mustered out in 1945, the law no longer tugged at him. In fact, nothing really did. Fred was a bit of a playboy in those years, a child of privilege casting about for something to do and enjoying his idleness, as his friends recall it. Fred's idyll didn't last long, and he never put his feet up again.

It was probably inevitable that Fred would end up back at the store. Barney wanted it that way from the day Fred was born, and all his browbeating had this as its end. Stop thinking so much about baseball, Barney would tell Fred when Fred was a young man crazy for sports; start thinking more about the store! Always the store. Until, much later on, the store was all Fred could think about, even when he desperately wanted to stop thinking about it, sometimes to get the decent night's sleep that so often remained beyond his reach.

Great retailers can be the most persuasive people on earth, and they are among the most doggedly optimistic. Barney had these attributes to their fullest; no customer could withstand the tidal wave of his gusto. As in so many of the great Jewish merchant families, the fathers trained the full bore of that gusto on their sons, and the sons usually succumbed. Many successful entrepreneurs who have created thriving businesses harbor dynastic ambitions, but retailers suffer the dynastic disease at its most virulent: They view their stores as extensions of their households, their merchandise as their treasure, and their children as stewards of a family legacy that encompasses every sock and handkerchief in the store.

This was particularly true among the prosperous Jewish families that had set their stamp so heavily on the retail business in this country. Jews didn't invent the department store. Non-Jews like Wanamaker of Philadelphia, Jordan of Boston, and Field of Chicago did. But the first wave of German Jewish immigrants in the mid-nineteenth century took naturally to peddling. "How much more I could write about this queer land," wrote Abraham Kohn, a peddler who had emigrated from Bavaria in the 1840s. "It likes its comfort extremely."

The most enterprising of these men ultimately found a ripe expression for their business genius in big, wonderful stores. Their names conjure rich images of the comfort and plenty that intoxicated Kohn: Bloomingdale's, Neiman Marcus, I. Magnin, Filene's. Behind each of these institutions stood a family, often very publicly through good works in their communities and a lordly presence on the floor.

Adolph Harris arrived in Galveston, Texas, from Prussia in 1859, prospered in the dry goods business in Houston, and later went on to found A. Harris and Company in Dallas. In his elegant history of notable Jewish merchant families, *Merchant Princes*, Harris's grandson Leon Harris, Jr., recalls his lockstep march into the store after college.

When, at the age of twenty in 1947, I graduated from Harvard, I went to work at the store as automatically and unquestioningly as the son of a medieval stonemason would have followed his father's craft. Or perhaps more accurately, it was as some minor noble's heir assuming his father's fiefdom, for despite the disadvantages of their religion, these Jewish merchants resembled the petty princes in their own localities. My uncle died in 1950, whereupon his son and I ran the store until we sold it in 1961 to Federated Department Stores. (New York: Kodansha America, 1994, p. xxiii.)

Store, family, family, store—the boundaries between them are often meaningless, so that when a father asks his son how the double-breasteds are moving, he is sending a message of love and fear and pride. The son knows this perfectly well. Which is why, in later years, if Barney came into the store that Fred was now running, Fred would leave. There are some things sons don't want to tell fathers, even if they say them with suits.

Children brought up speaking this inarticulate retail tongue are often subjected to a particularly crude kind of parenting. In his memoir, *Minding the Store*, Stanley Marcus tells the story of how his brother Edward reluctantly came to work at Neiman Marcus in 1928.

It was inconceivable to my father that any of his sons might even contemplate any other line of endeavor. . . . I doubt if my father ever gave thought to the problems that he might be creating by forcing all of his sons into the same business, or the conflicts which might eventually surface as the result of differing levels of capabilities, ambitions, or seniority. I think he was such a supreme egotist as far as his sons were concerned that he sincerely believed that since they all had his genes, they would all turn out to be equal in all ways. (Denton, Texas: University of North Texas Press, 1974, p. 65.)

Many in Fred Pressman's social and business circles were living out the same generational drama when they entered their own family businesses after the war. They knew it, too, and for the most part were not overly troubled by it, except insofar as it raised a host of practical problems. New York was still the hub of the garment manufacturing business and the end of the war signaled the beginning of the second generation's rise in hundreds of small family-owned businesses in the region.

"We'd all have dinner, oh, once a month or once every two months," recalls Harvey Weinstein, the tuxedo man. "Just ad hoc dinner without agendas, and we'd swap stories, because we were all second-generation guys—Irwin, myself, Jerry Tarkov, and Robert Hall were there; Sam Eisenberg. Fred. We were almost all college educated, and most of us were World War Two veterans, so we shared a lot. And it came from fathers who had fought tooth and nail, who had had to go to work. Self-made men. And we'd ask one another, you know, how do you handle your dad? Somebody would say, you know, you're handling all of the New York accounts. How did your dad happen to give them up? And we just thought through what our responsibilities were, how much authority we had. There was this great feeling of comradeship because of this. None of us were really fighting one another."

You couldn't really call Fred Pressman a handsome man. He was a head taller than his father and stayed a slim size 40 regular until he died, a point of immense pride. But you could also see in Fred a softened edition of Barney's goggly eyes, rounded further by dark shadows that got progressively darker over the years. A caricaturist would zero in on this feature, making great quizzical circles in the middle of Fred's face and crosshatching mournful pouches underneath them, and people who knew him would say, oh yes, that's Fred. His Pagliacci impression was only underscored by his habit of slouching deeply and looking at you sideways. He made a strong impression.

Fred lavished a great deal of attention on his appearance, which he masked by managing to look like hell. His clothes always exhibited the finest workmanship. His suits were usually made by Oxxford, a company he adored, and his sports jackets—camel hair or navy blue—by the Italian artisans of Fred's beloved Belvest. Occasionally he wore a gray chalk-stripe suit—the stripes always three quarters of an inch to an inch wide. Toward the end of his life, he sometimes had his suits made by the great Neapolitan tailors da Venza or Abla, but with special Fred touches—a softened shoulder and vents. That toned down their Latin-lover, "Soave Bolla" side, as Fred's protégé, Peter Rizzo, calls it. The shirt was a blue end-on-end with a tab collar. His tie was invariably black knit. When he traveled, he always carried his lucky hat, but he never wore it. And over his arm, inside and outside, he carried a bunched-up tan Burberry trench coat, which had nothing whatsoever to do with the weather.

Well made though they were, Fred's clothes were often frayed and invariably rumpled and creased. He wore his suits a size too large— size 41 regular—and he wore his pants too long. Other arbiters of fashion pride themselves on looking pulled together. Fred worked hard at looking pulled apart. And somehow, it all worked. Fred managed to make his scruffiness both chic and singular, and not remotely self-conscious, which was what he was aiming at all along. Peter Rizzo: "He wore the same thing every day, so it got a little mangy at times. And it was a little off center. It was kind of Gary Cooper off center, versus David Niven, a different kind of peacock. That was Fred's style, and he was great." Combined with his sad-sack posture, it also made Fred look deeply forlorn. In the end, you came away thinking that Fred stood above the hurly-burly of fashion, even as he orchestrated it. Yes, style is delightful, Fred's carriage seemed to say, but, ah, so fleeting.

This he learned from his mother, Bertha, who, more than Barney, forged Fred's sense of style. Bertha Pressman, née Gewirtz, was a grande dame in a milieu from which grandes dames did not often spring. She was tiny and wiry, but managed to project a regal presence for all that. In her dress, she favored Hermès, and mid-length skirts from Paris, which legend has it she smuggled back to the States in a false-bottomed suitcase twice a year. Also cashmere—cashmere blouses and a cash-mere scarf panel, which she wore day in and day out. Cashmere for Bertha was the kind of personal fashion manifesto that must have influenced Fred's decision to adopt his own unvarying outfit.

Always she wore three pieces of jewelry—a ruby brooch with diamond spray points, which she attached to every garment, whether it looked good or not; and a massive diamond-and-ruby bracelet on each wrist. She finished off her singular ensemble with thick, black glasses, like the French designer Pauline Trigère, and stiffly laquered black hair, like a Japanese Kabuki actor's. The gay boys who worked downstairs alongside her in later years revered her as an icon of style, and she watched over them maternally at a time when it was almost unimaginable to encounter openly homosexual salesmen in a respectable clothing store.

"She was a woman of phenomenal style," says Donald White, who worked in Barneys Underground, the unlikely neighbor to Barneys' Boys Town department in the late 1960s. "She was every bit as stylish as the great style-setters that we know and love. She literally had the aura of a Diana Vreeland. If anything, she was the more modern of the two because Bertha, unlike Vreeland, had a look that was neither overly stylish nor passé. She had a wonderful gravelly voice, and she'd say things like, 'It's the latest thing, it's the latest . . . it's fabulous!' But she was actually quite a refined character. She wasn't one of those crude monsters.

"She was the reverse of the husband in a way, and yet you had a feeling that's what kept him in line. And maybe that was the balancing act, you know, between the two of them. She was the one with ambition and taste and she was the one, I feel, who is responsible for the son turning out as he did. Without her influence, it would have been too far-fetched."

It was Bertha, for instance, who brought the first imported garments into the store—a line of boys clothing from the Dutch manufacturer Van Gils. That was long before anybody in the clothing business gave much of a thought to looking abroad for everyday garments. Bertha appreciated the workmanship, even though her customers probably couldn't have cared less. And this she passed on to Fred, too, and it would prove the making of the store. "She'd be very happy to know that, because she must have suffered mightily, having no outlet for her taste and discernment," says Donald White.

But that was all to come later. When Fred first joined the store, he needed to serve his own kind of apprenticeship. Fred got his primary schooling from the round and wily Ira Weiser, Barneys' shrewdest clothing man. Weiser arrived at Barneys in 1937 and worked his way up from the stockroom to vice president and merchandise manager. He was plenty tough and the best buyer around, which called for a different range of talents than the job of salesman. "If you took the best salesmen in any store, and you say buy the line, you are going to blow yourself up," says Martin Greenfield. "Salesmen do not know how to buy, because all of the things that they think they could sell, they can't sell. But Ira knew what they could sell. That's a good buyer. He knows what is safe to buy, what you must repeat, and he knows what is new and how far to go with new items, because basics you must always have in the store. He knows the inventory required. He knows how much they sell during the season. Today, that's all computerized. Ira didn't need any computer.

"When I first knew Barney, Freddie used to come along to buy with him and Ira, and he would sit on the side," remembers Greenfield. "They could buy and size up an order faster than anybody you ever knew. They started out with, like, twelve hundred blue serge suits. You can't go wrong with blue serge suits—because the first thing someone is going to buy is a solid blue serge suit, whether it's a bar mitzvah, whether it's a funeral, whether it's a wedding—so they would buy all the sizes, because you couldn't come in there and not be able to find portly and extra short. They sized it up. They finished it up. And Freddie would sit there on the side."

Weiser was the Falstaff to Fred's Prince Hal, and he reared the lad in the clothing business. In the end, though, he met Falstaff's unfortunate fate. Fred dumped Ira after he had remade the store, and there are many who say it was not Fred's nicest moment. From there, Ira went to work for Sy Sym's, a huge discount clothing business that suited Weiser's style. Says Alan Katzman: "Ira bought with a shovel, not a pencil." That was the way Barney wanted things.

Barney and Bertha also planted in Fred the seed of good taste, which would later ripen into the best taste anybody who worked with Fred had ever seen—before or since. Barney, it turns out, was no slouch in the taste department, either. He may have run a cut-rate suit store with all the finesse of a longshoreman, but Barney always had an eye for the finer things, which he passed on to his son long before Fred came to work in the store. Barney frequented auctions with Fred in tow, looking, fondling, seeing through the dust to the treasure hidden beneath it. He collected things, often without purpose but with an instinct that something so wonderful would come in handy someday. When the old Ritz Tower closed in 1926, and was torn down, Barney picked among the artifacts and bought much of the brass hardware and fittings from the old hotel-room doors, which he stowed away.

Chester Kessler walked by Barney's office one day and found it loaded with old, musty chair frames, the seats punched through and sagging. "Barney, what the hell are these?" Kessler asked, astonished. "What the hell do you know about anything, Kessler; you're not even a good clothing man," Barney shot back, waving a hand in disgust. "These are beautiful chairs. You watch. I am going to put them in a warehouse, and you will see one day."

And so Kessler did. Some twenty years later, Barney and Bertha bought a piece of property in Greenwich, Connecticut, and started building a home on which they lavished their native instinct for the impeccable. The swimming pool went into the ground before the house had even a foundation. Every weekend, Barney and Bertha would sit by their pool on the hilltop and watch this home take shape. It was not a grand home—just one bedroom. Barney presided over it from the pool like Tut surveying his pyramid-in-progress. A German carpenter hand-worked every molding, not over the course of months but of years. And, of course, into this house went the fine brass hardware from the Ritz, not to mention the beautiful chairs.

In much the same way, Fred fussed over the Seventeenth Street store later on, constantly changing departments and displays, tweaking the decor until it passed his maddening scrutiny, and then tweaking it some more. There was never a time when one department or another wasn't undergoing a makeover. As soon as he had brought one part of the store up to his standard of perfection, he would start in on another that had only recently gone through its own upgrading, and so it continued.

It was also in much the same way that Fred's sons fussed over their Madison Avenue and Beverly Hills stores in the early 1990s, but by then it was no longer a private passion. It had mushroomed into something much bigger and much more ungainly, until the vaunted Pressman perfection became its own undoing. What they got in the end was a $500 million *folie*, built with money borrowed against profits yet to come. In the end, those profits would never, and could never, come, precisely because the Pressmans had exalted their taste into a kind of personal religion.

It all started with gloves and shoes. Fred came to love them above all other garments. Watching Fred with a pair of gloves exposed the inner workings of a man who spent his happiest hours peering through the microscope of fashion. There, questions of what looked good were left far behind as Fred plunged deeper into the wilderness, pulled along by his own impulses, rather than some larger purpose he could explain to you if you asked him. Fred would dissect a pair of gloves for the better part of an hour, examining the quality of the skins, and then turning them inside out to pore over them some more. The inside of a man's glove! In later years, Fred would wander over to wherever Tom Kalendarian was working in the store, because Kalendarian had the bad fortune to buy the gloves, which meant spending time at the factories in Italy where the gloves were made. "In the evening, he would come over and he would corner poor Tommy, and they'd be there forever," recalls one of the salesmen with relief over having escaped Fred's iron-gripped attentions. " 'The lining, look at this lining. Look how they did the stitching on it.' He was very, very meticulous about all of these tiny, tiny, tiny details to the point of its almost being a little psychotic. Stuff that the average person could never possibly notice."

As Fred's education progressed, so did his preoccupations with the deep structure of clothing. You did not want to engage Fred in a discussion on the related subjects of point-to-point and half-back measurements of suit jackets, for instance, unless you wanted to make a short conversation very long. The point-to-point measurement spans the width of a jacket at the shoulder blades, while the half-back runs from the jacket's center seam to just under the arms where the sleeve meets the body. Together they govern the way a jacket hangs off the shoulder, and the way the jacket breaks under the arm—both as crucial to a jacket's architecture as the lintel of a door. Men's jackets don't change much from year to year in most respects, barring a few periods of violent upheaval in lapels that clothing men remember with a shudder, the way stock traders remember bear markets. The point-to-point and half-back measurements, however, gyrate wildly.

And so Fred treated them, always worrying about whether to adjust the measurements from one season to the next, and monitoring the progress of one season's point-to-point against the last, based on how jackets with two different measurements sold. It afforded Fred endless opportunity for disquiet and rumination, which he loved. "Fred was a man possessed when it came to this," says a former salesman.

Out of these early obsessions, Fred started shaping his own ideas about what Barneys should stand for and what kind of merchandise it should sell. Those ideas were as different from his father's as Harris tweed is from gabardine. For all the grave respect Fred had for Barney, he came to despise the business his father had founded and built.

Fred found Barney's showboating vulgar. He found the wheedling unseemly. He hated the discounts, and he hated the sales, despite the huge volume of business they brought in. He didn't really like the odd sizes that Barneys was famous for, and he didn't even like the idea that people with size 56 bodies were walking around his store looking for size 56 suits. It disturbed the unforgiving aesthetic Fred was forging, an aesthetic that, in the next generation, would reappear as outright contempt for the common man. Fred never felt that way, not least because the common man paid most of the bills at Barneys even after Fred had finally buried the legacy of the "cut-rate clothing king."

*   *   *

Crazy Fred was not, and he never lost sight of where the dollars came from. Also, down deep, he remained a clothing man, like his father, and he loved nothing better than a classic, well-cut suit until the day he died. Nonetheless, a nagging sense of shame was gnawing away at him. He would watch as Barney sidled up to a customer to kibbitz, as he did to a fellow named Emanuel Berger one day in 1963. Berger never forgot it. "I was perched on the tailor's pedestal being fitted when Mr. Barney (as the salesman called him) wandered over to me, gave my suit a slow, admiring once-over while appraisingly rubbing one of the lapels between thumb and forefinger," Mr. Berger reminisced recently in a letter to *The New York Times*. "Then looking at the price tag, in a loud voice the diminutive Mr. Barney shouted, 'Moe—how do we do it!'"

You can almost see Fred cringe, hunching deeper into his wrinkled suit. By this time, Fred held the official title of vice president of operations at the store. More to the point, he was starting to push his weight around. He never made a formal announcement to Barney that he was taking over, but that's what it amounted to. In retrospect, you could consider that famous ad from *The New York Times* to be Fred's semiofficial declaration of independence. In the top half of the photo, a liveried chauffeur opens the door of a parked Rolls-Royce as a prosperous businessman steps onto the curb. One look tells you: This man is not Jewish. The headline reads, WESTCHESTER TO WALL STREET . . . VIA BARNEYS. This was Fred's grab for the man in the gray flannel suit, the out-of-towner, the button-down, traditional Gregory Peck type of guy.

One thing this man was not was a Barneys shopper. He shopped at Brooks Brothers or J. Press, or one of the other uptown stores that peddled what they called the Ivy League look, which was the reigning style in American men's fashion during the 1950s and much of the 1960s. In suits, that meant natural shoulders, a baggy, shapeless kind of fit, and a silhouette that conveyed only vaguely the impression that there was a man inside it.

Brooks Brothers cleaned up with something it called its No. 1 Sack Suit, which, despite its formlessness, had its own kind of social rigor. "The whole business was driven by Brooks Brothers," says Peter Rizzo. "If you were a smart guy and you wanted to be a chairman of the board, or senior level management in finance or any corporate environment, you wore Brooks Brothers."

Fred wanted to attract not just the social outcasts who, after all, had been shopping at Barneys for years. "He was enamored by WASPs," says Rizzo. "He was caught up in wanting these WASPs to come to his store. He didn't want to be referred to as the ethnic store, or the fashionable store that WASPy people did not shop in." He wanted the real thing, and accordingly marked off a section of the store for something he not so subtly called the Madison Room—Madison Avenue being the street on which Brooks Brothers did business. The name was important to Fred, and he successfully defended his right to use it against a company that made Madison shirts. The Madison Room was devoted to natural shoulder clothing. More important, it was Fred's first experiment with what today is clumsily referred to as "lifestyle selling." At the time, no one else was really doing this. Stores sold the kinds of clothes they sold, and you patronized the store that embodied the style you sought. When Fred added a new department for an entirely different kind of customer, it was still a fresh idea. Who was this person? "A guy that's pissed off at Brooks Brothers," says a former salesman. "That type of gentleman wants to come in, get to the area, look at the clothing, possibly buy something, and get the hell out. He doesn't want to know about fashion."

The Madison Room was only the beginning. In 1965, Barneys took over the second floor of the building, which had been occupied by apartments. That gave Barneys roughly double the thirty thousand square feet it used to sell menswear (the boys department downstairs used up another thirty thousand square feet). The added space gave Fred room to pursue his own ideas about how to sell clothing. For one thing, he wanted above all to shift toward a better class of merchandise, which was the way the business was going anyway. Already, Barneys sold more suits at over $95 than it sold for less, and it sold very little under $75. Fred planned to leave the cheap stuff on the main floor and use the second floor as his personal domain for selling the kind of clothing he loved.

Off to the left on the second floor, Fred later scooped out a space for the English Room, where he contrived a way to make some real money. There Fred identified and catered to all the ethnic guys who had started shopping at Barneys after the war, and were looking for clothing with a bit more class to match their growing stature. Roger Cohen, a protégé of Fred's, is more blunt about it. "That's where we got the Jewish wannabe Anglophile," says Cohen matter-of-factly. "You know, if you're trading in New York, this is a very important market, okay?"

The heart and soul of the English Room was a line of clothing called Kilgour, French and Stanbury, a name with deep roots on London's Savile Row, where it was a noted bespoke tailor. Except that Fred was having Kilgour's ready-to-wear clothing made for him by Friedman and Calender in Canada and later, after Fred got the American license for Kilgour himself, by Greif. Basically, Fred had to make this all up as he went along, which was not so easy given that no one else was doing anything quite like it at the time. It meant that Fred was, in essence, the clothing designer, as well as the merchant.

"You really had to develop your own perception of what the Englishman looks like," says Alan Katzman, who was there shortly after the creation. "Maybe it should have a hacking pocketed coat. Maybe it should be a three pocket, not two pocket. Maybe in a gabardine, it should have a welt seam in the Madison shop. In the English shop, it should not have a welt seam. Maybe the pads on the Kilgour suit should have a side buckle, rather than the belt look. You have to give Fred the credit for figuring out whether it should look like this, because this is the English shop, or it should look like that. There were no parameters, no guidelines."

The second floor also housed the Imperial Room—the name was later changed to the Oak Room, and it was moved to an even larger space on the third floor as Barneys grew. That's where Barneys carried the most expensive merchandise, brands like 3Gs and Oxxford, neither of which would sell directly to Barneys until much later. Here again was another lifestyle. Suits here cost over $100 and ran as high as $200, which, in 1964, was an awful lot of money to pay for a suit. But once again, Fred had identified a distinct type who would feel more comfortable buying clothing in a separate boutique with others of his kind.

"The Imperial Room customer was kind of a New York wise guy— you know, cuffs on the sleeves," says Roger Cohen. "It was a unique customer, not price-conscious. And there was an interesting mix of salespeople up on the floor. The manager had a pinkie ring, and he knew George Steinbrenner and the bigwigs who all came down on Saturday mornings, and it was kind of a cliquey kind of a thing."

At the other end of the spectrum lay the New Yorker Room. "Meatball stuff," Cohen calls it: cheap suits at even cheaper prices, but nonetheless a big draw for Barneys still, despite Fred's embarrassment at its existence and his refusal to spend much if any advertising money to call attention to it. "It didn't intrigue Fred, and it didn't intrigue me," says Cohen, "but it made money, okay? It was a lifestyle."

It was clearly Fred's store now, and Barney accepted the rightness of that—at least in principle, although some people say it took Bertha's firm support to overcome Barney's initial misgivings. "People thought Freddie was crazy," says Irwin Grossman. "Compared to what his father had built, he was lavish. It was done in typical Freddie style, which, to put it mildly, was somewhat above the taste level of the average rag man. People said, 'Barney, this kid is going to ruin you.' I'll never forget, I used to take my kids up there, and I'd see Barney occasionally, and I would say, 'My God, what are you doing now?' He said, 'Look, it takes one kind of a guy to start a business; it takes another kind of a guy to build a business. I started it. Freddie's building it.' And it was true."

Would that it had been so simple. Barney meant what he said, of course, but he often didn't do what he meant. He dogged Fred, needling him mercilessly. He walked five steps behind, questioning this decision and that decision. Not trying to overrule Fred, nothing like that, but finding that his good intentions alone didn't quite give him the strength to bury the instincts of forty-odd years. During those forty years, Barney Pressman had managed to make Barneys into the single biggest menswear store in the world, with sales of over $6 million in 1964, the year before Fred expanded the store the first time. And here Fred was, turning that business upside down. In the end, it took the diminutive Bertha Pressman to face Barney down. "She said, 'How are you going to observe what Fred is doing with the store when you're dead,'" is the way Roy Kramon, founder of the Majer Company and an old family friend, remembers it.

Chester Kessler marvels that Barney let it happen at all: "You know, when you think of the old store compared with the new store, in terms of the appearance of the store and in terms of the marketing of the store and the products, and the mix of the products, the type of audience, and the way they were treated—these were all tremendous changes. It took a tremendous amount of courage, on the part of Barney and Bertha, to permit this to happen. If you look at families and business, you don't see that happen very often. Most infrequently. They let him do it, and do it his way. At least whatever went on, as they say, in the privacy of their own home, I'm not privy to, but I can report based on whatever conversations I had with Barney, riding in the car.

"I'm not saying that Barney was happy every minute of the day. When I would ride with Barney, sometimes he would say, I don't know why we're doing this, but listen, what the hell do I know? But he let him do it, and when Freddie wanted a marble floor, he put in the marble floor. When he put in a staircase that he wasn't happy with, and he had another one made in Paris, and it didn't come, the store didn't open, because Fred wanted that staircase to be a dramatic part of the store. They waited for it. They let him do it. And when Fred made the first big alteration in the store, he spent an awful lot of money, because everything had to be right. Business turned lousy, and there might have been a problem, when they got short of cash. If there was any second-guessing, I'm not aware of it. I don't think anybody was. Barney figured, look, this is what we did, we'll come out of it, and of course, in a very short period of time, business turned around."

It didn't stop Fred from resenting his father's intrusions terribly. Fred swore that when it came time to pass the torch to his own kids, Gene and Bobby, he wouldn't interfere. "When the kids have it, the kids have it," he told one of his protégés at the store. "I am not going to be five feet behind them."

Eventually, whenever Barney came looking for Fred, Fred took evasive maneuvers. If Barney tracked Fred to the second floor, Fred would head down to the first. If Barney was holding forth on the first floor, Fred might hole up in the store's office across the street at 106 Seventh Avenue, refusing to enter the store at all while Barney occupied it. The two of them played a strange kind of chess game—strange considering that Barney wasn't really trying to restrain Fred at all, even though, not without reason, it often looked that way to Fred. "I could be in an office with Fred, and Barney would walk in, and Fred would say, 'Let's go.' But that was business," remembers Roger Cohen, who headed buying for international fashion later on.

Fred's personality differed enormously from his father's. In many ways, you could say he rejected everything he found in Barney Pressman's manner, even while he retained many of the virtues Barney espoused, above all, the gilt-edged assurance of his word. Outwardly, however, the two could not have been less alike, as if Barney had set a pattern for Fred to avoid. Where Barney was voluble and explosive, Fred was controlled. He could lose his temper, and often did when he found a scrap of paper out of place or a suit hanging on the wrong rack. God was very much in the details for Fred, and in the store, Fred saw himself as God's vicar. But Fred channeled his anger and leveled it at you in a focused beam, while Barney just started blasting, scattering the buckshot of his displeasure all around him.

Where Barney was doggedly intrusive, Fred was detached. Where Barney purged his frustrations in a cathartic outpouring of bile and humor, Fred nursed his cares silently and largely alone. A dressing down from Barney Pressman was an experience everyone who knew him underwent at one time or another. Barney Pressman was a *schreyer*—a Yiddish word that invests your normal howl with an added level of imprecation, calling down the wrath of heaven on injustice. But for all Barney's schreying, the smoke always cleared quickly, and with it, Barney's memory of the mayhem he had caused.

Not Freddie. When a buyer irked Fred Pressman, there would often be no rumble and no thunder—no outburst of any kind. Fred just wouldn't say good morning to the man; that was all. In fact, he wouldn't speak to him, period. "He had a habit different than his father," recalls Martin Greenfield. "He would come in, and all the buyers had to be on the floor, in their different departments, and the things that didn't sell good, I don't think Freddie would say hello to the buyer. Barney would scream. Freddie would never scream. He just ignored them."

The cold shoulder treatment could last for a long time, as Fred chewed over his resentment. Sometimes, Fred's resentment lasted forever, and the only thing to be done for it was to leave and find another job. This was rare, but it did happen. "I remember, we were in Paris at a very chic restaurant after I was with the company just two years," says Peter Rizzo, who until recently ran Barneys' menswear department and was something of a surrogate son to Fred. "We had just hired a new buyer for boys clothes, and he got very drunk at dinner. No one knew it until he was asked to comment about a business-related issue, and Fred asked him about the profitability of the business relative to margins. And the kid said, well, I think the margins are such and such. So Fred said, you're not going to make a lot of money with those margins, you know? And then the kid came back with something like, 'You want margins, Jack?' You know, in a very streety kind of way. And I saw Fred look at him. And I looked over to some of the other buyers who were with me, and we all looked at each other. And we said to ourselves, it's over. And it was over. The kid lost his job within six months. I don't think Fred ever talked to him again. Barney would have kicked him in the behind and picked him up again the next day. Everybody who worked for Fred Pressman went through spells when he didn't speak to you for long periods of time. But with Fred, you don't get picked up at some point, you're finished."

In his way, Fred was just as demanding to work for as his father, maybe more so, since Fred's bite was worse than his bark. As a result, he inspired, if not terror, then trepidation and anxiety among the salesmen on the floor when he surveyed his domain. Fred's laser vision missed almost nothing. So managers knew that Fred would immediately spot the blue blazer that was hanging out of sequence with the camel-hair sport coats. And they knew that they would hear about it from Fred. "Freddie would walk in the store and find chewing gum on the floor and bite his lip. Why is that window so dusty?" Alan Katzman remembers his early exposure to Fred. "As a kid growing up, you would say, gee, this guy is insane, and that was my opinion of Fred Pressman when I started working there. This man is sick. He's crazy. Then you begin to realize, you know, maybe he is not so crazy."

Fred also never asked a question he couldn't answer, and employees learned at their peril that it was far safer to confess ignorance than to try to snow Fred. "He would test you all the time," recalls Rizzo. " 'What do you think about this? And what do you think about that?' Something that he spent the whole night on. He probably wouldn't sleep over it, but he would figure it out by the time the morning came. You could not bullshit Fred Pressman. He wouldn't permit it. And he didn't want those kinds of people around him."

Fred usually arrived late at the store, say around 10:30 A.M., but as soon as he came through the doors from Seventh Avenue, the muffled drum signals would begin, alerting each tribe within the store to Fred's whereabouts and where he could be expected next, like an all-day weather report. No manager wanted to be caught unawares by Fred.

"Everybody wanted to make sure everything was in place when Fred came onto the floor," says Mark Woodcock, who ran the Polo department at the Seventeenth Street store in the 1980s. "So the moment that he came walking in the front door, the hostess that was sitting at the front door would immediately pick up the phone and call the second floor and say Fred's on his way up. And then when he got there, somebody else would call to say that Fred was on his way over to the English Room. His whereabouts were always totally plotted, so within thirty seconds, you knew where he was."

There was even a secret code to warn of an incoming Fred. The code name for Fred was Mr. Saunders. When a customer was waiting for service, a hostess would often page a salesman by name to meet that customer in a particular section of the store. When a salesman heard the hostess page Mr. Saunders, and ask this putative Mr. Saunders to meet a customer in, say, the Oak Room, the salesman knew immediately where Fred was heading. Everybody figured this was very clever; it proved an invaluable way to ensure that Fred never caught you with your feet on the ottoman, without alerting Fred that he was being tracked. Until the day that Fred passed one of the senior buyers, and, almost as an afterthought, turned and said, "This Mr. Saunders, he sounds like a pretty nice guy; I'd like to meet him one of these days," then smiled and walked away.

Unlike Barney, Fred could be furtive in his watchfulness. In later years, when the Oak Room had moved to the fourth floor, Fred would stand facing the private elevator in a small alcove that served his priciest department. He wouldn't actually take the elevator, but would just stand there looking at it, causing great wonderment among the sales staff. Until, much later, Chris Ryan figured out what Fred had been up to. The alcove was lined with a map of the store etched on a glass mirror. "All of a sudden I saw the mirror image off the glass on the map, and I said to myself, he can see here, here, and here. Then I went out and stood where he stands on the floor, and looked at the fitting mirrors. You could stand on the front of the floor and see back to where the overcoats were through the mirrors. This man was watching you twenty-four hours a day. Who needs cameras? This guy had his eyes."

The expansion in 1965 was only the beginning of Fred's single-minded mission to efface his father's imprint from the store. By 1968, Fred, now president of Barneys, was building again, doubling Barneys' space a second time to around 100,000 square feet. To house the expansion, Fred gobbled up still more apartments in the main building, pushing upward to give the store four floors in what would now be called America House. Fred also bought an adjacent five-story building on the corner of Seventh Avenue and Seventeenth Street, to be called International House, which would serve as the springboard for Barneys' boldest leaps into high fashion. Here Giorgio Armani's startling vision of the well-dressed male made its first appearance in the United States. Later still, young Gene Pressman, ponytail flying, used it as the laboratory for his experiments in a new alchemy of women's fashion: Can you transmute flimsy black garments into gold? The answer, it turned out, was no.

At a cost of $3.5 million, the new International House was also the Pressmans' dress rehearsal for profligate renovation on a grand scale. Its stunning success—far beyond anything Barney Pressman ever dreamed of (in later years, he would wander through the new store picking garments off the rack and muttering to salespeople nearby, "You mean people really pay this kind of money for *that?*")—only encouraged wilder excesses afterward. Among the architects who worked on the project for the designers George Nelson and Gordon Chadwick was a young man named Peter Marino, whose long association with the Pressmans would establish him as one of the most fashionable store designers in the world. It also made Marino the instrument for the Pressman family's most capricious splurges, which ultimately bankrupted them. The triumph of International House, which threw off staggering amounts of cash, led directly to the family's formulation of what could be called Pressman's law: Whatever you spend on interior decoration, you will recoup through higher-priced garments. The linear thinking behind this equation postulated a straight line sloping upward to infinity. The law has, of course, since been disproved.

*   *   *

But when Fred first bought the building, the future looked as palmy as the pear trees he successfully petitioned the city for the right to install out front on Seventh Avenue. "We didn't go into this expansion program just for volume alone, although we do expect to do more business with the added space," Fred told *The New York Times* when the store opened. "We did it to further the concept that New York City needs a large store to offer a fantastic variety of clothing to please everybody's taste."

The new store certainly did that. The International House was divided into separate boutiques dedicated to the leading design houses of Europe, including names like Cardin, Christian Dior, Brioni, and Givenchy. Such an idea was pretty much unheard-of in this country of drab suits, whose prices reflected better or worse fabrics and workmanship but never a particular designer's idea of how clothes should shape the man. That kind of peacockery had yet to make an appearance in the land of the Puritan, and Fred more than anyone else ushered it in. "The showcasing of men's fashions hasn't moved ahead at the same speed as the new inputs of fashion for men," intoned Fred.

Barney Pressman's seedy storefront, the women wearing bottomless wooden barrels, the chest-thumping signs out front—HOME OF FAMOUS BRANDS; CUT-RATE CLOTHING KING; NO BUNK, NO JUNK, NO IMITATIONS—were all gone. The world Fred was imagining—a world of well-dressed men whose getups, like the duke of Windsor's, formed part of their identity—didn't exist yet. But Barney's world was dead, at least at Barneys.

Not everyone acknowledged this. Barney himself still bestrode the sales floor, *hondling, hocking* Fred's *chinek*—literally, banging his teapot—and making Fred's life generally miserable. And with Barney were a boatload of fellows Barney called housemen—the stout, sharp-elbowed loyalists from another era who still lived by Barney's bygone verities: buy low—whatever it is—sell lower, treat the customer right, and never, ever, let him slip away empty-handed. They were Barney Pressman's roly-poly shock troops and could not be fired. Barney would never allow it, and Fred, for all the generational animosity he had stored up, would never even consider it.

That said, Fred was gently, and not so gently, nudging the housemen toward the door. First to go was Irving Parker, who had done so much to keep Barneys well stocked throughout the long embargo by the best manufacturers. By the middle 1960s, the embargo on trade with Barneys was cracking. The manufacturers realized that Fred was not only making Barneys respectable; he was making it impossible to resist. Besides, hard times had fallen on many of the retailers who had sniped at Barneys from farther uptown and pressured the suit makers to boycott it. That took the pressure off the manufacturers, and moreover, left them with some big holes to fill. Before long, Hart, Schaffner and Marx had started to sell to Barneys on the up-and-up. Hickey-Freeman finally came on board after decades of seeing its suits with the labels snipped out on sale at insulting prices. ("Moe, how do we do it!") Barneys no longer needed Irving Parker scouring the country for odd lots and overstocks to keep it supplied.

Barney tried to keep Parker busy—after all, he was the houseman's houseman. But times had changed, and Parker's style just didn't jibe with the new Barneys. "Parker would go out to buy regular goods and he was sent up to buy from me," recalls Kessler. "Now, usually, the buyers would come up, they would go through the line and make a selection, and somewhere along the line, Freddie came, and Freddie would review everything. Then the final selection was made, and the order was given. So Parker would come, and Parker would try to make a deal, and Parker was very tough. But he's not going to make a deal with me. I was not that kind of manufacturer. Once in a while, Fred would come up, and he would hear this going on, and eventually they wouldn't let Parker come to my office anymore." In 1966, Irving Parker resigned from Barneys after thirteen years there, although he continued to roam Georgia, Alabama, Mississippi, and Florida looking for suits to ship north to a Philadelphia company called Middishade, Inc.

Fred bought merchandise quite a bit differently from the way Barney bought it: He bought only what he liked, which was a novel concept at the store. With Barney, any merchandise was good merchandise at the right price. In Barney's day, for instance, Hammonton Park would iron out any billing discrepancies with suits. If, say, Barney had ended up overpaying Kessler because he had returned defective merchandise, Kessler would make good the difference at the end of the season with whatever he had left in stock and adjust the price accordingly. "It used to be very easy to make him even," says Kessler. "Ira Weiser would come up, and he'd go through the line. He'd always buy what he wanted, because he would buy everything. Ira liked the idea of running sales, or he liked the idea when something was available, to buy it. To buy it complete, not to pick."

This system broke down when Fred took over. "It got to be very hard to make them even, because half the things I would show them, they wouldn't want to buy. Fashion meant Fred's interpretation of fashion. Freddie didn't care if you gave it to him for nothing. You know, even with the shouldered pieces, if it wasn't Fred's thing, he would insult them."

There was a rage back then for iridescent sharkskin suits. The fabric was made by wrapping silk around worsted wool fibers; the blue silk wrapped around black wool gave the fabric a sheen that came off slightly sinister and, as a result, became immensely popular among the young dandies. Kessler calls it a dry fabric, meaning stiff on the hand. Kessler's piece goods buyer developed a way to get that sheen on the wool fabric without using silk, which made for a much softer fabric without sacrificing the shiny look. Hammonton Park had a field day with that fabric for nine years. "We sold thirty thousand suits a year of this one fabric; never had a markdown, never bought one yard of goods that we were not able to sell. Fred never would have it in his store, because he didn't think it was right for his store."

The transition from the old Barneys to the new took place gradually, resulting in some odd juxtapositions when the different worlds of father and son collided in the same part of the store. In the

basement, where Bertha, now seventy-two years old, still presided re-
gally over the old Barneys Boys Town, Fred took half the space for a
department he called the Underground. There Fred sold the most off-
beat fashions in the store—rock and roll plumage from places like
London's Carnaby Street. None of these fashions would be admitted
to any other reputable men's store, which made the Underground a
kind of hidden shrine for hipsters. Also for the salesmen who worked
there—and who did double duty fitting the pudgy bar mitzvah boys
from the neighboring Boys Town's Husky department.

The salesmen were almost all homosexual, often chosen for their
lithe good looks by the Underground's manager, a flamboyant queen
named Jimmy Nielsen. One of the salesmen specialized in giving initiated customers oral sex in the fitting rooms, which amused Jimmy
Nielsen heartily. A visitor who descended the staircase from Barneys'
main floor would come upon a surreal tableau: Bertha Pressman, ar-
rayed like the dowager empress she still was but propped shakily against
a clothing rack, since she had become too frail to stand unsupported;
a gaggle of plump adolescents on the threshold of manhood with their
anxious, high-strung mothers fluttering around them; and Jimmy and
his entourage, whom Jimmy would summon by crooking his finger and
commanding, "Italian queen [or Chinese queen], come here!" Jimmy
would have to bribe the Italian and Chinese queens with extra commissions to wait on the bar mitzvah boys, but their distaste was still
palpable. They much preferred to huddle in their own enclave, hung
with photos of Jean Harlow and The Supremes. Just to complete this
otherworldly scene, in comes an Italian tailor, one of the old-timers
who had spent three decades doing Barneys' free alterations.

"Sal Leviari commuted from Philadelphia each day to get to the
store, and Sal would serenade the customers with 'It's Impossible.' That
was his theme song during that period. 'It's *impossible*, da, da, da-da-
da, da-da, it's just impossible.' It was very sad, but he was a mainstay
there, and, of course, a whiz as a tailor," recalls Donald White, who
worked there as a salesman in the late '60s.

Bertha Pressman willed herself to stand like a tiny flagpole in her cockeyed kingdom, eight hours a day, for close to fifty years. Two years later, in 1972, Bertha Pressman died.

A year later, so did her daughter, Elizabeth, Fred's sister. No one ever speaks about Elizabeth to this day. The family's explanation for Elizabeth's untimely death is heart attack. Close friends of the family know Elizabeth committed suicide.

The odor of cut-rate clothing still clung to a few racks in the store for another few years, but in 1975, Fred purged it for good. Fred loved Oxxford clothes—Oxxford made perhaps the most prestigious and expensive American suit—and he wore them faithfully, but Barneys still couldn't legitimately sell Oxxford. Oxxford was a stickler for propriety and the last holdout when all the other manufacturers had acknowledged Barneys' reformed character. Barney Pressman had been a particular thorn in Oxxford's side, and Oxxford had a long memory. In the early 1960s, a top-of-the-line Oxxford suit might run $300, and cost an Oxxford store $160. Barneys would sell it for $125 to $150, because Irving Parker had snagged a few from other stores for $80, and Barney Pressman took a notoriously short markup on the merchandise. If other retailers hated Barneys, Oxxford retailers considered it "a cancer for the industry," remembers Neil O'Brien, the Irish kid first hired by Oxxford's Jewish owners to handle non-Jewish accounts.

The trouble was, Oxxford's fancy New York outlets were dropping dead. De Pinna had closed up, and so had Abercrombie and Fitch. Leighton's, which got the showbiz crowd, was on the point of expiring, chiefly because street crime was menacing the entire Times Square area around Leighton's and killing the business.

"So the Oxxford customer base had shrunk to virtually nothing in America's most powerful city," recalls O'Brien. "And all of a sudden one day in the trade paper, I read that Fred Pressman was taking over the Barneys business. And he was going to take them in a new direction and make them a so-called legitimate store. So I'm sitting over in the New York Hilton Hotel one day with Jack McDonald, who was then president of Oxxford, and he says, what are we going to do in New York? And I said, the people I talk to in the business say the only store to sell in New York now is Barneys. He said, are you nuts? He said, they're a discounter! I said, well, the rumor is that they're moving out of that. He said, do you know the kind of heat I would get if I ever sold Barneys? But he comes back to the hotel the next day, and he said, call Fred Pressman.

"So I called and I immediately got put through to his secretary, whose name was Miss Terry, and I said my name is Neil O'Brien, and I'm with Oxxford Clothes. She said, he's in Europe and isn't due back for a couple of weeks, but she says, I have a feeling he would like to talk to you."

A secret meeting was arranged for several weeks later between Fred and Jack McDonald—at a neutral site so no one could spot McDonald near the store. McDonald didn't succumb easily. "Of course, McDonald was all negative about the reputation of the company, and how damaging it could be to him personally—almost more than to Oxxford—to sell to Fred Pressman. But Fred was very low-key and not hard to like, particularly when he wanted to put on the charm. I found him exceedingly charming.

"So McDonald says, Fred, if I sell you Oxxford, you've got to promise me that you'll buy five hundred units a season, and that you'll never put any on sale. He says, no problem. So we sat down, and we did business. And for the next fifteen years Fred would come to Chicago twice a year with his buying team to buy Oxxford, even if he only stayed two hours. He would come out of respect to the product. He would arrive in the office at eleven, and he would look at the swatches for an hour, make a few suggestions. He was color-blind, but he would never admit it, and the way he dressed, you would say to yourself, my God, corduroy pants, some strange jacket, the suede shoes, a tie that doesn't match. He owned the most valuable clothing store in America! But he had an incredible sense of the expression of clothing. He would love to put on a coat and look in the mirror—not looking at himself, but to see how that coat looked.

"From then on, whenever I did a trunk show, he was there. Now here's the man, the president of a multimillion-dollar corporation on the clothing floor doing trunk shows. You don't see that anywhere else. We used to always have lunch down there, and of course we would always have dinner at night. He would bring the whole crew of fifteen or so people to Joe and Rose's steak house, where Fred liked to eat. The boys, too, Gene and Bobby, maybe two dozen times.

"He bought those five hundred units season in and season out. And finally in about 1986, I saw this incredible inventory of Oxxford building up at this store. So I finally went to McDonald and I said, there's something wrong here. They're not selling this product as well as they should. So Fred said, well, you told me I could never put it on sale. And I said, Fred, that's true, we did, but we only meant you could never promote it. He said, you mean you won't object if I get rid of the old inventory on sale? I said, no. He said, Jesus, you would do me the biggest favor anyone could ever do me. He said, I want to continue to buy five hundred units a season. He still always bought five hundred units. Might have been four-ninety-eight one season, five-oh-four the next season. Five hundred units. Until my days were over with him.

"But as soon as the boys started going off on different tangents, and apparently started the infighting among themselves, they were never to be seen. And when you did see them, you had to be reintroduced to them. They completely had forgotten—not that I was that important, but I was a very close friend of their father by that time. And it was like, I've never seen you before in my life, nice to meet you."

UNO DEI GRANDI MAESTRI

Whenever Fred Pressman discovered Italy in the 1950s, Italy was in pretty sorry shape. The war had obliterated much of Italy's manufacturing base, and much of its industry remained hobbled and backward. Italy stayed a nation of artisans and close-knit family businesses. That had always been the source of its creative strength, as Italians never tire of telling you with great pride. The so-called economic miracle that made Italy an industrial dynamo and, not coincidentally, helped make Fred Pressman a very rich man, still lay some years off.

In the 1950s, an Italian man bought a suit maybe once every four years. Close to 90 percent of those suits were made by a tailor hunched over a sewing machine. Ten years later, this had changed only slightly. In the 1960s, Italians bought a suit every two years now, and tailors made around 70 percent of them. The manufactured clothing business was virtually nonexistent.

Fortunately, the country was overrun by tailors. Back then, Italy could field an army of perhaps 100,000 tailors, each producing something on the order of seventy suits a year, or just over one a week. That hardly equipped Italy to compete as a power in the global clothing trade, but that mattered little, because there *was* no global clothing trade to speak of. Certainly, wealthy men of fashion might have their clothes made elsewhere, say by one of the bespoke tailors of London's Savile Row, or even in Rome, where many of the ingenious tailors from the south of Italy had migrated after the war. But for the masses, clothing was bought where it was made.

The tailors of Rome were perhaps the first to attempt to extend their influence beyond their native land in any serious way. The English tailors liked serving their elite clientele and were little tempted to court the rabble. When Fred Pressman finally convinced Huntsman, the great Savile Row tailors, to let him carry its ready-to-wear goods, long after he had made Barneys the premier merchant of international clothing, Fred had one request: Change the color of the red linings in Huntsman's blazers. "Then I would presume you don't want Huntsman after all," replied Ian Hunt, the head of Huntsman. No, no, protested Fred—I love the blazers, just take out the red linings is all. "You're saying you don't really want Huntsman," replied Hunt stonily. Fred said the red lining would do just fine, but Hunt's attitude typified that of many of the finest English tailors and held them back. As for the French, they had yet to make their mark on the world of men's clothing and would prove a brilliant flash in the pan. But as in so many things, it was the French who coined the word for it—*prêt-à-porter* ("ready to wear").

Giovanbattista Giorgini, an Italian clothing buyer, is often credited with putting Italian fashion on the map when he organized the first fashion shows for Italian couturiers and tailors at Florence's Grand Hotel in 1951. Shortly after, the Accadèmia dei Sartori held its first fashion show in Rome. Around the same time, a prestigious jury made up of Italy's star tailors bestowed its first Forbici d'Oro award—the Golden Scissors—on Saint Homobonus' Day to the best tailor under the age of thirty-five. Saint Homobonus, by the way, is the patron saint of tailors.

The first flowering of Italian fashion took place in Rome. The Eternal City both provided the stage set and made the costumes for La Dolce Vita, the city's day-to-day pleasure chase that Federico Fellini turned into one of his greatest films. Roman tailors like Brioni, Caraceni, Cifonelli, and Cucci cut the clothes for *la bella figura*—the splashy impression that scores more points on the Italian social scale than anywhere else in the world.

The Roman look was not an easy sell to Americans, even though the war had exposed so many of them to Italy's caress. The suits were often outlandish and overdone in the smarmiest kind of way—lounge lizard couture at its most reptilian. The jacket had sloping but clearly marked shoulders, tapering violently to below the hips, while the trousers hugged the pelvis insinuatingly and stayed scandalously close to the leg on their way down, ending abruptly with no cuff. It was a disreputable look for people clearly up to no good, albeit in the most winning kind of way. Ironically, the Italians had interpolated this look from the American GIs who sashayed through Rome in tight-fitting blue jeans and chinos. This, however, was not what we had in mind at all for business dress. It was all well and good for buzzing around Rome on a Vespa, but it merited censorious clucking on Main Street, U.S.A.

In 1955, Brioni, perhaps the most export-minded of the great Italian tailoring concerns, launched what it called the *Ordine Dorico*, or Doric column look. Brioni, named for a posh resort island off Trieste, was founded by Nazareno Fonticoli, the inside man who did the cutting, and Gaetano Savini, the business partner and outside man. The partners chose the name for its uniquely Italian resonance, a signal that the country would now trumpet its native traditions when doing business abroad. Their first show in the United States exposed Americans to a palette they had never seen before—at least in a suit: Mediterranean blue, Capri red, Venetian reddish-yellow, and burnt sienna. And still Fred Pressman bought, seeing in the painstaking workmanship and fine fabrics a whole new direction for Barneys, which became the first retailer to carry Brioni in New York.

"Fred made me a hero," recalls Joseph Barato, now president of Brioni in the United States. "He took the line, even though it was just terrible—awful! He just knew it had incredible tailoring and fabric, and that we would move it in the styling direction he had in mind. He was a pain in the ass, Fred; insistent, no compromise, but he always knew where he was going."

Sure enough, Fred soon started nudging the Italians in his own relentless way. "The other stores were just buying—they wanted, how you say, tchotchkes," says Pepino Pesci of Brioni. "Fred wanted a different expression—the Barneys touch." For instance, Fred took Brioni's Pincio model, named for the terrace overlooking Rome's Piazza del Popolo, and completely reworked it. "Our basic model was very narrow, with stiff shoulders, which you couldn't sell to anybody outside Italy. We absorbed many of Fred's lessons ourselves."

Not surprisingly, it took the French to translate this Latin version of American swagger into big business overseas. In contrast with Italy, France had almost no tailors: around ten thousand in 1955, and barely two thousand by 1967, according to Farid Chenoune's authoritative *A History of Men's Fashion* (Paris: Flammarion). But it had preserved a great deal more of its industrial base. More important, France had invented the job of fashion designer. Ever since 1858, when Charles Frederick Worth had set himself up in Paris as the first "man-milliner," the French had been telling women how to dress, and they had grown quite comfortable with their authority. It was a short leap of imagination to apply the same thinking to menswear. The first person to do this on a grand scale was someone named Pierre Cardin.

A short footnote here. Long before Pierre Cardin came along, Barney Pressman had the same idea. It was before the war, and Barney was, of course, fuming, because he was always fuming at something. This time he was furious at the 150 tailors who executed Barneys' free alterations—a big calling card for the store. "So Barney says, 'I'm having a lot of trouble with the tailors,' " Irwin Grossman recalls vividly. "I say, 'That's a problem.' He says, 'You know what? I watch them marking with a piece of chalk. Goddamn chalk is *this thick.* I'm sure the next day the customer comes back, he says it's too long or too short.' Barney says, 'You know, these goddamn tailors, they think they know everything. You know what I want to do? I'm going to hire designers to do my alteration department.' I say, 'Barney . . .' He says, 'I don't give a shit. I'm going to advertise it: Your alterations are being done not by a tailor but by a designer!' He wanted me to interview designers and so forth. Well, at least until I talked him out of the idea." And that is how men's fashion designers did not come to America.

Cardin launched his first menswear collection in 1960, and by 1965 he had turned himself into an international phenomenon. In retrospect, Cardin had a much keener head for business than an eye for line, and it is in business that his lasting influence is still felt. Cardin discovered the true leverage of licensing—making a name through showmanship and personal flair and letting others spread that name by putting up the money, making the clothes, and taking all the financial risks. The weakness here is that the licensor often maintains at best a tenuous control over the products that go out under his name, but Cardin didn't care much about that. He licensed his name out pro-miscuously, flooding the market with indifferently tailored clothing that acquired a cult following by virtue of Cardin's superb marketing instincts. Chenoune reports that by 1965, 500,000 men were wearing the Cardin label bought from 900 outlets—700 of them outside of France. By 1966, *The New York Times* had declared Cardin "the name to drop in men's fashion these days."

Like the Ordine Dorico, the Cardin silhouette fit columns better than people, or at least better than American people. This did little to slow down Cardin's "concept looks" with names like "cylinder," "stick," and "tube." Cardin had decreed that it should be so. "The he-man look is out of date," he pontificated in a 1966 magazine article. "Today's fashion is extra-slim in every sphere, from lighters to wallets, via husbands." This was youth fashion with a vengeance, but, for the first time, youth held the upper hand in determining what their elders should be wearing. To quote Chenoune: "There is no better proof of Pierre Cardin's enormous influence on the appearance of ordinary men than the proliferation of spare tires bulging out of highly tapered nylon shirts or the countless buttocks and hips squeezed into low-waisted, poorly-cut Dacron trousers."

No one cashed in on Cardin more heartily than Fred Pressman, who had already sensed a change in the prevailing winds of fashion. Bonwit Teller was the first store in the United States to carry a small selection of Cardin, and Barneys followed soon after with a much broader commitment to the French designer. Other stores carried a smattering of Cardin and Brioni, although, in truth, not that many. Bloomingdale's stuck Cardin in the basement at first. Fred staked the future of his store on Cardin, Christian Dior, and a handful of other European designers like Yves Saint Laurent and Gilbert Feruch—the much-reviled creator of the Nehru jacket. This was the foundation of Fred's $3.5 million dream for the International House back in 1968.

"In those days, there was no European fashion," says Peter Rizzo, one of Fred's most trusted lieutenants, and ultimately the head of all Barneys menswear business until he left the store in 1997. "There wasn't a well-developed cross section of European clothing. It was either low in a cheap way or very high. So Fred had all the top stuff and all the bottom stuff. There was no middle. No one else carried it. Department stores were all stocked with American goods in those days. No European clothing anywhere except for Barneys and maybe a handful at very small specialty stores. You had the market cornered. You had locked up all the big brands."

Fred gambled big not so much because he trusted Cardin's staying power—he knew better than any of his customers how shoddy many of Cardin's slinky jackets really were—but because he knew with certainty that designers like Cardin would replace manufacturers as the engine of men's fashion. He knew, too, that most of those designers, not to mention the clothes they made, would come from Europe—a pretty daring insight in a country that made 99 percent of its garments at home.

Barneys International House opened on the evening of September 29, 1970. In attendance were the fashion world's royalty: From

France, Marc Bohan of Christian Dior, Gilbert Feruch, Philippe Venet, and Hubert de Givenchy; from England, Hardy Amies and Lewis Stanbury of Kilgour, French and Stanbury; and from Italy, Bruno Piatelli. They were awaiting annointment by Fred. Pierre Cardin sent regrets. He was opening his own store in France the next day.

"Great designers have proven themselves," was the solemn quote from Fred on page one of the menswear industry's trade paper, Fairchild's *Daily News Record,* two months after International House opened. "And the whole menswear industry is watching," the trade paper added. "On the sidelines, there is a big audience of menswear retailers and manufacturers wondering how Pressman's plans for a total menswear department store will work out."

Predictably, Cardin waned almost as fast as he waxed. The French, it has often been pointed out, are lousy at team sports. They seem to mistrust one another almost as much as they mistrust outsiders. The clothing business is very much a team sport, requiring cooperation among a variety of sportsmen with complementary skills. The Italians, with their long history of interdependent artisans, adapted to this new global system with a silken ease that goes far to explain why they eclipsed the French so easily and so quickly by the mid-1970s.

Before Cardin's star fell for good, however, Fred Pressman made a mint off him—and vice versa. Pierre Cardin is not a poor man today, although he relies on the royalties from licensing his name for much of his income. In the early seventies, just after the International House opened, Barneys was selling ten thousand suits a season from Cardin and Yves Saint Laurent, who followed on Cardin's dandified coattails— a staggering number. Says Roger Cohen: "It was really rock and roll. Fred taught me how to make a lot of money for him."

The International House had also inadvertently spawned another cash cow for Barneys, which Fred regarded to the end of his days with an uneasy mingling of greed and regret. Like other, grander expansion schemes to follow, the International House opened late and over budget. When the store finally opened, half of it had still not been completed. Clothing inventory ordered for the new, bigger Barneys built up and sat around. At the same time, the bottom was falling out of the clothing business, and many of the entrenched New York specialty stores were forced to close their doors for good.

Times got very tough. Fred Pressman had pushed Barneys so far so fast that the downturn in the market left it reeling. It was then that the housemen hit on a plan straight from the store's heyday. Barneys would hold a five-day warehouse sale, with discounts as much as 50 percent—all sales in cash. To supplement the slow-moving merchandise it wanted to get rid of, Barneys would call on all its steady suppliers to ante up goods at distress prices. "Every manufacturer had to contribute something—not cash, merchandise," says Irwin Grossman, whose Austin Leeds label took a big hit in the sale. "The pain of sending out the bill was a real lesson."

The warehouse sale turned into a bonanza for Barneys and quickly became a New York institution. With discounts so steep, it seemed as if half of New York turned out for the sale. Lines wound around the block, and people waited as long as two hours in the rain behind police barricades just to enter. Inside, it was pandemonium, and so it has remained in the twenty-eight years since. Fred was furious: fire-sale prices, lines of drooling bargain hunters waiting to scavenge through his beloved merchandise like Visigoths looting Rome. This is the way Chester Kessler remembers it: "Every executive in that company had to fight like hell to get Freddie to accept that concept. He just didn't want to have it. He didn't come to work, because he couldn't stand to see those people standing in line around the block, waiting to get in to buy clothing. That is not the way he wanted this business to be."

First off, there was the problem of the white suits—thousands of them for a sale due to end Labor Day, the end of summer. Fred blew a fuse, and went gunning for Ira Weiser. For all the weight he carried, Weiser was not an easy man to outmaneuver. Weiser knew Fred was coming, and asked one of his old manufacturing cronies to page him at the warehouse just when Fred found him. The manager gives him the phone, and Ira screams, "Goddamn motherfucker, look what you did to me! You sent me all the white goods."

A few days later, Ira Weiser called Grossman. "The son of a bitch, he wants me to stop the sale!" Weiser fumed to Grossman—the son of a bitch being Fred. "We're going to get killed if we stop it." Reason prevailed, but not before Fred, who had fled to Puerto Rico rather than witness the barbaric spectacle taking place, had telegrammed three agonized words to Grossman: "End the sale!" The sale continued, but that was the beginning of the end for Ira Weiser, who finally resigned in 1975.

Nor would Fred ever feel tempted to end the sale thereafter, no matter how much he hated its vulgarity. He simply started making too much money off it. The first warehouse sale may have been intended to dispose of excess merchandise, but it didn't stay that way for long. Barneys' immense clout with manufacturers allowed Fred and his buyers to purchase goods specifically for the sale and still mark them up 100 percent—even at 50 percent off the retail price. Sometimes more than that. One salesman remembers buying Greif suits for $38 and selling them in the warehouse at $242. Basically, Fred was now in a position to exact tribute from manufacturers who wouldn't walk down the same side of the street with his dad.

"That's how good it was," says Tony Consulos, one of Fred's shrewd band of buyers for many years. "Why would vendors sell to the warehouse sale? Because we buy so much. No vendor ever walked away from us. Hickey-Freeman was one of the biggest contributors. And I would determine how they cut it: I would tell them what sizes we wanted, and I wouldn't have to take delivery of the goods—they would warehouse it. To a manufacturer, the most important thing, as I learned through the years, was to keep their production going."

In reality, that 50-percent-off figure is a bit misleading, too, because Barneys was not above inflating the purported retail price of some goods to cushion the blow when Barneys later swore that it had cut that price in half. Few people ever wondered, half of what? "The stuff that they could buy at off-price was actually priced higher than the comparable stuff in the store," says a salesman. "For instance, if, say, the comparable suit retails in the store at, say, $395, it would be marked at $495 in the warehouse sale, and then at half off it would sell at $250."

The salesmen cleaned up. It was a long day—from seven in the morning to ten at night—under the most trying conditions, namely, a bargain-crazed crowd of New Yorkers. Given the nature of the mission, only volunteers were called up. Barneys compensated these front-line troops with the haberdasher's equivalent of hazardous-duty pay. Commissions were doled out in cash, at least until the warehouse sale started accepting credit cards in 1988 and written records made this unkosher arrangement imprudent.

In the early 1980s, a salesman working in a two-man team would pocket $0.50 for every suit he sold, and $0.25 for a pair of slacks. After the sale period was extended, it was not unusual for a salesman to rake in $2,500 for a ten-day stint, a hefty take in those days. The bills got peeled off huge wads of cash that piled up in what they called the "money room." At the end of the sale's first day, that room might hold over a $1 million in small bills—"Fred's spending money," the employees called it. At its peak in the mid-1990s, Fred's spending money amounted to as much as $15 million, and Fred had probably forgotten that he ever barked at Ira Weiser to cancel the first warehouse sale.

Fred was also minting money at Barneys across the street. By 1975, the store's revenues had reached an estimated $34 million, and were showing no signs of slowing down. Fred's big gamble on the International House had paid off spectacularly. Most of the original designers were licensing their names, either to U.S. manufacturers like Irwin Grossman or to Fred himself, who would find factories to manufacture the licensed clothing directly. Fred got very cozy, for instance, with Maurice Biederman, a Parisian charmer who manufactured some of the Cardin goods, and later manufactured Yves Saint Laurent. Fred bought much of this merchandise directly from Biederman in francs.

This proved a godsend, since Fred could keep the price he paid for merchandise low and still charge a higher price for labels with the novelty of international cachet. Fred would purchase a boatload of Biederman's indifferently made suits, slap a continental-sounding label on them, and charge whatever he thought the market would bear. Oftentimes, a suit that sold in Barneys for $175 would cost no more than $60 from Biederman. Kilgour, French and Stanbury, later licensed to Barneys itself, brought margins over 70 percent—an unheard-of level of profit in the men's clothing business.

"Botany made Christian Dior, we made the better Cardin—all the designers' names were tacked onto a domestic product. And it did not differ much from what you would deliver under a nondesigner label," says Grossman. "But it was revelation to the retailer. We sold Barneys' Cardin and we sold our own labels, and in many cases they were similar. We used to laugh at designer labels because the first ones that were brought in were so damned tight and so small that the average American couldn't get into them. They don't laugh no more."

By the middle 1970s, Fred had assembled an eager cadre of Young Turks to do his bidding. The money they made was flowing freely, and they dressed better than anybody who made more. And they worshiped Fred as some kind of mystical clothing god who would mold them into merchants in his image. There could be no better model for a clothing man. Among the young men Fred hired to introduce America to European clothing were Eddie Glantz, Roger Cohen, and, a bit later, Peter Rizzo. All of them still look back on those years as being present at the Creation.

"Fred was a mentor to me, whether people liked him or didn't like him, because Fred wasn't an easy person to get along with," says Glantz. "But if Fred liked you, you could do anything—you were gold. He was able to see things in the future, and I was one of the lucky ones to be around that. I learned something new every day. I just picked up on it, ate it up, lived to do it better than I thought I could. I've always had balls the size of my computer, and besides, I was young and didn't really give a shit.

"The clientele didn't get it right away. But then, before I could even call anybody, my old customers from the store where I had worked uptown were slowly drifting downtown. I'd see them on a Saturday, or Thursday night. You know, Barneys was just getting to be known in fashion. And all of a sudden the salespeople are moving. Someone just came in and bought two thousand dollars' worth of shirts, ties, and sweaters. You know? That's the way they shopped. I would tell them what to buy—you buy the color line, for instance: You like the sweater, it comes in four colors, you buy all four. It's a whole different mentality than today.

"The people I hung around with had fathers who owned companies; the kids had money to spend. And they spent it on clothing. I had kids in their twenties, my age, who would buy things and I'd have to send it to their laundry so their wives or their mothers didn't know they were spending so much dough. Grown men who bought so much that I would send it to the dry cleaner, because I couldn't send it to their house, so it would come back in a dry cleaning bag. The men at that moment were becoming peacocks. All of a sudden, a guy would walk out on the street and somebody'd say, you look great, great suit! No one ever said that to him before. No one ever commented on this guy's clothing before. I mean, guys weren't supposed to get noticed for their clothing. And the moment someone says that to you, you go back and get about five more."

To supply this new breed of peacocks, Fred and Eddie Glantz were regularly scouring the northern Italian countryside, pulling piece goods out of the newly minted factories in the north for next to nothing and marking them up three, maybe four times. And still the clothes were a bargain at the price, so high were the standards of tailoring and manufacturing compared with suits made in the States. That, and of course Fred's own exacting specifications to improve them.

Fred was a hard-bitten negotiator, and he taught all his buyers that the huge profits he aimed to extract would come primarily from their skill in buying, because there is always an upper limit to how much you can charge for merchandise, but there is no lower limit to how little you can pay. No matter what price Fred got from a vendor, his face would contort sharply, as if an acute gas pain had struck him suddenly. One buyer calls it "the classic Fred wince." The startled vendor would lower the price, and Fred would wince again, "until you got it to like twenty-five points off the cost," recalls Patrick Gates, who got to know Fred well when he worked at the store much later.

"When I worked at Neiman Marcus, we would negotiate too, but we never negotiated like that. I mean there was a certain dignified level at which you did business. You don't act like you're at a flea market. But it became fun. Fred didn't believe in making the consumer pay for it. He wanted you to get it out of the hide of the vendor. Gene was not at that level. He would show up at the runway shows, he understood the product, and he had great taste, but he didn't get down to the nitty-gritty the way Fred did."

The devastation of the war proved an unlikely boon to the Italian clothing business, as it turned out. America's gift for industrial organization had led it to develop the means to clothe its masses while the rest of the world was still patronizing local tailors and seamstresses one by one.

By the end of World War II, however, much of the technology that America had been using for decades had grown old and hopelessly out-of-date. The problem was compounded by rigid union regulations that stifled whatever drive there might have been to rethink how clothes could be produced. Clothing came in six grades, six being the top of the line, according to a system developed by the Amalgamated Clothing Workers of America. If a manufacturer wanted a hand-sewn buttonhole on a grade-two suit, he found himself suddenly making a grade-four suit, since the hand-sewn buttonhole automatically boosted the suit two grades up. That meant that the manufacturer had to pay the workers who sewed the pockets at grade-four scale. The result: no hand-sewn buttonholes on the grade-twos.

The Europeans, and the innovation-minded Italians in particular, had neither the burden of outmoded machinery nor entrenched and powerful unions to contend with. What they did have was a hunger to learn and the aptitude to succeed. If they could make a cheap suit better by sewing the buttonholes by hand, then that's exactly what they did, without incurring a host of higher labor costs along with it.

Starting shortly after the war, American tailors, many of Italian descent, returned to the old country in a loosely organized lend-lease operation of their own. The know-how to build a modern clothing manufacturing industry in Italy came from the United States, but with the freedom to discard whatever was hidebound over here and start from scratch. Chester Kessler's own factory in Hammonton Park, New Jersey, saw one of its prized technicians answer the call and return to Europe after the war to lend a hand.

Within fifteen years, the Italians had built up a superb manufacturing base of their own. They already had the finest woolen mills in the hills around Biella and Prato, up north where the mountain water runs off the Alps. Many of the woolen mills, like those of Carlo Barbera and Ermenegildo Zegna, were starting to weave their own plush woolens and buttery cashmeres into suits themselves. And farther east, along the corridor that runs from Milan to Venice hugging the Dolomites, factories were springing up for less expensive commercial goods.

Fred and his young scouts had a field day. Fred met Mino Nicoletto, owner of a small company called Belvest at Florence's Grand Hotel in 1972. It was love at first sight. "I knew when he took the jacket in his hands that I was dealing with *uno dei grandi maestri* [one of the great masters]," says Ivaldo Marchiore, now Belvest's head tailoring technician. "He was never in doubt. I said to Zopito, my teacher, Zopito, see this guy, how he takes the jacket in his hands."

Fred was what the Italians call a *pignolo*—a tough nut. "It's not true he was difficult—he only got furious if you didn't give him what he wanted. He wanted the jacket to flow when you bent over—he hated when the jacket would ride up. For me, it was always a pleasure to work with him, because he always made you try to do it better. He was a *punto di riferimento*—a point of reference. Not like his son Gene. *Troppo veloce*—too fast."

It's easy to overlook Gene's presence at Barneys during the years when Fred was transforming the character of the store Gene would inherit along with his brother, Bobby. Many people did. Gene graduated from Syracuse University in 1973, and, like Fred after his Army service, enjoyed a brief interlude when he batted around the fantasy that he wouldn't end up working for his dad. First came an obligatory four months extending the wild partying that had occupied most of his time at school. Then it came time to buckle down to some serious self-delusion: Hollywood, the movies.

"I had no intention of working for Barneys," he told the *Daily News Record* in a remarkably candid 1979 interview. "I was working at Paramount, kind of gofering and trying to be an assistant director. I was twenty, and no one wanted to hear about some young whippersnapper of twenty doing anything in Hollywood, so that lasted about six months. I didn't like L.A. I didn't even like the weather, so I came back to New York and kind of contemplated what I was going to do. I hung out in Westchester for a few months doing nothing, and I got very bored. I had always thought Barneys was a nice store. I mean, I respected what my father and grandfather did, and I'm one of those people who fall into things. So I started working here and I've been here for seven years."

Gene's early years at the store differed markedly from Fred's. "Well, basically, I could do anything I wanted, so I went into the management end of the business first," Gene recalled with the kind of breathtaking guilelessness that only people who believe they truly deserve their good fortune display. "For the first three years, I sort of revamped the operation and changed a lot of the management. I guess I brought the basic operating philosophy of the store up to date. I had done pretty much what I set out to do with the operations. So I said, Okay, it's time, I guess, to move on to the next thing."

"Gene joins the store, and he comes to Europe. Fred says, take him with you," Eddie Glantz picks up the story. "He didn't say, okay, put him under your wing and teach him the business. Fred's the teacher. I was still the pupil. But I took Gene. In Paris, we used to stay at the Paris Hilton, which is right near the Eiffel Tower. For me, Paris is Paris, and a hotel is a place to sleep. We arrive at ten o'clock at night—Gene's first trip for the store—and all the luggage doesn't come off the plane. Gene's bag was missing. We got to the hotel at twenty after twelve, and they didn't have our rooms, and we needed a place to stay.

All they had was one big suite, so I said, fine, we'll take it. Gene takes the bedroom, I'll sleep on the folding bed, and Alan Katzman, the other buyer, will sleep on another folding bed. I'm opening my bag and taking out my toothbrush to brush my teeth, and Gene is on the phone and he says, my father wants to talk to you. Okay?

"I said, Fred, I don't control the airline. Yeah, they had no room. The best I could do. He said, okay, make sure Gene calms down. And Fred was calm at the time, you know. It's very easy to get excited on the phone. I mean, I'm doing the best I can. If you wanted me to take him and you rely on me for my judgment and my expertise, then you have to rely that I'm doing the best I can. It's not that I put him in the single room and took the suite. Or I was sleeping in the bedroom and I'm making him sleep on the sofa. Or I lost his bags on purpose. What do you want from my life? Shit happens, as they say.

"Next morning, Gene gets up, and we have an appointment, but he disappears—runs out and buys a couple of suits so he'd have new clothes to wear. And of course his bag comes at ten o'clock the next morning, anyway. That night we go to dinner. Gene, not naive, just a poor little rich kid with a tradition that he's thinking of following. He takes me to L'Orangerie—great restaurant. And it was a great experience, and he gets the check and he says to me, Ed, do me a favor. Don't tell my father we went here. I thought it was very funny. He could spend it because he understood it, but he doesn't want me to tell his father. And Gene and I became friends. A good heart—and I say it fondly—but it was the silver spoon that got in his way. Hey, God bless him. I was never that fortunate."

Around this time, Bruno Piatelli's daughter Barbara was being kidnapped by Italy's Red Brigade. What the Red Brigade didn't know was that Bruno Piatelli was not a wealthy man. He was successful, certainly, but he essentially ran a small, exclusive clothing shop in Rome. When the kidnappers looked at all the clothing bearing a Piatelli label in flowing, reddish script, they were really seeing Fred Pressman's handiwork. Fred had cultivated a warm friendship with Piatelli, who licensed his name to Fred. Fred then commissioned whatever he wanted made from Mino Nicoletto at Belvest.

"There was probably a document, not very long, and not very involved, where we guaranteed X amount of money, not a big fee, to Bruno, and we could execute the goods any way we wanted to execute them," says Roger Cohen. "It had nothing to do with what he carried in his store. So if we had a tie maker that we had a good relationship with, or we had a shirt maker that we had a good relationship with, or a suit maker, then we went and we put the Piatelli label on these products. And he really didn't review it, because he trusted our integrity, which is very important."

The kidnapping shattered Piatelli, and for over a year, someone manned the telephone twenty-four hours a day so as not to miss a call from the kidnappers. "This was an Italian kidnapping," points out Eddie Glantz. Ultimately, Piatelli paid the ransom and Barbara was returned safe and sound, but it was Fred Pressman who fronted much of the money to secure her release. Those were the kinds of relationships Fred formed over there.

Italy bestowed on Fred a kind of peace that slipped through his fingers in New York. He still never slept, but the tension and worry that hung from Fred's face would lift. He was doing what he loved best, splashing happily in the pool of pure taste, his true element. Dinner in Italy would last until well after midnight, at which point Fred would profit from the six-hour time difference to call the store in New York, which wouldn't close until 3:00 A.M. Tuscan time. By 7:30 that morning, he would be at breakfast with his lieutenants, happily mapping out another day of ties, shoes, gloves, and shirts, his lucky loden hat packed away for the day's journey to the next hill town. He once told Peter Rizzo, "I wish I could turn it off sometimes, do something else, but I can't. My mind just works twenty-four hours a day, thinking about the same things." Says Rizzo, "He had the single-mindedness of a great religious person."

Fred's success did not go unnoticed. Some years later, just before

Bergdorf Goodman opened its men's store in 1991, Ira Neimark, Bergdorf's chairman, flew over to Italy to woo Mino Nicoletto and contract Belvest to make private-label goods for his new store. Jeremy Hull, an Englishman who represents Belvest abroad, advised in favor. It would have been a big score for Belvest. "Mino said, 'I just can't do it and be embarrassed in front of my friend Fred,' " recalls Hull. "Neimark knew he had to respect that."

In Biella, Fred romanced Luciano Barbera, whose father, Carlo Barbera, founded the mill that made the finest grade of cashmere—the one they call white cashmere, even though it comes in any shade. Chanel buys Barbera's brown cashmere, a lower grade. Together, Fred and Luciano Barbera munched dozens of the cream-filled wafers that Barbera had made especially for him by a local baker. And while they ate, they reveled in their shared habits, like wearing thick gray flannel trousers in the heat of summer, just because they adored the feel of the thick fabric.

Barbera, still tall and slim, has the natural authority of a practiced aristocrat. You can easily picture him with a jacket of heavy Biella wool draped around his shoulders, his Biella wool cap at an angle: a duke of wool in a region whose whole economy flows from the clear streams that run through the mills, because, they say, it's the quality of the local water that makes the whole valley rich. The Barberas, the Zegnas, the Loro Pianas, all grew immensely wealthy in the years after Fred arrived and from their genial hauteur, you can tell they have no doubt they deserved to.

You can tell that Barbera loved Fred because Fred loved him, or loved his wool, at a time when Americans couldn't tell Biella wool from burlap. "Fred always used to say that my work was like the fountain of clear water—the source," says Barbera with hushed appreciation for Fred's discernment. "Yes, Fred was color-blind. Not important. The fabric—it can be any color. Fred could feel its weight in *grams*. Sometimes, it only takes a glance with the eyes to communicate with someone from the same club."

Meanwhile, Eddie Glantz, Roger Cohen, and Peter Rizzo were

mining the real gold of Italy's postwar economic miracle in towns like Vicenza and Asolo. Italy had finally managed to mechanize the hand-sewing traditions it had passed down through generations of tailors and bring it within reach of a middle-class market around the world. Glantz, Cohen, and Rizzo were locking up all the production they could get their hands on, buying dirt cheap in staggering quantities.

This put Barneys in a class by itself when other stores were still flogging shabby suits from the French designers. "The French—the fucking French, that's the only thing I can say—they weren't changing their quality concept. They didn't have to worry about the guts, the interior, or anything else, because people were buying it, and it was flying off the rack." Roger Cohen still gets irritated remembering it. "But we could see that there was a trend that was different. People wanted quality. They wanted better piece goods."

In Corona San Marco, between Vicenza and Asolo, Cohen and Rizzo bought San Remo. In Mantua, they bought Lubiam. In Arezzo, they bought Marzotto. Always, they negotiated Barneys' exclusive right to sell it in the United States, which gave Fred extraordinary control over the price he charged. "That's how I built my reputation with Fred, because I was buying suits for one hundred dollars from government factories—the Italian government had nationalized the entire industry back then—and I was selling them for three hundred fifty to four hundred dollars," says Peter Rizzo. "Four times! Selling them out—no markdowns. When you have exclusive brands you determine their value, because no one can find them anywhere else. I had this discussion with Fred. I said, how do you want to do this? We were getting rid of the moderate designer business by then—the Cardins, the Saint Laurents—because every department store and discounter was carrying them. We used to be a discounter ourselves, so we knew all their tricks. So I said to him, no one knows these names in America, and maybe we can establish them like designer names."

Before long, Barneys was selling some three thousand San Remo suits a season. Add in the other lines Cohen and Rizzo bought, and Barneys sold maybe eight thousand suits and another three thousand sports coats, season in, season out, from Italy's commercial factories. "We were so successful at this that each of those brands opened up their own offices and started marketing that brand in America," says Rizzo. "And they used all of the merchandising that I gave them and the models that I developed for Barneys to get them started. None of these guys, when they talk about Fred, say, oh yeah, that's the guy who ripped me off. I mean, they all sort of venerate him. They knew they were getting a good deal at the time, and what they got in return was enormous!"

What a business it was: Ingoing margins for the entire store hovered around 65 percent, which is what Fred demanded, and the maintained margin ended up between 55 and 60 percent, which means the margin after accounting for sales and markdowns. No other store could come close. Compare that to the average department store at the time, which aimed at a 40 percent maintained margin as its magic number.

In the late 1970s, Barneys was turning over upward of $50 million of inventory a year, with almost none of it left unsold at the end of a season. Most stores carry over 20 to 40 percent of their inventory each season, so on sales of $1 million, the retailer must carry over as much as $400,000 worth of goods he has already paid for. At Barneys, that number was closer to 2 percent, or $1 million in clothing that didn't find a buyer out of $50 million Barneys sold. That's why Fred never imposed a ceiling on what his buyers could spend—what they call an "open to buy." The two floors of the International House that sold the merchandise Fred had made in Italy held maybe 4,000 suits, and moved between 12,000 and 14,000 suits a season. In other words, the entire inventory turned over perhaps three and a half times. Most stores average less than one inventory turn a season.

"There was an extraordinary amount of cash pouring out of the business in those days—an unbelievable amount," says Rizzo. "And I'm not even counting the warehouse sale, which was throwing off another three million cash." What happened to all that cash? "I don't know," says Rizzo blankly.

Fred made one other crucial discovery in Italy during those years, and that discovery profoundly changed both Barneys and the way men dressed from then on. When you talk to people in the clothing business about Fred Pressman, at some point they all ask, did you know that Fred discovered Giorgio Armani? In the history of modern fashion, that gives Fred a status something like Christopher *Columbus's*. Had Columbus not come along, America would simply have waited to be discovered by somebody else. But it wasn't somebody else who discovered America; it was Columbus; and it was Fred Pressman who discovered Armani.

It is difficult to say this without snickering. People who tend to take fashion seriously tend to take it much too seriously, and almost everyone else doesn't take it seriously enough. A perfectly good adjective seems overstretched and bombastic when applied to an article of clothing, or to the person who designs it. Certainly, the fashion industry bears responsibility for much of this, since it specializes in the art of overstretching adjectives. But allowing for fashion's essential frivolity, it's fair to say that Fred did something historic in his own not-so-trivial world of taste, and no one who inhabits that world would underestimate it.

Giorgio Armani was born in 1934 in Piacenza, about forty miles down the road from Milan. His parents wanted him to be a doctor, but it was not to be. Three years in medical school and a three-year stint as a medical assistant in the army couldn't dislodge the wonderful childhood memories of his grandfather's small shop and the ornate, nineteenth-century-style wigs Ludovico Armani made for the theater. In 1954, Giorgio settled in Milan, the hub of Italy's fashion industry then and now, making fanciful window displays for Milan's Rinascente department store. Too fanciful, it turned out. He was soon exiled to Rinascente's style department—in those days, the store's equivalent of Siberia. For Armani, it was the beginning of an education. It anchored him to the real world, a locale that designers like Cardin disdained to inhabit. "It's one thing to design clothes, but it's something else again to hang around the salesrooms watching the public react to them," he told *Time* magazine in 1982. Fred Pressman might have spoken exactly the same words.

His stint at Rinascente led Armani to textile magnate Nino Cerruti, who was launching a line of clothing with the faintly ridiculous name of Hitman (the Italians like to appropriate zingy Americanisms as brand names, which often end up sounding slightly off-key). "I fell in love with textiles and began to understand the work behind each yard of fabric," Armani recalled. "That is why today, when I see anyone throwing away a yard of fabric, it is like cutting off my hand."

By the time he left Cerruti in 1970, Armani knew pretty much everything there was to know about the structure of a man's suit jacket. Whatever acclaim he has won since, he will always be remembered as the man who took apart the suit jacket and put it back together again in a way no one had really imagined before. From 1970 on, he experimented with this notion as a freelancer for a variety of clients. In the early seventies, you would often see his name on the back page of *Uomo Vogue*, but always as a designer for some other label: Giorgio Armani for Hilton; Giorgio Armani for Bagutta; Giorgio Armani for Allegri.

The way Armani's partner and lover saw things, this was always one name too many, and besides, Armani was beginning to get a reputation as a man to watch. Sergio Galeotti was a canny Tuscan with a sharp head for business and an even sharper nose, which prompted his nickname, Il Becco, "The Beak." Galeotti worked as an architect but he soon gave it up to take charge of Armani's fledgling career. The Beak and Gio—Armani's nickname—opened their business in 1975. The story goes that the two sold their used Volkswagen for start-up money and took space on Milan's Corso Venezia. They had $10,000 working capital when they opened for business.

It wasn't too long afterward that Fred came across them when the pair still didn't have two lire to rub together. Galeotti had flown over to New York on business and dined with Fred shortly before flying home. "Listen, Mr. Pressman, he says," according to Ed Glantz, who was there at dinner. "I can go back to Milan tomorrow with a five-dollar gift from Bloomingdale's, or a five-dollar gift from Bendel's, or a five-dollar gift from Bergdorf Goodman for my friends, and they say thank you very much for thinking of me, I really appreciate it. Or I can go with a fifty-dollar gift from Barneys. Who's Barneys? What does Barneys mean? And I agreed with him. At the time it meant nothing. They had no money at the time—zero, nothing. But it was the principle of what they wanted, because Galeotti had the vision, and he knew exactly what Armani could do and where Armani would be."

Fred outlined what Barneys could do for Armani, and Fred and Ed Glantz flew over to negotiate further in June 1976. Fred arrived in his rumpled tan jacket—now doubly rumpled from Fred's suitcase—corduroy pants worn at the knee, a blue shirt with holes in it, and, of course, the black knit tie. "Fred never felt the need to impress anyone," says Glantz. They met in Armani's office, a room about fourteen feet by fourteen feet. From the first, Fred knew he had stumbled across something very special. And then he started in on Armani, the way he always did with everyone. If only the lapels were just a bit narrower, if the collar on the shirts was just a little bit higher—everything Armani wasn't. And through it all, both Armani and Galeotti realized that Fred understood.

Plus, they needed the money, and Fred, knowing instinctively what he was looking at, was prepared to shell out much more than Armani and Galeotti had ever seen since they started in business. Fred offered the pair 20 million lire a season—about $10,000 back then, and around $40,000 today. In return, Barneys would get the exclusive right to use Armani's name and designs in the New York area, plus the right of first refusal to license a less expensive line of goods if the business would one day support it.

Done. Fred paid them for the full year up front, and although the two were prepared to finish the deal with a handshake, Fred insisted on drawing up an exacting contract. "It was probably twice the amount that both of them earned for the year before, and it started them well," says Ed Glantz. "That's why the relationship between Armani and Barneys was always so strong. Fred saw the potential in it, and he wanted to lock it in—which he did. That meant Saks won't get it, Bloomingdale's won't get it, Bergdorf couldn't get it, the specialty stores couldn't get it. He had it. It was a real coup."

To Armani's ultimate regret, it turned out. Much later, when Armani and Barneys had both achieved worldwide renown, Armani wished he had had only a handshake to bind him to the store. In 1994, a Swiss court affirmed that Fred had drawn that first contract much too tightly for Armani to wriggle out of, squirm though he did.

By July of 1976, Glantz was sourcing Armani's first shirts and sweaters for Barneys—Laura Biagiotti, known for her luxurious cashmere knits, made the first Armani sweaters. Armani had no hand in the manufacturing during those early days. He executed the sketches, and Fred had the clothes made. The first merchandise appeared in the store in September, celebrated with great fanfare under a tent Fred had raised in Barneys' parking lot on Seventeenth Street.

The impact was extraordinary and immediate. No one had seen anything quite like it before. Out came the padding from the jackets; stiff lapels sagged; trouser legs swelled and relaxed their vise-grip on the crotch. It was as if the men's suit had been holding its breath for a hundred years and suddenly exhaled. The general relief was palpable. Suddenly, middle-aged men could hold up their heads again in the fashion world—and they could breathe, too. The spare tires and ample buttocks that had suffered so cruelly under French rule found a far more forgiving monarch in Armani, who would one day earn the sobriquet, King of Milan.

The looser structure of the suit allowed Armani to utilize a wider range of lighter fabrics, many of which Armani had a hand in developing. His grainy blends of wool and crepe, for instance, simply wouldn't have supported the rigid architecture of more traditional men's suits. And in place of the sober palette of banker's gray and navy blue, Armani dug into the Italian hills and came out with a fistful of mauves and taupes and olives that one American critic wrote off as "mud." That did not displease Armani one bit. In a commemorative retrospective on Armani's designs published in 1990, Richard Martin, curator of the Metropolitan Museum of Art's Costume Institute, calls that "a canny and not at all disparaging description."

In its own way, it was an American-inspired look, by way of Hollywood and Harlem, with a passing nod to the zazous who brought that fashion to Europe. Armani had idolized Hollywood movie stars like Joseph Cotten growing up, and patterned his own outfit of jeans and T-shirt on James Dean, whom people said he resembled, except he really didn't all that much. Armani synthesized his memories of all that and sent it back to America.

At the time, however, the clothing men were mortified. "I looked at those first Armani suits, and I said to Fred, 'Man, they look like somebody cut up some curtains or drapes,'" says Irwin Grossman. "I mean, to the eye of a clothing man, it was unheard-of!" But the clothing men were done for. When Cardin came on the scene in the late 1960s, America had twelve hundred suit manufacturing concerns, ranging in size from $10 million to $100 million. By the end of the seventies, that number had dwindled to several hundred firms. In a suit business that started the decade almost exclusively American, one in every three suits sold now came from abroad. The vision of a designer-driven suit business that led Fred to build the International House had been vindicated in spades.

Armani did a lot more than just put Barneys on the same map as the fancy uptown department stores; it redrew that map altogether. "Now, all of a sudden, there was a new fashion guy on the block that everybody wanted, and he was tied to Barneys," says Glantz. "It brought Barneys into a whole different era. And the people who wouldn't sell Barneys because they had their ties with Bloomingdale's or Saks now wanted to sell to Barneys. Barneys owned it. You had Armani linen suits, linen shirts; roll up your sleeve, flip up your collar, put your hand in your pockets—that's attitude, that's fashion.

Everybody had to come down there, and it happened so quick, it was frightening. It took the old style of the store and threw it out the window very quickly."

Armani sold $90,000 worth of clothes his first year in the United States—pretty much all of it at Barneys. By 1982, when *Time* magazine made Armani only the second fashion designer to grace its cover—Yves Saint Laurent was the first—U.S. sales hit around $14 million, roughly 10 percent of Armani's worldwide total. A 1980 movie called *American Gigolo*, starring Richard Gere in the title role, helped propel Armani out into the hinterlands and make him a household name. In the movie, Gere's Armani wardrobe, on which he lavishes as much attention as on the women he romances, made a sizable splash. From then on, the slouchy Armani suit became the uniform of choice for swashbuckling 1980s capitalism. It is a testament to Armani's abiding influence on fashion that his designs survived a decade that came close to making them a caricature of their times.

For this, Armani paid grateful tribute to Fred Pressman in an obituary after Fred's death from cancer in 1996. "He was the first person in America to treat me and my clothes as if they were something important," said Armani. "He was a man who loved his métier, and I think he recognized in me someone who shared that with him."

5

"HEY, WANNA FEEL MY STOMACH?"

Gene just kind of popped into the office when he felt like it," recalls Peter Rizzo. He popped in on Nick DeMarco one morning in the late 1970s, while DeMarco was selling the Cardin line to a group of Barneys buyers. There were six earnest clothing men sitting around a table and the radiant Gene, his insolent ponytail hanging down the back of his jeans jacket. Gene leans back in his chair, props his cowboy boots on the table, and, folding his arms, smirks at DeMarco's merchandise. "What is this shit?" DeMarco gets up, says, "Gene, this shit pays for your store," and walks out the door. Gene caught up with DeMarco halfway down the hall. "Take it easy, don't get so mad. I didn't mean anything by it. It's just . . . It's the way I . . . What are you doing tonight?"

That's how Gene and Nick DeMarco got to be very close friends. That first evening together was a revelation to DeMarco, who grew up in Brooklyn, where his father owned a garbage route. DeMarco had just moved back to New York from Kansas City and was fresh out of his marriage, and here he was in the back of a black stretch limo with this newly minted prince of fashion. DeMarco had his head screwed on right. He was a tough street kid who had played college football and served as a lieutenant in the Army; a father and a dedicated churchgoer. DeMarco's street credibility made him particularly appealing to Gene. Eugene Pressman has always tried to camouflage his privileged suburban roots by playing the "momser," as Barney might have called it—to the point of inviting one woman employee into his private boxing ring to hash out a difference of opinion with the gloves on.

Down-to-earth as he was, DeMarco was dazzled. First stop, Madison Square Garden to watch the New York Rangers lose a hockey game, which always put Gene in a foul frame of mind. "He was really angry," says DeMarco. "He doesn't like it when any of his teams lose. They're in New York, they get paid top dollar, you don't lose, you know?"

Gene's mood lifted quickly. "After that, he said, come on we're going out. My date had to work the next day, so we dropped her off. We dropped Gene's date off. I didn't know where he was taking me. And we get in the limo, and we drive to this place called Studio Fifty-four that I had only heard about slightly but never even dreamed of going into. We pull up in front. There was a mob outside. The minute Gene opened the door to the limo and I came out with him, it was like salt and pepper. I was in a suit and tie. He was in his ponytail and jeans. It was like Moses parting the Red Sea. We walked right through the crowd into Studio Fifty-four. And all of a sudden for the first time I saw dancing and lights and disco, and a whole new world opened up. And it was all based on one meeting with Gene, and me telling him to screw himself and walking away."

In that way he has of falling into things, Gene Pressmen fell into fashion at a most propitious moment for a young man of his tastes and temperament. Just as Gene arrived on the scene, fashion assumed the mantle of real power in the cultural life of New York, which means to many people the cultural life of the world. The days of hippie insouciance were over. People were starting to take their clothes very, very seriously. In a few short years, the people who designed those clothes, sold them, and modeled them suddenly vaulted ahead of the people who bought them on the social scale.

"The decade from 1978 has been decisive for fashion, as important as the 1950s were for the motor industry and the 1970s for computers," writes Nicholas Coleridge in his book *The Fashion Conspiracy* (London: William Heinemann, Ltd., 1988). "Designers like Ralph Lauren, Calvin Klein and Giorgio Armani have created from nothing fashion empires on a scale and with a speed that seemed impossible in the mid-1970s . . . designer money has transformed the social status of designers."

When Gene parted the waters outside Studio 54 that night with Nick DeMarco, he felt no need to give thanks once inside, either to God or Fred. Privileged access to the hottest club in New York was his due as the man who ran the small, seventy-five-hundred-square-foot boutique within Barneys that anointed the designers who clothed the models who inspired the envy of every young woman in New York.

Gene had been dabbling in different areas of the store since the middle 1970s, first the warehouse, then the selling floor, but his influence never quite matched his arrogance. When Barneys installed a sportswear department on the third floor of the International House, it was Gene's inspiration to put the dressing rooms in the middle of the floor in a kind of homage to the free-standing pissoirs of Paris. Most of these suggestions were never implemented. "Fred was the merchant and he watched over the business, while Gene was the guy throwing shit on the wall and seeing what stuck," recalls Roger Cohen.

Gene's inspiration to sell women's clothing in Barneys started sporadically with a few things he picked up in Europe on his grand tour with Eddie Glantz in 1976. As Gene diffidently told the *Daily News Record*, "I kind of sat in and watched him pick swatches . . . it's kind of difficult to watch someone pick swatches, immediately you want to start picking them yourself."

In fact, he did more than pick swatches. He picked designers—but only the top designers, like Armani, who had branched out into women's wear after several years, Missoni, Sonia Rykiel, Gianni Versace. Unlike Fred, who continued to do a steady, highly profitable business in bread-and-butter men's suits long after he had brought fine Italian threads to the United States, Gene didn't want to waste time on women's clothing most women could afford. Coats ran around $400, a simple blouse upward of $100, and skirts around $140. In the late 1970s, this was a great deal of money. Before long, Gene had seventy-five hundred square feet atop Barneys' International House to play with, and that was clearly only the beginning. "The whole thing was Gene's idea," Fred told an interviewer in 1986. "One day, he came to me and said, 'Let's open a women's store.' I told him, 'That's a great idea,' and then I said to myself, 'That's not a great idea, and I hope he forgets it.' "

Gene didn't forget it, and, in truth, Gene couldn't forget it. It was his one shot at the fashion stardom he craved. No one in Hollywood would give Gene a movie to make in the six months he labored there, but back in New York, someone would give him a store of his own. Rarely do fathers and sons collude as cheerfully in the oedipal murder, and murder is literally what some of Fred's friends call the cancer that killed him. The way they look at it, it was as if the malignant cells started dividing the day the women's store opened.

Even people with a more benign view were taken aback by the nervy opulence of Gene's new venture. "Gene was a little difficult, but Freddie had great respect for his talents," says Irwin Grossman. "I'll never forget, when they opened up the women's department on the top floor, everybody wondered whether Freddie was crazy. But he liked this kid, and he wanted to keep him in the business, and the only way he could keep him in the business was to let him run things his way. He says, I've got to leave him alone. Gene's got his own idea of where he's going, and I don't want to . . . upset him.

"I once went in that store after going through the ladies' thing, which was beautiful, and I came down, and I said, Freddie, the stuff is gorgeous, but man, the prices are ridiculous! You know, I said, in your store you've got Hickey-Freeman, you've got Oxxford, but you've also got me, and you've got guys below me in price. You go to that ladies' store—it's not just that the sky's the limit, the sky is all there is. And Fred said, That's what he wants. And I'm going to let him have it.''

No one knew at the time that the women's business would never make a dime, if you figured in the interest on its various borrowings to finance expansion; not when it opened, not after Barneys built its lavish women's store in the mid-1980s, not when it moved to Madison Avenue in 1993. For all the notoriety it won and the glitter it sprinkled on the enterprise as a whole, it relied on financial life support from the men's store, which is something very few people at the store knew and even fewer acknowledged. Fred had established an unfortunate precedent for Pressman infallibility when he wrested the soul of the store from Barney, and it came to be expected that things would always work out somehow.

"Barneys went from a secondhand clothing store that his grandfather opened up to a discount store to a fashion store," says Eddie Glantz. "Gene's only mark was to make it into a woman's store. That was all Gene's baby. And his father allowed him to do it. Everything they touched had turned to gold, so why would he not believe his son?"

Fred told Chester Kessler that he expected Gene to lose several million dollars at the outset, but he figured that Barneys would ultimately spread its gilt-edged aura over less costly women's merchandise that would sell in greater quantities. That was not exactly what Gene had in mind, however. In time, the rich prices Barneys charged for women's wear did get diluted by somewhat more affordable goods, but never to the point where Barneys could ever be accused of wooing the hoi polloi. A Barneys television commercial comes to mind that hints at how the store preferred to view itself. A stunning young couple is strolling down a picturesque boulevard, speaking, we gather, of love. The city is Paris. The couple is speaking in French. One comprehensible word pops out of their discourse. That word is "Bar-*nees*."

Gene extended Fred's distaste for the big-bellied, penny-pinching schleppers who bought from Barney Pressman until that distaste included just about everybody. Barneys hosted a promotional event sponsored by Chanel some years later in the hope of drawing more uptown shoppers to the store. It was a discreet, well-heeled crowd, chic but decidedly not hip—"ladies who lunch," in the words of one of the event's young organizers. "All through it, I can remember Gene fuming, 'When are those ladies going to *leave*.' I tried to tell him that the whole point was to get them there in the first place."

The considerations that went into making a stable business were far from Gene's mind as he set about building his empire within an empire. Taste was all that mattered—the best taste. Oh yes, Gene did have that in spades. He had gotten it from Fred, and he hired only people who met the exacting standard he inherited. He chose well, too. Several came from Bergdorf Goodman, and it must have given Gene particular satisfaction to toss a harpoon or two at his white whale uptown. Barbara Warner ran the women's store, taking over from a woman named Louise Ohm who was Gene's first mentor in the women's business. And under her, Richard Lambertson, Connie Darrow, and Mallory Andrews, who was the mastermind behind a publicity apparatus that was as important to the store as its clothing.

From the beginning, Gene made Barneys more daring, more provocative, and more fun than any other women's store in New York. Gene himself discovered a diminutive Tunisian named Azzedine Alaïa, and brought his clothes to New York for the first time. Alaïa usually dressed in a black Chinese outfit and black rubber shoes, and slung his pet Yorkie, Patapouff, from a black saddlebag on his shoulder. He had studied sculpture at the École des Beaux-Arts in Tunis, and learned to sew from his grandmother. Both skills were abundantly evident in the clothes he created when he moved to Paris; only a woman with the physique of a marble Venus could squeeze into the exquisite, form-fitting sheaths that are Alaïa's hallmark. But if you were one of the seventy-three or so women who could, you could paralyze a room, which was all that really counted. Equally important, Alaïa had a devoted following of lithe French actresses and slinky celebrities like Grace Jones and Tina Turner.

"Alaïa made you feel like a sex bomb," says Loren Ezersky, a willowy New York fashion critic who scrimped to buy one of every Alaïa Barneys sold. "You slithered into that dress and it made your tits look like apples and your ass look like melons. I had a lot of dates back then. Sure, it was really expensive, but look at it this way—you saved by not needing a girdle or a bra."

Gene expected similar discoveries of his underlings. Their mission was to unearth the next trend while everyone else was cashing in on the current one. This they did with a vengeance, fueled by Gene's infectious boosterism and his giddy excitement at their finds. "It was like a big candy shop for everybody," remembers a young woman who worked in what Barneys called the Co-op, a separate department that opened later for its most frolicsome fashions. "It helped us find unique people, because where else could they buy things that they loved and adored personally? There I was, on a Friday night, rolling the racks myself from the warehouse across the street, so I could get my clothes on the floor. Everybody did that."

She remembers the day in the early 1980s when she was taking Gene on her rounds of young designers who would kill to get their merchandise into Barneys. If you were an unknown and trying to build a following, there simply was no better calling card, and that remains true to this day. "It was our last appointment of the day, some people I had never heard of who kept calling me and sending postcards. I liked the look of the postcard—just the words, 'Sleek, Modern, and Sensual.' So I thought, let's give Gene a shot at this. And we get to this funky little red door—it was on Thirty-seventh Street next to the fire station. We open the door, and I'm thinking to myself, oh my God, this is embarrassing. The staircase is just dripping with crud, it's filthy.

"But I was there, so we had to go. And we got to the door, and this really huge, jovial black character comes to the door, and he's wearing a crown on his head and screaming at the top of his lungs. It's Isaia, who is no longer with us. But he is one of the most talented young people I've ever met in my life. And in his showroom, he's got a little top called the 'sex top,' and he's got a little skirt called 'the sex skirt,' and a little legging called 'the sex legging.' And it's all black Lycra and black-and-white-striped Lycra. No one was really doing stretch clothing at the time. And Gene went nuts. He just went berserk. Maybe I would have bought a couple of them just to try it, because the guy was such a riot. But these things weren't cheap—ninety dollars for the sex leggings, and one-twenty for the sex top, which is pretty expensive for a little top in 1984.

"Gene negotiated exclusivity on the spot. He starts telling Isaia, we'll give you a little area of your own, we'll do this, we'll do that, and I thought, oh my God, he's lost his mind. But you know what? He was right. From that point onwards, I was selling hundreds of sex sets a week out of the Co-op."

When it came to the serious study of clothing, however, all the kids in the candy store went to the guy who owned it. "All you wanted to do was be close to Fred because you learned so much. He taught me professionally how to put your thumb and index finger together and feel a fabric. He would spend two to three hours talking about every single detail on a raincoat, from the lapel to the buttonholes, to the quality of the button—every last stitch. And he'd ask you whether you have any raincoats coming in and you'd say, well, yes, Mr. Pressman, actually I have some raincoats coming in for fall. Well, can I see them? I'm like, errrr. And you'd line them all up and go through them, and he'd bring down the raincoat he'd been thinking of, and lay it out, and go through it. It was like all your hard work with all these raincoats just went out the window."

Those were wonderful, carefree times at the store. Barneys quickly developed a reputation for seizing upon the hottest designers of the moment and either locking in their wares exclusively or buying them with infinitely more panache and chutzpah than its rivals. Comme des Garçons, Thierry Mugler, Jean-Paul Gaultier, Yohji Yamamoto, Ann Demeulemeester, Anouska Hempel: The women on intimate terms with these names associated them inextricably with Barneys. As did other retailers, who looked upon Barneys as a fashion laboratory and often repeated its more successful experiments—at half-strength.

"Women went crazy," says Marina Crispo, a vivacious Italian woman who managed the selling floor at the women's store from 1982 to 1995. "I was coming from Bergdorf's, which had all the respect at the time. Bergdorf's is a beautiful institution, but at the time it was like an old lady compared to a trendy young woman, and all of a sudden I went from this old lady walking slowly to a disco with young people jumping up and down."

Fred had shown how this was done in menswear, "editing" the designer lines in a way that made them as much a statement of Barneys' taste as the designer's, which is the essence of what makes a great merchant. Gene's buyers did the same thing in women's wear. Even if other stores carried the same designer's merchandise—and Barneys did everything in its power to ensure that they didn't—it rarely produced the same éclat. This was show business as much as it was retailing, and often more: For a mere $12,000, you could buy a jacket from Romeo Gigli, another designer associated with Barneys, woven out of spun-gold thread. If you had to ask what woman would ever buy such a thing, you clearly missed the point.

Barneys was using clothes like this to make a statement about what it stood for aesthetically. Heidi Baron, a buyer for Barneys in the late 1980s who was married at the time to the graphic artist Fabien Baron, brought an unknown designer named Christian Francis Roth into the store, along with Roth's M&M jacket. This was a bright orange thing, plastered from top to bottom with M&M candies and a $1,200 price tag. "It was simply, like . . . hideous in a way, but I thought it was pretty interesting and very Barneys," says Heidi Godoff, who has since re-married. "Everyone loved it. It wasn't really even bought to sell. It was just the kind of thing that was unique and special."

Gene functioned more like the impresario of this spectacle than its hands-on maestro. He applauded, he goaded, he cursed, he turned thumbs up or down; he supervised the gestalt, but from a distance. None of this required his presence in the store all that much. In this he differed markedly from both his father and his grandfather. From Barney, Fred had soaked up the wisdom that running a store meant being around, and Fred was always around. You couldn't pry him away from it. Not Gene, who came in late and left early.

Gene's passion, during daylight hours anyway, was his own body. He spent hours exercising in his private gym across the street in the Barneys offices at 106 Seventh Avenue. Employees were often summoned to meet Gene in the gym, and just as often found him naked, toweling off after a shower. That appeared to cause Gene no embarrassment whatsoever, unless, perhaps, his own nakedness was the point. In any case, word of Gene's formidable penis did manage to get around.

Gene did take great pride in the firm muscles that resulted from long hours on the weight machine. He had a habit, while talking to you, of touching himself distractedly in a way that was half nervous tic, half winsome appreciation. In the middle of a meeting, Gene might suddenly raise his shirt and say, "Hey, wanna feel my stomach?" This often caused employees some consternation. What exactly is the correct protocol in a situation such as this? Does one demur politely, or is it considered bad form not to stroke the boss's rippling abdominal muscles under the circumstances. "It made me very uncomfortable," says a former employee who worked closely with Gene in the early 1980s. "If I have one image of Gene in my mind, it's Gene rubbing his belly. He was obsessed with it."

Gene had an outlet for his vanity, and that outlet was women. He styled himself a lady-killer, and he used his rangy good looks and buoyant charm to maintain a steady flow of casualties. He had always idolized Jim Morrison, rock and roll's patron saint of preening narcissism who drank himself to death in Paris in 1971. Gene was always humming Doors tunes and hung a poster for the movie *The Doors* in his office. It's a style that never strays too far from self-parody. But the women who didn't find Gene absurd often found him devastating, although there were many who found him both. And he was persistent. "He would always go for the best-looking women, but he was like a child with a parent, never taking no for an answer," says a close friend from Gene's college days who often went nightclubbing with him in the late 1970s. Gene had a patented seduction line when a woman rebuffed his initial pitch: "Come *on!*" Back at the store, the gay employees in Barneys Underground would giggle over stories of Gene's high jinks, like taking college girlfriends for a spin in the country, coaxing them out of the car, and leaving them stranded on the side of the road.

The early years of the women's store, around the time that Gene and Nick DeMarco got close, were the glory years of New York nightlife, a time when single-minded hedonism still seemed fresh and guileless: Weimar washed pure. In college at Syracuse, Gene had gotten chummy with Steve Rubell and Ian Schrager. The pair would put a deeper, if briefer, stamp on the times than Gene not long after graduation. While Gene was bumping around the store after college, Rubell and Schrager had marked out the unformed world of nightclubs as their turf. Rubell was the short, bubbly, ingratiating one, always eager to be liked and usually successful at it. Schrager, tall and taciturn, played the straight man.

On April 26, 1977, they opened Studio 54, the club that defined the era that sent Barneys into its high-fashion orbit. Studio 54 brought together all the different tribes that would coalesce into Barneys' new clientele and piped the tune that set them all dancing under the light of the artificial moon: the simmering gay subculture that Barneys had catered to in its Underground; the well-born European refugees, still too fresh on the scene to have acquired the New York moniker, Eurotrash; uptown socialites who were dipping their toes in the dangerous waters of downtown, the way an earlier generation of swells would go slumming up in Harlem. At Studio 54, they glimmered together, they danced together, they sniffed cocaine together in the club's DJ booth, and they had sex together on its much-abused banquettes.

And, of course, they all looked closely at what everybody else was wearing. "The fashion business was the engine and inspiration," Ian Schrager told Michael Gross of *New York* magazine. "Giorgio, Halston, Perry, Calvin, Norma were the movie stars of the East Coast."

*   *   *

Studio 54 made notorious another New York ritual: the velvet rope. The rope started as a kind of cordon sanitaire to keep out the prostitutes and pickpockets who inhabited the seamy neighborhood around the club's location at Fifty-fourth Street off Eighth Avenue. But it soon came to represent the withering social Darwinism that was dividing fashion-conscious New York into two classes: the cool and the uncool. All through the long night, the crowd surged toward this red velvet rope, hoping to win the approval of the gatekeeper on the other side and gain admission. Bribes were often proffered, both financial and physical. The gatekeepers were adamantine, having learned from cold experience an essential truth: The right people would keep coming only so long as the wrong people couldn't.

Studio 54 hardly invented the idea of social engineering, but it did help make it acceptable to practice it openly, without shame and without pretense. For the most part, the rejects accepted their fate stoically, and slunk away. An absolute judgment had been rendered. Did Gene Pressman absorb these lessons from his old college friends? That seems like a bit of a stretch. The Studio 54 mentality lived on at Barneys, however, long after Schrager and Rubell were sentenced to three and a half years in jail for tax evasion in 1980. Barneys had no actual velvet rope, but it did have a new breed of salespeople with their own velvet ropes in their brains. Gene encouraged them to think this way. Customers who didn't make the cut might as well have been trying to get into Studio 54, for all the attention they got from the sales help.

Gene went to the club often—three, four, sometimes five times a week—with his close comrades, Nick DeMarco and Steve Hansen, a friend from Gene's hometown of Harrison who owned several restaurants. "Three gorgeous guys making every model there was—all the girls looked alike," says a woman colleague from the fashion business who hung around with the three of them. "Gene was truly cool—obnoxious, arrogant, something of a jerk—but cool in his very bones. I remember being frightened of him. He just seemed mean. I never thought he deserved to win, and yet, somehow, he always won. But he did have exquisite taste—taste so cool you didn't even understand it."

Was he worse than any of the other merrymakers? Probably not, although he was certainly every bit as bad. If you point the accusing finger at Gene, Nick DeMarco says, you're just another hypocrite. "I don't look back and relish the things that we did, but at the same time, it was the entire family of the fashion industry. We try to pinpoint Gene for his attitude and for his style, for his role, and for his character. And you look at him today and say, look what you did, look how you treated me. You attack him now, because he's vulnerable. He's lost his power base. But at the time, everybody was like that."

By the time disco fever subsided in the early 1980s, Barneys had launched several new businesses that had done much to establish it as the arbiter of taste in New York. As befits a Pressman, Fred's wife, Phyllis, was a gifted shopper. Phyllis Pressman had long had the habit of brightening up the store with some of the trinkets she would bring back from Europe. Who knows how Pressman taste rubs off? Suffice it to say, Phyllis got the full brunt of it from Fred. Once again, shoppers at Barneys found themselves looking at objects the likes of which they hadn't seen in any local stores, objects of such beguiling charm that they had to possess them. What was to become Chelsea Passage, the gift and housewares business Phyllis bought for and managed, started as a trickle of requests to buy Barneys' own decorations.

Chelsea Passage opened officially as a department in the store in October 1980. It was an instant success. "She would literally travel all over the world looking for things," says a salesman who worked closely with Phyllis for years. "Some of them were artisan-done things. Some of them were by companies that had not yet been introduced into this country that she was able to persuade to start there. And whatever we carried was really the best of the best. We had select Limoges china in patterns you wouldn't see everywhere else, many of them hand-painted. We had fine Christofle silverware before anybody else. We were the only outpost for Li-Lac chocolate other than the Li-Lac store, the only other place it was sold at that point."

It wasn't long before Chelsea Passage outclassed all other gift departments around town. Phyllis would prowl the dank passageways of Paris's famed Marché aux Puces—flea market—with Nancy Klein, Chelsea Passage's chief buyer. On one occasion, they discovered a French ceramist who led them to a warehouse with no lights on the outskirts of town. They examined the mosaic tables they found there by the yellow headlights of their car. It was impossible to tell what colors they were looking at, but they bought the tables anyway, so enchanted were they by the design. This kind of aesthetic risk taking made Chelsea Passage unique.

Like all the other Pressmans, Phyllis ruthlessly practiced what Stanley Marcus called the "tyranny of taste." She browbeat Porthault, the nonpareil French linen manufacturer, into reviving several designs from the 1920s and '30s—Phyllis's favorite period. Over half the items sold were done so exclusively to Chelsea Passage, and woe betide the artisan who even thought of selling to Bergdorf Goodman. There was one rule: Please Phyllis. It was not difficult to tell whether that had been achieved. "They expect a new design with each reorder," one artist told *Connoisseur* magazine. "If not a new design, then a new color or shape. It's slightly holding you by the hair. But it is how they have something new and exciting in the store all the time."

But there was a ghost hovering over the Chelsea Passage's overstocked hallway on the Seventeenth Street side of Barneys: It was the frail ghost of Bertha Pressman, propped against the Christofle candelabrum and nodding knowingly. "Phyllis told me that the reason she got into the business at all was because she never saw her family," says a former salesman who worked closely with Phyllis Pressman for many years. "She was lonely. And so the only way she got to see Fred was to come and work at the store. And, you know, I thought that was incredibly sad. I don't think she was telling it to me in a sad way, but I found it extremely sad that the only way she saw her husband was to come and get involved in the business."

Gene had launched another business, too. In the late 1970s, he had decided he could design clothes as well as sell them, and so he had started Barneys' All-American Sportswear Company, or Basco, which would sell its sportswear line wholesale to other stores as well as to Barneys. Gene brought in his friend Lance Karesh to make the designs, although Gene would be listed as a designer, too. Later, he asked his old high school buddy Jeff Klein to come in. Gene needed to surround himself with people he felt he could trust, and he didn't give his trust easily. And always there were the extravagant promises of a huge score when the new business triumphed, as it inevitably must. Karesh had a piece of Basco, and Klein, too, was told he would get a cut of the profits. Gene conveyed the myth of Pressman infallibility with such verve that those around him were usually carried away in his high-spirited undertow. Looking back, it's hard to see why so many lost their footing, but that's exactly the menace of a strong undertow: It's treacherous.

Things started inauspiciously. At the party to celebrate the new line in November 1979, fourteen guests got stuck in the Barneys elevator for forty minutes. Guests arrived to the wail of sirens and the flashing red lights of fire trucks summoned to the rescue. As some of the partygoers munched hot dogs in keeping with Basco's Americana theme, firemen used their axes to pry their trapped comrades loose. Far from being a social disaster, this only underscored Gene's loosey-goosey aplomb. In those days, nothing dented Barneys' high spirits. "While it may not have been exactly what Gene Pressman had in mind when he was planning his Americana party, it was certainly very Hollywood," chortled the gossip columnist for the *Daily News Record*.

The symbolism of the busted elevator stuck, however. Basco would turn out to be the first bruise on Barneys' unblemished skin. Not a big one, nor a very painful one, but the first inkling of something feeble in the body. It wasn't the clothes. Everybody agreed that Basco managed to turn out lively, tasteful sportswear, although it added nothing terribly new to the clothing scene. Gene simply never devoted the attention to Basco necessary to give it any hope of succeeding. Basco was one of Gene's first toys, and he tired of it quickly—the first sign that his conspicuously short attention span could undermine his lofty ambitions.

Managements came and went. Jeff Klein left early on. He had signed on reluctantly out of friendship, having no experience in the clothing business. Gene said they would all have a lot of fun, but this was no fun at all, and instead there were hard feelings that ultimately led to a falling-out. Gene was saddened by this, but he had already turned his attention to the grand new women's store that was starting to go up, so he really didn't give it that much thought. "Sure it was his ego," says Klein, "but it wasn't killing him."

The business floundered. At one point, two thirds of the staff worked out of a showroom on West Fortieth Street, while the rest worked downtown on Twenty-second Street. "When I got there, there was no infrastructure whatsoever," says one executive who passed through Basco in the late 1980s. "If a customer called on the phone for order status, he couldn't get one. If a customer wanted to place a reorder, nobody in the company knew what was available to sell."

At its height in 1990, Basco was approaching $20 million in sales, but it still could only deliver 65 percent of its orders. "We were leaving thirty-five cents of every dollar on the table," says the former Basco executive. "It was terrible." At the same time, Gene and Bobby were taking out annual salaries of $75,000 apiece as Basco directors, which irked Lance Karesh no end. It was their money, of course, but Karesh owned 30 percent of the operation. He felt that every nickel taken out of Basco was a nickel that wasn't being spent on making the business profitable. Today, Barneys still owns the Basco trademark, but outside of a tiny licensing business in Japan, distributed by Wrangler, Basco is a worthless shell. Over the years, it managed to lose in the neighborhood of $15 million.

Basco did manage to touch Gene deeply in a completely different way, however. Gene Pressman had always mixed business and pleasure, chasing—and catching—many of the models he met on what are called "go-sees," when models audition for assignments. In 1979, Gene met a model named Bonnie Lysohir (pronounced "lee-sore") when Bonnie was doing some modeling work for Basco, and they started dating. Bonnie differed from so many of the good-time girls in the modeling profession. Her look was more winsome than feline, and her manner was as restrained and demure as Gene's was tempestuous.

But Bonnie was no pushover, either. From the beginning, she made it clear that she wouldn't stick around while Gene pranced his way through the disco scene. She followed through, too. The pair broke up several times during their first few years together. By this time, Gene was hitting the cocaine pretty hard, too, say his friends. Finally, she kicked Gene out, and gave him an ultimatum: Clean up or get lost. Gene cleaned up—he even went so far as to cut his ponytail at Bonnie's insistence. They married in 1982. "He always used to say that Bonnie saved his life," says Scott Kraft, who socialized frequently with Gene and Bonnie. "She was reticent, beautiful, and sweet."

Settling down with Bonnie was a kind of watershed in Gene's life. It was time for him to do what a previous generation of Pressmans had done before him. "The marriage was a stabilizing factor in his life," says Nick DeMarco. "Instead of channeling his energies socially, he channeled them back into the store. Gene always wanted stability. You know, as long as he can come home to stability, he can do the edginess thing in the store. Don't forget, he patterned his marriage and his life after his dad."

Gene presided over a two-level women's department, called the Duplex, atop Barneys' International House. It soon became clear that the 5,500-square-foot Duplex would never contain Gene's ambitions, and indeed it did not. Even before the Duplex was up and running, Gene was badgering Fred for a full-blown women's store to complement Barneys' men's business. It wasn't a harebrained idea, either. Even in the late 1970s, it was clear that Barneys would have to do *something*. The law of inertia applies to stores, too: Stores in motion tend to stay in motion, while stores at rest tend to get stale. Standing still has a number of pernicious effects, even for a successful store. For one thing, it frays exclusive relationships with designers, and those relationships are the lifeblood of a store that has decided it will live and die by the whims of fashion. For another, it puts undue pressure on profits: Costs increase constantly, but there is always a ceiling beyond which prices can't be raised to cover them, and Barneys would eventually hit it.

Gene wanted a bigger women's store because his ego demanded one, but for all his misgivings, Fred also knew that a thriving women's business would help Barneys in a number of ways. "You're either in the women's business or you're out of the business," Fred told *New York* magazine in 1986, and he was right. Women have always shopped for their men—by one estimate, their say-so governs almost half of all menswear purchases. If you bring more women to Barneys to shop for themselves, you almost automatically boost your menswear business at the same time. Nor could Barneys consider expanding as a men's store alone. Despite the new male peacockery Fred had helped encourage, men just don't shop aggressively enough to support a string of Barneys in other places. Without a women's store, the Pressmans would remain tastemakers, but Barneys would find itself stymied as a business. But a successful women's store would make Barneys something unique—a fashion temple with a mixed-gender congregation. Such a thing did not exist, and would give the Pressmans a way to keep their business growing well beyond Fred's death.

Ed McCabe, whose ad agency, Scali, McCabe, Sloves, worked on the Barneys account back then, remembers telling Fred how important it was for him to build a full-scale women's store, and Fred would give Ed the patented Fred wince, which McCabe imitates by pruning up his face and sucking in his breath in a sharp whoosh through tightly pursed lips. It would be a big, big gamble, said Fred. No one really knew anything about the women's business, Gene's flirtation with women's fashion notwithstanding. And it would cost an awful lot of money.

Barneys was very rich: The men's store was throwing off between $5 million and $6 million in profit every year in the early 1980s. But the investment needed to make the women's store the kind of showcase the Pressman family had in mind would soak up a great deal of cash.

Fred winced, Fred waffled, and then Fred would say to Ed McCabe, "Ed, you wanna buy a tie?" And McCabe would say, "How much?" And Fred would say, "Well, what does it say on the price tag?" And then Fred and the man who ran his ad agency would start haggling over the price of a tie. In the end, Phyllis Pressman played the Bertha role in this recurring melodrama and carried the day on behalf of her favorite son, Gene.

Fred did make a run at a suitable location in 1980. Genesco, Inc., which owned Bendel's, said it was looking to sell the elegant Bendel's flagship on Fifty-seventh Street, smack in the heart of the uptown shopping district and just across the street from Barneys' old nemesis, Bergdorf Goodman. It would have been perfect: Bendel's, which opened its doors in 1896, was an architectural jewel. A former executive says Barneys actually had a contract to buy the store but saw former president Geraldine Stutz, who had the right of first refusal, snatch Bendel's away for $8 million. It was a fire-sale price and would have guaranteed Barneys a huge profit just on the real estate even if its women's store there had failed miserably.

Fortunately, the Pressmans had been trading astutely in the real estate around its own Chelsea neighborhood, which, though still an awkward journey for many shoppers, was gaining a reputation for low-key chic. Barneys owned the International House outright and benefited mightily from a low lease on the space it used for the America House. Barneys paid Treger Realty only $200,000 a year for sixty thousand square feet of space—an absurdly low rent of $3.33 per square foot—and the lease wasn't due to expire until 1996. Fred owned the parking lots across the street directly through a subsidiary called 147 West Seventeenth Street, Inc., and the parking lots paid regular rent.

More important from a Lebensraum standpoint, Barneys also bought up the six 100-year-old tenement buildings adjacent to the store in the late 1970s and early '80s. Those buildings ran east along Seventeenth Street toward Sixth Avenue. The cost of the buildings was negligible, but Barneys suddenly found itself a New York City landlord with four buildings full of rent-controlled tenants (two of the buildings were unoccupied when Barneys bought them). There are easier things to be than a New York City landlord.

The Pressmans' first attempt to convert what they grandiloquently called "the town houses" into a women's store ran smack up against an outraged community that wasn't about to let Barneys literally bull-doze them. Barneys needed a zoning variance to convert the residential space into a commercial enterprise. Chelsea neighborhood partisans stood up for their rights, although what rights exactly they were de-fending remains unclear. The Pressmans, like the British at Bunker Hill, marched in woefully unprepared for this kind of guerrilla wran-gling. The locals whacked them squarely on the snout. The ragtag irregulars won the first round.

In 1984, it was time for a second try, and this time the Pressmans entered the fray with eyes wide open. Barneys hired a battalion of community relations consultants, politically connected lawyers, and building renovation specialists. They "built bridges to the community," a euphemism for throwing enough money at local charities and com-munity projects to mollify the restive populace. Negotiations remained contentious, however. An ad hoc group with the unwieldy name Chel-sea Coalition on Housing and Block-Eye on Barneys, staged rousing street demonstrations. Barneys was portrayed as an insatiable beast, gobbling up the local housing stock, displacing the tenants, and oth-erwise disrupting the serene atmosphere of shabby gentility that had enveloped the quarter for years. "Gentrification" is the rallying cry usually employed to villainize the kind of predatory beautification Bar-neys was engaging in, and it was employed here with a vengeance. "We need apartments, not high-priced clothing stores!" one community board member shrieked.

To no avail, as it turned out. Barneys won final approval from the New York City Board of Estimate in March 1985 to knock down an interior wall and move forward with the project. It cleared out the tenants on the first floors of four of the buildings it planned to annex, relocating them to other apartments in the neighborhood and subsidizing the difference in their rents. A fifth building closer to Seventh Avenue was cleared out entirely. One lone holdout—a dotty, stiff-necked women with an apartment full of cats and little more than a mattress for furniture—refused to budge, threatening the whole project. As a last resort, Barneys petitioned a civil court judge to appoint the local parish priest as the woman's guardian and have her removed in his care when, lo and behold, she moved on her own.

The path was now clear for Barneys to tackle its grandest building project to date, and under the most trying conditions: seventy thousand square feet in six ramshackle buildings with a dozen or more tenants whose electricity and plumbing facilities would have to be maintained without interruption for the duration. Out of this hodgepodge, Fred and his family intended to create nothing short of the most beautiful women's clothing store in the world.

There was one other engineering complication that made the project even trickier. Barneys could take advantage of a city tax credit if it managed to preserve the facade and exterior walls of the empty building close to Seventh Avenue. This required shoring up the entire structure from within with temporary wood supporting beams, erecting a steel frame around the entire building, and reattaching the exterior walls to this new frame. Doing this while maintaining the structural integrity of a building close to one hundred years old proved Herculean, not to mention horrifically expensive.

Meanwhile, another construction nightmare was unfolding in the basement. The plans called for Herbert Construction, the contractors on the job, to excavate fifteen feet below the basement. The first five feet down was easy going through soft dirt. Then the workmen hit rock, which meant blasting. As they blasted, they discovered that the entire store was sited above an underground creek—you can find it on some city maps—which ran through the rock veins beneath Chelsea and out to the Hudson River. As soon as the workmen had blasted out a hole, the creek would surge in, creating a series of indoor swimming pools in the middle of the construction site. A plan to siphon off the water and run it as coolant through the air-conditioning system was judged brilliant but unworkable. In the end, there was nothing to do but divert the stream altogether and channel it around the site and back into its original course to the Hudson. That soaked up lots more money.

All this time, the tenants on the upper floors were shuddering with each new blast and waiting for the interminable completion of the most beautiful store in the world. "Well, it was an incredibly complicated project not only because they were excavating and digging underneath where they were building, but because there were people living upstairs," says Dick Blinder, head of Beyer Blinder Belle, the architects of record. "The infrastructure for those people had to be retained, and it was hanging down like entrails from a dying horse—pipes hanging into this space and stairs coming out for the people to get into their apartments. It was an incredibly messy project."

Construction headaches posed only one set of obstacles to the smooth running of the women's store site. In normal circumstances, Barneys would have made a list of the designers whose boutiques it planned to include in the new store, and drawn up its plans with those designers in mind. Instead, that list kept changing throughout the construction, requiring the architects to change the plans on the fly to incorporate new entrants and scratch the dropouts. "We were building the store while all that stuff was happening, because the business was driving the design, which drives the construction, but the construction was already moving forward," recalls one of the architects on the store. "So, it was a constant chase to keep up with the design changes. Every week there would be a new set of drawings out in the field."

Complicating matters further, Barneys had assembled an international all-star team of architects and designers to put their individual stamps on the interior of the store. A voluble Frenchman named Jean-Paul Beaujard served as the consultant to Phyllis Pressman for her expanded Chelsea Passage on the first floor. Beaujard was not an architect himself, but he did have taste galore. It was often a frustrating process, however, to translate Beaujard's Gallic outpourings into concrete plans. Beaujard would make great sweeping gestures with his arms and

spout lyrical instructions like, "The ceiling—it should be more . . .
blue." The architects furrowed their brows and tried to encapsulate this
in some sort of a directive. "I would have to meet with Jean-Paul, and
he would say, 'It should look like *zeese*,' and I would have to turn that
into a drawing you could build from," says the architect.

In contrast, the Japanese member of the team, Setsu Kitaoka, was
as taciturn as Beaujard was expansive. Kitaoka spoke virtually no English, so all conversation took place through an interpreter. The interpreter, however, could be maddeningly unforthcoming. "You'd ask
a question and Setsu would speak to his interpreter and they'd go back
and forth in Japanese for a while, and the interpreter would turn around
and say, 'No.' And that would be it." Rounding out the crew was
French savant Andrée Putman, one of the most revered names in interior design, and while she contributed, no one was ever quite clear
what exactly her role was. Another vaunted name in interior design,
Philippe Starck, dropped out when the shoe company whose boutique
he was to create suddenly fell off the list of suppliers. And so it went.

But by far the thorniest element in this mare's nest was the Pressman family itself. The quest for absolute perfection prompted innumerable design changes. Each Pressman individually could hold wildly
contradictory ideas at the same time, and would flit between them like
hummingbirds in a spring garden. It was bad enough when each was
alone, but this was an eight-person family affair: Fred and Phyllis; Gene
and his wife, Bonnie; younger brother, Bob, who had joined the business after getting his MBA; and his wife, Holly; and the two Pressman
daughters, Elizabeth and Nancy. Together, their contradictory points
of view multiplied exponentially. Family meetings had all the decorum
of a prison riot: They were clangorous, violent, and seemingly ran-
dom. By the time the women's store was completed, the Pressmans'
caprices had generated close to one thousand change orders in the
construction—about ten times the normal number of changes on a job
that size.

Nor did the family make any attempt to conduct its brawls behind
closed doors. "I go into this meeting, and they ended up in a screaming

match with each other—Fred and Gene and Bob. There I am, this junior architect, meeting this wealthy, prestigious new client, and I just wanted to flatten up against the wall and disappear because I was so embarrassed for them. I don't come from that kind of family background. After a while, I got used to it, but I was really taken aback that these people would abuse each other in public, not just in the privacy of their home but in front of their consultants. They didn't care. There was such a collection of huge egos, you just couldn't contain them in the same room together. I really don't think I could actually say that they hated each other, but they were so competitive."

While the family screamed, the meter ticked. The dramatic centerpiece of the store was an art deco–style spiral steel staircase that climbed six stories to a skylighted atrium. That stair was indeed a marvel, with its marble treads and marble risers. It gave the whole store an open, airy atmosphere that instantly made Barneys feel less cluttered than other stores. (It also removed a large chunk of the selling space on the main floor, where cosmetics are sold—the most profitable real estate a store has.) The staircase was considered such a distinctive feature of Barneys that a version of it was incorporated into several of the bigger, better Barneys that the Pressmans built later. It also cost a cool million dollars.

The original design for the staircase was a little different from the staircase Barneys ended up with, however. It called for the staircase to be encased by eight massive steel columns. The columns were duly incorporated in the shop drawings, and the steel had been ordered from the foundry. Construction had reached the stage where the concrete footings for the columns had already been poured in the building's basement. That was the point at which Fred looked at a rendering and professed astonishment that it included eight columns he claimed he knew nothing about. A decree was issued: The columns must go.

Not so simple. Taking out the columns meant compromising the entire support of the building and starting from scratch on the structural design. The footings would have to be buried and huge beams

Barney Pressman soon after Barneys opened its doors in 1923. They say he hocked his wife's engagement ring for $500 to bankroll the store, but Barney occasionally embellished the truth. He wouldn't be the last Pressman with that predilection. (AP/Wide World Photos)

By the 1950s Barneys at Seventh Avenue and Seventeenth Street had become a cherished New York institution. If the cabbie he hailed didn't know the address without asking, Barney Pressman would storm out of the cab and hail another one. *(Archive Photos/Frederic Lewis)*

Barneys sold more suits than any other single store in the world and employed 150 tailors to make alterations on them. *(Archive Photos/D. Gorton/New York Times)*

Barney Pressman's son, Fred, transformed the store into a temple of European fashion and changed forever the way American men dress. He could tell you the weight of a fabric with his thumb and forefinger—to the ounce. (UPI/Corbis-Bettmann)

Barneys opened its new International House next to the original store in 1970. Fred staked the store's future on his belief that fashion designers would one day rule the menswear business. He won. *(Archive Photos/Barton Silverman/New York Times)*

Giorgio Armani opened his own business in 1975. Fred Pressman discerned Armani's genius immediately and brought him to the United States before anyone else could. It was a historic partnership. *(Archive Photos/David Lees)*

A customer trying on an Armani suit in the late 1970s. No one had seen men's fashion quite like this before. Fred's colleagues in the garment business thought Fred was a little nuts. (Archive Photos/D. Gorton/New York Times)

The lion in winter: Barney Pressman, eighty-four years old, in 1979. He didn't really understand what his son, Fred, had done, and he often didn't agree, but he backed off anyway. It was the right decision, but a terrible precedent. (Archive Photos/Jack Manning/ New York Times)

The third generation arrives. Barney and Fred Pressman flanked by Fred's sons, Gene (right) and Robert. (Archive Photos/Fred R. Conrad/New York Times)

Fred in Barneys' "Penthouse" in 1978, where expensive women's clothes were sold for the first time since Barneys opened its doors. Gene wasn't wasting any time exerting his influence. (Archive Photos/William E. Sauro/New York Times)

The clan matriarch, Phyllis Pressman. Phyllis adored Fred, but she stuck up for her firstborn son, Gene, as he pushed Barneys further into women's wear. In the same way, Fred's mother, Bertha, had stuck up for him a generation earlier. (Archive Photos/Keith Meyers/New York Times)

These daring creations by the English designer Anouska Hempel typified the style of Barneys new Women's Store, which opened in 1986. For all the attention it got, the Women's Store never made a dime. (Archive Photos/Robert Levin/New York Times)

Gene married former Ford model Bonnie Lysohir in 1982. It didn't take long for the marriage to hit the skids. (Robin Platzer)

Tunisian designer Azzedine Alaïa, whose ultratight sheaths got some of their earliest backing from Barneys. "They made your tits look like apples and your ass look like a melon," said one devotee. (Roxanne Lowit)

Phyllis Pressman, here at a New York flea market, started Barneys giftware department to be closer to her store-obsessed husband. Before long, she had made her Chelsea Passage as chic as Barneys' fashion business. (Archive Photos/Michelle V. Agins/New York Times)

Simon Doonan over-saw Barneys' windows and made their displays the ambassadors of the store's sensibility: wry, ironic, and often quite cruel. (Andrew Eccles/Outline)

Two examples of Doonan's handiwork: "Heaven's Buffet" and a Father's Day display. (Archive Photos/Top: Jim Estrin/New York Times; bottom: Jack Manning/New York Times)

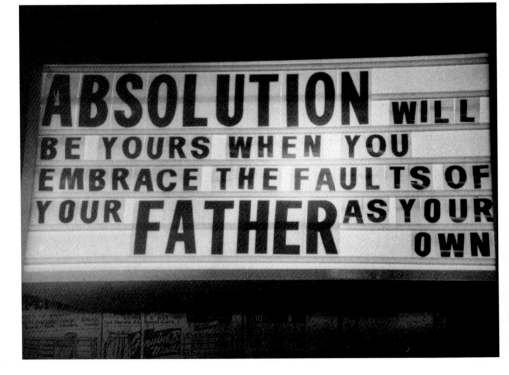

Barneys' arch style extended to its advertising. "Thought should be lofty, thought should be deep" reads the caption to this photo of supermodel Linda Evangelista and Kyle Maclachlan. These Jean-Philippe Delhomme illustrations pioneered fashion advertising without photography. The caption reads: "Sometimes luxuries are necessities."

The Pressman women (left to right): Bob's wife, Holly; Phyllis; Gene's wife, Bonnie; and Phyllis's daughters, Nancy and Liz. (Andrew Eccles/Outline)

Barneys' downtown store in its glorious heyday, not long before the company filed for bankruptcy protection in 1996. If only the Pressmans had just stopped there. (Archive Photos/Mike Segar/Reuters)

Kuniyasu Kosuge, the vibrant scion of the clan that built Japan's giant Isetan retail empire. Kosuge committed Isetan's resources to Gene Pressman's dreams in 1989, and came to regret it soon afterward. (PANA/JIJI/Morikawa)

The Pressman boys with Kazumasa Koshiba, who took over as head of Isetan after Kosuge's disgrace. There is a reason Koshiba's smile looks forced. (Robin Platzer)

It's all down from here. Gene and Bob Pressman just after the opening of the uptown Barneys, which ruined them. (Andrew Garn)

extended on the ceilings, which no longer had the columns to support them from the middle. That is exactly what was done.

As you would expect, the Pressman family marked many of its emotional milestones with its stores. Fred staked his claim to the future of the business when he first expanded the store in the mid-1960s, and seized it from Barney with the building of the International House in 1970. Similarly, Gene, the putative prince regent of Barneys since his first Alaïa sheath, claimed the throne halfway through the women's store.

Fred had hired Dick Blinder to design the women's store. Blinder's firm, Beyer Blinder Belle, specialized in historic preservation—a key skill given the need to maintain the original facades of the six buildings Barneys was converting on Seventeenth Street. Beyer Blinder Belle also had a long history of work in the Chelsea neighborhood, and both Fred and Dick Blinder had grown to love the area around the store. Dick Blinder had restored the old Fitzroy Houses on West Twenty-third Street, a charming row of gaslit town houses. That's how the Pressmans found him. Blinder first worked with Fred and Phyllis on their house in Southampton—a "funny, old Hansel and Gretel house" that Blinder was at first going to restore and ended up redesigning.

He and Fred saw things very much the same way, and the relationship between the two men was a warm one. "I was working very closely with Fred, who was an incredibly wonderful person in terms of wanting to do something of great spirit and character, and wanting to feel very intimately involved in the whole process. Fred and Phyllis didn't read plans very well, which was a problem in the sense that very often when they saw something coming close to reality, they weren't completely aware of what it was going to be until it started appearing in the flesh, in three dimensions. But for me it was a great experience, because they cared so much. They wanted to do the right thing."

Gene had a soul mate of his own on the project, a young designer named Peter Marino. Marino had worked for Fred as a junior draftsman with George Nelson and Gordon Chadwick, Barneys' primary architect. When Chadwick died in 1980, Marino volunteered to fill Chadwick's shoes. He first designed a two-by-four-foot glass display case for the Li-Lac chocolates Phyllis sold in her Chelsea Passage. But it was really Gene who found in Marino a kindred spirit.

Marino graduated from Cornell University in 1971, making him Gene's contemporary. Unlike the avuncular Dick Blinder, Marino also had the flashiest of downtown credentials. In 1969, when he was twenty, Marino took a year off from school and fell in with Andy Warhol and his crowd of drugged-out hangers-on. During that period, Warhol often held court in a club called Max's Kansas City, where Marino paid his dues and emerged a certified member of the city's subterranean elite. His reward came in commissions to renovate Warhol's town house and the Factory, the studio on Union Square where Warhol housed his twenty-four-hour-a-day art party.

Even without the Warhols that now line his office wall, Marino got more than his money's worth. Warhol, who always knew the true value of social coin, duly registered the transaction in his diary. "I can't figure Peter out," he wrote on September 29, 1977. "He's nutty. I told him how he owed his whole life and architecture career to us—how we gave him his first job—took him out of his business knickers and gave him his long pants and he said that well now he was in Armani suits and we sure didn't put him in those. He was funny (cab $4)."

Of course, it was the Pressmans who quite literally put Marino in Armani suits—and kept him in them, too. Marino tacked adroitly as the winds of fashion shifted. "In the late sixties and early seventies, Andy was quite a good calling card," he told HG magazine in 1989. "As times changed, however, and our clients became more social and at a certain economic level, it actually became rather a liability to say you had worked for Andy Warhol."

Peter Marino is a professional pleaser—one client, asked why he used Marino, answered, "His charm." He doesn't adhere to any particular visual style, as he is the first to admit. Whatever his client's aesthetic leanings, Marino prides himself on adapting to them and distilling them into their most rarefied, most expensive form. His commissions usually require skills that leave the formalist concerns of architecture far behind and run much closer to interior decoration.

Marino has compared himself to Stanford White, who often accompanied his Gilded Age clients on blowout shopping sprees through the Old World. It is an apt comparison, at least in that sense. Like the Pressmans themselves, Marino has a knack for tracking down the perfect object, whatever its price. An interviewer asked him to confirm a rumor, then making its way around the salon circuit, that the bill for the contents of a living room he designed came to roughly $57 million. Marino paused briefly while he punched numbers on his mental calculator and replied, "Only if you include that little library next door."

When needed, which is often, he will also design for his clients the furniture, the fabrics, the light fixtures, even the dinner plates. "I don't do ready-to-wear," he has sniffed in several interviews. "Mine is very much a couture house." This is very profitable work. For his custom creations, he usually tacks on a commission of between 25 and 35 percent over the cost, which is always steep. Former employees of Marino claim that the commission Marino makes on the things he buys and the things he custom-designs brings in far more profit than his architecture fees.

Gene took to Marino immediately, hiring him to design his new home in the New York suburb of Larchmont, which Gene bought in 1982. Marino went on to spruce up the homes of Gene's brother, Bob, and his two sisters, Liz and Nancy. They made a perfect pair of bookends, Gene and Peter: the rich kid from Westchester who tried to sandpaper his privileged background by sounding like Bayside, Queens, and the architect from Bayside, Queens, who had wiped his own ethnic vowels with velvet until he sounded like Shropshire. "I would look at Peter and find it impossible to imagine what he might have been like as a child," says a Barneys executive. Both Peter and Gene shared a mutual objective, however, which was to embody the best taste money could buy.

Together they commandeered the women's store and made it very much their own. "As the project was sort of halfway done, they began making a transition from Fred to Gene and Bob," says Dick Blinder. "They appeared on the scene and started to assert their own point of view and perspective, changing things. Gene had his own relationship with Peter Marino, whom he liked and felt a lot of confidence in. I never had a very good relationship on the design side with him."

Marino ended up designing the second through the sixth floors of the women's store. Original furnishings by twentieth-century masters like Ruhlmann, Porteneuve, and Josef Hoffmann reflect Gene's affection for early art deco and Wiener Werkstätte—two styles that keep appearing in future renovations for Barneys, all of which Marino oversaw. French artisans were flown in to hand-paint trompe l'oeil motifs on the walls. Another set of artisans applied costly silver leaf to the elevator doors, square inch by square inch. Dick Blinder had designed an oculus window for the sixth floor. Gene had it ripped out.

"Honestly, money was no object," says one of the architects on the projects, still amazed by the heedless spending more than ten years later. "They really were not concerned about the bottom line. Most owners, the bottom line comes first, you know? The Pressmans really had no concern for it. Honestly. They would say that they wanted this to be the most beautiful store in the world. That really was their goal in the women's store, and later on Madison Avenue, and then it carried over into the other stores as well."

Many people say they succeeded stunningly. For all the caprice and chaos that accompanied its construction, the store was a jewel when the Pressmans finally finished it—two years late. The women's store stood out for its unfussy elegance and a level of taste that immediately made its competitors look shabby by comparison. It wasn't just a matter of unbridled extravagance, either. Merchandising considerations incorporated into the store's design have ended up exerting a profound and lasting influence on the way other retailers display their wares. In the standard department store design at the time, for instance, showrooms were bordered by what was known as a "curtain wall," with merchandise lit from fixtures hidden behind it. In Barneys, Marino brought the ceiling right to the wall, and he lit the merchandise through incandescent spotlights. That was much more dramatic, much more impressive, and much more expensive.

"If you go into Bloomingdale's or Saks today, a lot of them are now doing the same thing," says the Barneys architect. "They've eliminated the curtain wall, and they're spending the money on this other idea. Peter and Barneys initiated this, although a lot of the ideas were Fred's. Fred was a master at presenting merchandise."

But the final price was truly astronomical. When the family was first planning the women's store, it commissioned two consultants to estimate the costs. The estimates came in at $8 million and $6 million. Bob Pressman, who was taking control of Barneys' finances, was shocked that anyone could imagine the cost mounting as high as $8 million, and so plans were drawn up according to the lower estimate. The final bill for the women's store: $35 million.

6

BLACK

Connie Darrow liked Patrick McDonald's guts. Darrow had just laid out an array of Chanel jewelry in a display case—Gene Pressman had hired her out of Bergdorf Goodman to run the accessories department at the women's store. An eager shopper was inquiring about the price of a pair of Chanel earrings, and Patrick, who managed the fourth floor where the eveningwear was sold, was matter-of-factly reeling off some shockingly high numbers. The woman replied that she could get the same Chanel earrings at an uptown store she knew for half the price.

"I said, 'Well, why don't you?'" huffed Patrick McDonald. "I mean, really, if I have to explain Chanel jewelry to you, then you shouldn't be buying Chanel jewelry! Oh, I don't know, I was in one of those moods. And that's how Connie and I became friends. Connie liked my guts because we'd get certain people in and I didn't give a shit."

Patrick and Connie lived for fashion. He wore his black hair slicked back and tight on the scalp, and long sideburns that swooped down to two pencil points on his jawline, and heavy black eyeliner. On the right side of his powdered cheek, he drew in a beauty mark, like Madame du Barry. Connie rimmed her entire eye with dark brown makeup on a base of white paste, raccoon-style, and cut her hair like

Louise Brooks, with a straight bob across her forehead. She asked Patrick to call her Lulu, after Louise Brooks's best-known role. Even on a sweltering summer day, she would wear a floor-length velvet ball gown by Anouska Hempel, a London designer she was instrumental in bringing to Barneys.

"She was a freak, like I'm a freak," says Patrick. "And I appreciated that." David Rubinstein, who once worked with her and doesn't like her at all anymore, treasures a memory of the time in Paris when Connie Darrow, in a winter-white Chanel cashmere twin set, white gabardine Bermuda shorts, white crocodile shoes, a white Hermès bag, and white kid gloves, stumbled in a pothole and fell in the mud. I mean, can you imagine a worse thing happening? To this day, a big grin spreads across Rubinstein's face when he thinks back on it.

Three months after Barneys opened its expanded women's store in September 1986, Barbara Warner resigned as general merchandise manager for women's apparel. She had been there five and a half years. No one knows exactly how Connie Darrow did it, but boy, did she do it. She had risen steadily since she joined the store in 1984, from accessories buyer to buyer of designer apparel to Warner's job. "Kicked ass and took numbers, okay?" says a woman who worked under her. But even the walking wounded will all say this: Connie Darrow had the best eye and the best taste of anybody working that side of the street in New York.

The fashion business is not a nice business, and the women's end of it is especially not nice. Nice scores no points in fashion, and it certainly scored no points at Barneys. For the rest of the decade and a bit beyond, Connie Darrow reigned as the raccoon queen of women's fashion retailing in New York. If Connie said it was cool, then Barneys said it was cool, and if Barneys said it was cool, it was most definitely cool. Cher knew it. She stopped in whenever she came through town; Susan Sarandon and Kathleen Turner knew it; Elizabeth Taylor knew it, and she never even came into the store—it came to her. Patrick McDonald would bring over a handpicked selection of merchandise so La Liz could be spared the indignity of shopping with . . . other people.

For a certain kind of woman, a woman with a pronounced persona to bedeck, Barneys was the ultimate, and when it had a sale, it was super-duper ultimate. "Suddenly on the phone is this woman who called me directly to say, hi, this is Lee Radziwill," says Patrick McDonald. "I was like, oh my God! Is this *Princess* Lee Radziwill? I didn't say that to her. I thought to myself it was a trip that she only called me maybe three or four times, but she always wanted me to call her when Barneys was having a sale. It was just sale, sale, sale."

The Pressmans reveled in their newfound celebrity. If Fred was in the office building across the street, he would sometimes call over to the store just to see if anyone noteworthy was shopping there, and was thrilled if someone was. Patrick remembers: "When he found out that I knew Elizabeth Taylor, and I was doing clothes for her when she'd be in town, he'd go, 'Can you try to get her in here? Can you try to bring her down to the store?' "

Gene, of course, adored the limelight and chased it tirelessly. Barneys' parties were legendary and did much to establish the store as the foremost outpost of chic. No detail was too small to merit obsessive attention, down to the stamps on the invitations, which were chosen from a stamp sampler to match the ink on the envelopes.

Soon after the women's store opened, Barneys threw a charity bash for AIDS research. In many ways, it was a typical Barneys party. As the guests gaped, Madonna, Andie MacDowell, and Susan Sarandon sashayed down Peter Marino's elliptical staircase, each wearing an outfit designed for the occasion by the likes of Jean-Paul Gaultier and Chanel. Nell Campbell, who had recently opened the trendy nightspot called Nell's down the street from Barneys, descended the stairs in a pair of Manolo Blahnik pumps with heels so pointy they looked like they could pierce the marble steps. At each landing, Nell executed a perfect half-turn and kicked her leg high above her head—not an easy maneuver in Blahniks.

Guests bid for denim jackets Barneys had sent out to be decorated by designers and downtown artists like Basquiat, the Warhol protégé who later died of a drug overdose. Down in the café at the bottom of the stairs, the café where Fred went for the same lunch every day—tuna fish, it was—Marianne Faithfull, onetime girlfriend of Mick Jagger, sang her world-weary dirges. The bar pushed the vodka: Vodka doesn't stain.

Led by Connie Darrow and Gene Pressman, Barneys soon made its particular notion of stylishness into a new kind of uniform. Barneys dressed the quintessential New York woman of the 1980s, which meant arming her for the kind of sexual and economic combat the time and place provoked. The look popularized by Barneys came in different versions, but it was usually tough, austere, and unflouncy. There was a horror of appearing "bourgeois," a class of people it was mandatory to *épater* even while it produced almost all of Barneys' customers.

In the case of Rei Kawakubo, that meant loose, asymmetrical layerings that often made the wearers look like they were headed for a soiree of nuclear holocaust survivors, which was not an unintended image. Suzy Menkes, the venerable fashion journalist, described Kawakubo's 1983 collection thus: "Down the catwalk, marching to a rhythmic beat like a race of warrior women, came models wearing ink-black coat dresses, cut big, square, away from the body with no line, form or recognizable silhouette." The point here was not to please.

For Thierry Mugler or Jean Paul Gaultier, it often meant designs with fetishistic overtones—leather corsets, say, or, in the case of Gaultier, conical brassieres. The clothes often had a military menace to them, expressed in exaggerated padded shoulders and wasp waists in the jackets. They were meant to bring to the boardroom and the nightclub the same kind of don't-fuck-with-me authority a uniformed cop conveys on the beat. A *New Yorker* cartoon from 1990, after this sort of thing had exhausted much of the public, underscored the rigors of the style. "You're home now, Adele," says the husband to his wife. "Why don't you take off your shoulders."

"This was hard for most women to understand or appreciate," writes Valerie Steele in her book *Fifty Years of Fashion*. "Socialites fretted that it was too severe and unfeminine, and housewives saw it as ugly and irrelevant." Neither group, it should be noted, tended to shop at Barneys, which was just fine with Gene Pressman.

Perhaps the most important element unifying its disparate styles was a color, and that color was black. If there's one thing associated with Barneys and the women who swore by its sensibility, it was their rejection of God's whole rainbow. "Everybody always said there was too much black," huffs a former Barneys publicist. "There was. So what?"

In the hands of Gaultier, it was the black of the sadomasochist; in the hands of Ann Demeulemeester, a gifted Belgian designer introduced by Barneys, it was the black of the tragic poet. In a less challenging context, it was the classic black of Chanel's legendary "little black dress," a style that reappeared in hundreds of variations and soon became de rigueur in every New York woman's closet. Black has its practical side, too. It makes everyone look slimmer, for one thing. And it doesn't show stains.

"Gene hired me on the spot for that kind of minimalist sensibility," says Heidi Godoff, who worked there as a buyer in the late 1980s. "It's the kind of aesthetic that someone has or doesn't have. It's whatever is most pure, without any frill or anything added. It's all in the cut and the quality, whether it was discreet and subtle, or completely daring and over-the-top. I mean, there just aren't that many colors that I like. Connie's philosophy was never to buy safe. Barneys put black on the map, and they put that severe silhouette on the map as well. I don't know that any other store thought like that, even when another store had the same designer, like Moschino. Bergdorf had Moschino, too, but it was bought in a different way for Barneys."

If it couldn't be bought differently, Barneys insisted that it be made differently. Barneys was famous for insisting that designers modify their creations to its specifications, often functioning as a design consultant itself. Fred Pressman set the precedent for this, and he continued to impose his demands unhesitatingly on the vendors who supplied the men's store. They grumbled, of course, and then gave in, later admitting that Fred was probably right in the first place. The women's store did the same thing, although its demands often got far more fanciful and bordered on caprice. That might mean changing the buttons, or it might mean adding a velvet trim. Whatever it was, most designers were hard-pressed to refuse, such was Barneys' power and leverage in the women's fashion business. More often than not, it worked.

"Connie had a huge influence, and she had that kind of eye," recalls Heidi Godoff. "She was part of the reason why a lot of designers didn't like Barneys—you would come in and almost try to redesign their whole line. We were always reworking whatever they had to fit into the Barneys look."

Fabrice—his only name—had just such a relationship with Connie Darrow. Fabrice was an eveningwear designer whose collections sold at better stores around town. When it came time to sell Barneys, Fabrice would sketch and Connie would criticize, and together they created a line of flapper-style dresses in chiffon fabrics with georgette and light jet beading, and, of course, dark colors. It was a big hit for Barneys. "She wanted a certain look that no one in town had," recalled Fabrice, "so I did the very special things they requested, no matter how hard they were. I would sketch them and then show her what I was doing, and that worked very well."

To work at Barneys back then, if you were one of the fashion-mad kids tapped by Gene's magic wand, well, it was like you'd died and gone to heaven, except in fashion heaven, the angels wore black. The clothing men of Barney Pressman's day took their satisfaction from the sheer abundance of suits they sold, which encompassed every conceivable style and every conceivable size, and moreover cost less than you would pay for that suit anywhere else, provided you could even find it. At the women's store, it was exactly the opposite. Pride bubbled up from a rich but shallow pool; there was very little merchandise, and what merchandise there was came in a narrow and unforgiving selection of sizes at prices that would just break a secretary's heart. One fashionable woman went shopping at Barneys some years ago and found a dress she loved, only to be told that the buyer for the department had decided not to carry any sizes from 12 on up—12 being pretty close to a statistical average for women. "I was thinking of writing a note to someone, but then I said, oh, fuck it," she says. "I mean, who would you write a note *to*."

During the fashion shows in Europe, you could spot the Barneys crew a mile away. They strutted in close formation, anywhere from eight to twenty of them, and they radiated the tinny confidence that comes from knowing absolutely you're the hot thing du jour except you don't know how long that jour will last. In Paris, you might see them trooping out of l'Hôtel, just around the corner from the Beaux-Arts, and *the* place to stay in Paris in the late 1980s. In London, it was Blake's, the hotel Anouska Hempel owned, and in Milan, the Principe.

"We were happy campers, you know, but we worked twenty-four/seven," says Beverly Wilburn, who did the first women's line with Dries van Noten for Barneys, and brought in Galliano, too. "But you were getting to stay in the best places; you got to eat the best food at the best restaurants. We had group dinners mostly every night unless Gene had something really, really executive important that he and Bonnie were going to, like dinner with Pierre Bergé of Yves Saint Laurent or somebody like that. Then we would have a free night, but other than that, we had to be there. And when you saw your friend that bought at Bloomingdale's, or you saw your friend that bought at Bendel's, you said hello and you kept going. We really were like a commune, and we didn't break ranks.

"There was a sense that we were creatively superior, and I think we really were. You know, at the time I weighed about one hundred twenty pounds, I had black hair with massive curls, and I wore only Alaïa, Isaia, and these little black dresses. And I was forty then, okay? So you can imagine. And Wendy Burke is like this hot little thing with the little haircut, sort of the Winona Ryder kind of look, all in Chanel. David Rubinstein, this dweeb in Gaultier, he was just so visual. And of course, Connie—ninety-five pieces of jewelry, and brown around the eyes, with two pink spots on her cheeks.

"And after dinner, we'd hit the clubs. We'd go to Bains Douches in Paris; we'd go to Fred in London. But we always went as a group and we stayed as a group. And we left as a group. All the women in the group knew the rules: You don't pick up anybody. You came alone with your group and that's how you go home. Sort of an unwritten law. We were like an orphanage full of well-treated orphans. Every single one was really kind of an outcast, really idiosyncratic in their own way. You were the chosen, you know? And Gene was almost like, you know, Moses. But I never got over it. I just never got over it. You know?"

All was not quiet in the orphanage. Beverly went early on, in 1988, and she never knew what hit her. Connie had talked her out of quitting the week before she was fired. Patrick and Connie would do everything together. In the quiet afternoons, they would get drunk on white wine in the Café des Artistes, and later on, when Connie's husband, Howard, walked out, Patrick slept beside her to calm her frazzled nerves. But that friendship, too, fell away, and before you knew it, Patrick and Connie were no longer even speaking, who knows why. He quit without giving notice, so he couldn't be fired in the interim.

One by one, the Jacobins of fashion faced the guillotine themselves. David Rubinstein, the dweeb in Gaultier, knew his time would soon come when he happened upon a young designer named Isaac Mizrahi, and Connie said absolutely not, never. So Rubinstein went over Connie's head to Gene, and Gene flipped for Isaac, who is known for fun and splashy colors and is anything but austere. Rubinstein dodged the executioner, too, and went to work for Isaac Mizrahi after he quit. Barney Pressman had his "housemen," the core of faithful employees whose long years of service at the store made them virtually untouchable long after they had passed their prime. Suddenly, everyone was touchable.

Fabrice didn't realize he had been dispatched until he was already dead. It was Fabrice's last fashion show, in 1993, and Connie Darrow was due to attend, as she always did, along with two of her assistants. They were late, but given the importance of Barneys, Fabrice held up the show. Finally, after half an hour, the crowd was getting restless, and the show went ahead—without Connie Darrow. She never did show up, she never called, and she never bought from Fabrice again. "That's the way it is in fashion," said Fabrice philosophically. "You have to be able to take all that shit." Fabrice recently died of AIDS. And then the fashion revolution consumed its Robespierre: Not long after, Connie Darrow resigned.

The frenzy that Barneys whipped up in the late 1980s came from more than the merchandise it sold. While Connie Darrow and company were working their black magic, Barneys was also overturning the staid conventions of retail marketing. As long as retailing borrows from stagecraft to make shopping fun, reasoned Barneys, why not borrow from the inspired absurdity of an Ionesco instead of the rigid formality of a Racine? There was no rule that said store design or advertising needed to be decorous or conventional, although a look at most stores made it seem that there was. The accepted thinking went that since every passerby encountered the store's display windows, it would be foolhardy to alienate anyone who might be tempted to walk into the store by thumbing your nose at his or her sensibilities. That thinking obviously didn't sway Barneys, which never missed an opportunity to put thumb to nose.

The person Barneys tapped to do this was another of Gene's inspired hires—an acerbic young Brit named Simon Doonan. Doonan joined Barneys from the Metropolitan Museum of Art's Costume Institute, where he had worked with Diana Vreeland, then the city's reigning fashion personage. But Barneys wanted Doonan for the work he had done before that for a tiny but terribly trendy boutique out in Santa Monica called Maxfield Bleu. Maxfield Bleu had a cult following among rock stars like Elton John and Tina Turner, who had no money at the time and so was forbidden to sign for anything on the strict instructions of Maxfield's owners.

Maxfield turned Doonan loose on its window, and Doonan took full advantage of his license. A mannequin would show up dead and reposing serenely in a coffin, for instance. During a local scare over marauding coyotes, Doonan posed a mother casually watering her lawn while a stuffed coyote made off with her baby. "Oh, we got horrible

phone calls," Doonan recalled in a 1987 interview. "But we were top-
ical and shocking and the windows helped put the store on the map."

That is exactly what Gene Pressman wanted Doonan to do for
Barneys. While Doonan's freewheeling style flew in the face of prevailing wisdom, it actually harked back to the early days of store window display at the end of the nineteenth century. Perhaps the foremost
theorist of the art of window display was L. Frank Baum (who also
wrote *The Wonderful Wizard of Oz* in his spare time). Before Baum
came along, merchants tended to cram their wares together in their
display windows with little thought as to how they were arranged.
Baum changed all that forever when he published the first issue of his
monthly journal, *The Show Window*, in 1897. A year later, Baum
founded the National Association of Window Trimmers, aimed at "the
uplifting of mercantile decorating to the level of a profession."

In his approach to store windows, Baum was more than a little Oz-
like himself. As a young man, Baum was captivated by the theater, and
had spent his early years in the 1880s traveling up and down the Midwest performing with his wife, Maud, in theatricals that he wrote himself. It was a short jump from acting to selling, which Baum pursued
in a variety of business ventures, some more successful than others.

Eventually, he made enough money as the top salesman for a leading Chicago wholesaler of glass and crockery to settle down on Chicago's North Side and turn his attention to his two favorite
occupations: children's stories and commercial showmanship. As
editor of *The Show Window*, Baum preached religiously against the
frumpy merchandising practices of his day, urging the unbridled use of
wild fantasy and spectacle to "arouse in the observer the cupidity and
longing to possess the goods."

"In page after page it recommended new tactics to attract consumer
attention, especially Baum's strong personal preference, 'spectacular'
moving electrical displays of revolving stars, 'vanishing ladies,' me-
chanical butterflies, revolving wheels, incandescent lamp globes—anything to get the customer to 'watch the window,'" writes William

Leach in his superb study of the roots of merchant capitalism, *Land of Desire*.

Simon Doonan couldn't have said it better himself. Like Baum, Doonan pursued the jaw-dropping effect, but he overlaid it with the thick irony of his own fin de siècle. Doonan's topicality, irreverence, and nasty-minded wit all tumbled out in Barneys' Christmas windows. A twisted take on the zodiac, for instance, featured grotesque caricatures of Margaret Thatcher and Tammy Faye Bakker. Fat targets, to be sure, but that didn't stop Doonan from blowing them to smithereens with a cannon anyway. The Tammy Faye Bakker window featured the disgraced evangelist next to a Christmas tree made from a large mascara brush—a reference to the rivulets of makeup that streaked her face during teary interviews. Not subtle, but wickedly apt.

Before long, the unveiling of Barneys' Christmas windows turned into a New York ritual, and crowds would gather to see the latest victims of a Doonan skewering. A Magic Johnson Christmas window featured a tree festooned with condoms. Queen Elizabeth held photographs of her children with their spouses, a tiny saw through each one. Former Vice President Dan Quayle was represented by a Mr. Potato Head doll in front of a sign that read, TODAY'S SPECIAL—POTATOE, a reference to one of Quayle's more embarrassing public gaffes. When a staffer suggested the need to make the visual reference more pointed, Doonan suggested a dunce cap. "I tend to like the more absurd, overextreme and vaguely hideous things," Doonan told *Women's Wear* in 1992. "And though I'm drawn to a certain grotesque quality, I also understand the aesthetic." For this Doonan was richly rewarded with a $600,000 salary, not to mention unrivaled influence within the company; more than anything else, his painstakingly flip sensibility defined the public face of Barneys.

There was nothing flip about the production values, however. As in all Barneys endeavors, the level of craftsmanship was astonishing.

Doonan and his staff would start planning the Christmas windows a full year in advance, and they continually scoured the country for just the right artisans to execute their arch downtown take on life. Steven Johanknecht, who ran Barneys display department, responsible for both the windows and the visual presentation in the store, found an artist named Ellen Karen, who was some kind of genius at painting faux finishes. Karen would design a faux wood dress in different tones of marquetry that she would then paint to match the actual woods used architecturally in the store.

Barneys also designed its own mannequins, instead of relying on the zombielike models out of a manufacturer's catalog. Johanknecht himself created a mannequin known as Spike with an elongated neck that was patterned after a Scandinavian candlestick Johanknecht had seen. To assure that he got exactly what he wanted, Johanknecht regularly traveled out to the mannequin factory in Brooklyn to work with the sculptor on a clay model of Spike. Before the factory poured a fiberglass mold of the clay Spike, Johanknecht wanted to make sure that the mannequin's body posture enhanced the appearance of the clothing it would wear. Believe it or not, there are a lot of mannequins with bad posture.

"I've seen mannequins where the shoulders are sort of slouched, so when you put a jacket on it, the jacket buckles," says Johanknecht. "The mannequin manufacturer isn't necessarily thinking about what clothing's on it. These were subtle things. If you get it wrong, the customer doesn't really understand it, but the clothes look bad. Were we more of a pain in the ass to work with than other stores? Absolutely, but then the manufacturer has the reputation of doing Barneys."

That reputation counted for plenty. By 1994, Barneys' uptown rivals were slavishly imitating its visual presentation, and particularly its Christmas windows, to the point that Women's Wear Daily dubbed the phenomenon "keeping up with the Pressmans."

"Barneys—and the senior vice president and creative director Simon Doonan—have simply stolen New York's Christmas Show and everyone else's thunder," wrote Women's Wear. "The shock value worked and in recent years, other stores have strayed far from their own traditions and tinkered with the edge." Not altogether happily. In 1993, Macy's decided it, too, would skewer celebrities in Barneys' sour Yuletide spirit, although one critic derided Macy's efforts as "half-hearted papier maché heads on regular mannequins."

"It would kind of drive me crazy when I would go out to other stores, and see people copying us left and right," says Johanknecht. "I thought, why did they want to do that? And it always kind of baffled me that other people would want something that would be so identified with Barneys."

As with all gifted agents provocateurs, it was inevitable that every so often Doonan would stir up more trouble than he bargained for. Such is the nature of dancing on other people's outrage. In 1994, Barneys stubbed its toe badly on the grandest spectacle it had mounted to date—the so-called red windows. For this event, Barneys enlisted 36 designers and 300 artists to create works of art using the color red. The artists chosen included pillars of the modern art establishment like Robert Rauschenberg, Jasper Johns, and Ross Bleckner, along with the usual assortment of momentary celebrities on the downtown scene.

The mix followed Barneys' tried-and-true recipe: Take equal measures from high and low society and shake vigorously. The resulting cocktail would enliven uptown pastiness with a downtown kick, while it cut downtown's gritty aftertaste with the syrup of money and privilege. After Christmas, the works of art were to be sold off in a silent auction run by Christie's. The proceeds would go to benefit the Little Red Schoolhouse, a progressive school in Greenwich Village for well-to-do downtown children, and the Storefront School in Harlem.

Among the undiscovered artists was one Tom Sachs, whose Nativity scene was intended as a scathing indictment of commercial exploitation. Sachs's Nativity, made largely out of duct tape, featured overexposed icons of popular culture in place of the traditional participants. Madonna (the singer, that is) represented Mary, and a popular cartoon cat named Hello Kitty played the infant Jesus, while Bart Simpson and the McDonald's logo appeared in supporting roles.

Roman Alonso, who worked in Barneys' publicity department at the time, remembers the public relations nightmare that followed: "There was nothing hideous about it. It was rather adorable, right? But the way that it was described in the press was with the purpose of blowing it up into this huge thing. Well, I mean, it just completely snowballed. It was enormous.

"The next day when I got out of my house and I walked down the street, I looked at the newsstand and on the cover of the *New York Post* was a picture of the Nativity, and on the top it said 'Away with the Manger.' I still have it, because I just couldn't believe it. And that was the beginning of a very horrible two weeks where every hideous tabloid show just completely wanted to pick at this. I'm a Catholic, but I never for a minute thought this would offend anybody. None of us did. Very naive. That was the one thing that everybody hung on to, that goddamn Nativity scene. And it's like, Jesus, what about the rest of the stuff, how amazing this was? It really hurt us."

Soon after, the death threats started coming. "Most of the calls and letters came from people who had never seen the piece. They had just heard about it on the radio or read about it, or somebody had told them about it. So you can see what the media is doing here. They always loved to do that. We had to stand by the artist. We could not censor it. And we only removed it from the window when it became dangerous, when the calls and the letters and the people that were coming into the store kept complaining and we thought that it was dangerous to keep it in there."

In Barneys' glory years during the late 1980s and very early 1990s, missteps of this kind were uncommon and, when they did occur, largely irrelevant. Barneys had taken the peculiar pulse of its time and place more perceptively than any other store. It had harnessed the extraordinary, if volatile, talents it had gathered around it. And the Pressman family, for all the noise its members made, functioned in a synchronized way, giving the best each had to offer and managing to keep their worst impulses more or less in check.

For a short period—maybe as long as five years, maybe less—the

Pressmans hit their high-water mark. Barney Pressman, seemingly immortal, still called the store every day—collect—from Florida, where he lived with his second wife, Isabel. He was in his nineties, but each day he checked the sales figures. Occasionally, he would offer helpful advice. "Are you advertising the free parking? You should advertise the free parking more," he would hector Neil Kraft, vice president of advertising.

That at a time when Barneys was sending out promotional booklets with a photograph of supermodel Linda Evangelista in a leopard-trimmed chapeau and actor Kyle Maclachlan, wearing a Maine lobster on his head. The whimsical caption, written by copywriter Glenn O'Brien, read: "Thought should be lofty, thought should be deep." (Evangelista and Maclachlan fell for each other on the shoot). Other Barneys ads listed a few of "our favorite things," among them, cellular phone sex and strip poker with wild cards.

Still, the family had fulfilled all the dreams Barney Pressman always had for it—even if Barney would have scrawled "free parking" on Maclachlan's lobster headdress. By the end of the 1980s, Barneys New York was pulling in around $95 million a year in sales in 170,000 square feet of space. That worked out to almost $560 a square foot, with overall gross profit margins approaching 50 percent. Not too many stores could come anywhere close to that.

The women's store had set a new standard for chic in New York, and its influence among other retailers knew no bounds. The men's store, meanwhile, continued to churn out money. Armani set the tone for the whole store, but Barneys' dirty little secret was that it sold far more suits by Hugo Boss in the $600 to $900 range.

Hugo Boss made big-shouldered, faux Armani clothing for strivers on a budget. Hugo Boss was *not* Barneys, except (surprise!) it was. Gene was mortified and only disclosed this to one of his ad agencies in strictest confidence. On the other hand, Barneys sold $3 million worth of Hugo Boss a year. For all its faults, the women's store had also managed to goose Barneys' sales of men's accessories, the most profitable part of a men's store. Even the woman who couldn't squeeze into that size 6

Alaïa would often leave with a tie or two for her husband or boyfriend; it shouldn't be a total loss.

At the store, the employees were known to refer to the Pressmans as the Royal Family. That sort of thing is not unusual. The great family-owned retail dynasties often inspired—even encouraged—a primitive kind of fealty among their workers. In the case of the great stores, their owners were often present on the selling floor, where their lordly bearing shined forth for all to see. And all around lay the magnificent trappings of ownership, the ermines and rubies that, if you winked at reality a little, might have been brought from the Indies and laid at the family's feet.

At Bergdorf Goodman, employees called founder Edwin Goodman and his wife "Dad" and "Mom." In the days before automatic elevators, Bergdorf's had a standing rule: If any member of the Goodman family stepped into the car, the elevator operator would immediately convey that Goodman to whatever floor he or she wanted to go, no matter where it had been previously headed with its load of paying customers. It was considered an acceptable gesture of deference, and almost no one, customer or employee, protested.

What was unusual in Barneys' case was the anachronism of this patriarchal attitude at the end of the twentieth century. The great days of family retailing had passed many years before. Most of the legendary family-owned enterprises had sold out to large, publicly held retail conglomerates, which tended to homogenize their quirky personalities even while it bolstered their financial stability.

At Bergdorf Goodman, the store the Pressmans always envied, "Dad" and "Mom" were long dead. In 1972, Andrew Goodman announced that the family would sell out to the Broadway-Hale department store chain—later Carter Hawley Hale—for $11 million. Andrew Goodman, known to all as "little Andrew" in his youth and "Mr. Andrew" when he assumed the mantle from his father, would be the last in his line to run the store. The men of the third generation—a son, Eddie Goodman, and two Goodman sons-in-law—did join the store like they were supposed to. But one by one, they dropped out to follow their destinies elsewhere. Eddie Goodman went to run a radio station with a politically radical bent, while the two sons-in-law pursued the disparate paths of insurance and forestry.

In 1971, *The New York Times Magazine* chronicled the passing of the Goodman clan from the store. To a man, the third generation professed relief at its liberation from the terrible burden of expectations. But the article sounded a melancholy note for the end of an era. "Not long ago, a candy manufacturer approached Andrew Goodman with the idea of setting up a street-floor chocolate boutique at Bergdorf's," wrote author Stephen Birmingham. "Andrew took a box of chocolates home, tried a few pieces, and didn't like them. So there was no boutique. In the Broadway-Hale conglomerate, who will taste the candy? Who will even care?"

At Barneys, Pressmans still tasted the candy, and they meant to go on tasting the candy long after that tradition had withered everywhere else. Each Pressman reigned semiautonomously over his or her respective fiefdom. The men's store was still Fred's exclusive domain, and he continued to oversee it personally. Increasingly, however, he retreated to the two spots where he felt most at home—the Madison Room and the Oak Room, each one a clothing man's castle. There he continued to wait on customers, without announcing who he was, like a medieval baron wandering incognito around his realm.

"Fred had Barney's ability to sell," remembers Chris Ryan, who managed the Oak Room at one time. "You would watch in amazement when this man took a customer. He would not tell the customer who the hell he was. Here was this guy with a Burberry raincoat coming up to a customer, saying, can I help? Some customers would turn around and say, Who the hell are you? Well, I'm the president of the company. He would never say he's the owner. He would romance that customer, and you prayed to God that you had that jacket or that suit in the size that customer needed, because that customer was going to buy it."

Fred's wife, Phyllis, held court in the Chelsea Passage, which by the late 1980s had grown into a $5 million business. Fred could eviscerate an employee when he felt the employee deserved it—within the store, the shell-shocked victim was said to have been "Fredified"—but Phyllis's rages came far more erratically. Her employees lived in utter terror of her wild and random tirades.

"She could be the most gracious, lovely, wonderful, fun woman to be with, and she would turn on a dime, and go for the jugular, for no obvious reason in many cases," says an employee who worked with her for many years. "We always had tables that were set up as part of our crystal and flatware displays, set for fake occasions. Normally, it would be the display department's job to take care of that, but she would come in and do her thing because she had her vision and it had to be her way. The next day she would come in and start screaming about who did the table; it was horrible. In fact, she was the one who did the table. I was one of the few people who could say, 'Mrs. Pressman, you know, you did the table.' And she would get this look on her face that said, 'Okay, whatever,'" and then just slink away and not say anything."

At least the rages helped remind Phyllis who was working for her. Often she didn't remember at all, and would simply draw a blank that employees found oddly unnerving—at least the first few times it happened. It helped to have a sense of humor. "Dozens of times, I would take care of things for her, like spending hours choosing a dress for her daughter, and she would turn to me and say, 'Are you new here? I don't recognize you.' And I would nonchalantly say, 'Oh, I've been here seven years,'" recalls a saleswoman in the women's store.

At day's end, with the selling and the screaming done for the night, Fred would come down from the Oak Room and call for Phyllis at Chelsea Passage, and the two would leave for dinner together, often arm in arm—the king and queen of this royal family as Goya might have painted it. But not one of their subjects would say that Fred and Phyllis weren't deeply in love. "She was in awe of him, and thought he was the most brilliant thing that walked the face of the earth," says a close associate of Phyllis's for many years. "His word was gospel as far as business, and since business was the only thing that family was about, that was everything. His life was the store, and so it became her life, and in their own weird way, she loved him."

Barneys always billed itself as a family operation, and the Pressmans never failed to point this out in press accounts of their golden touch. This meant not just Gene and Bob Pressman, nominally executive vice presidents but clearly in full control by now, but their wives, Bonnie and Holly, and Fred Pressman's daughters, Elizabeth and Nancy. The daughters were never inclined to treat the store as more than a casual way to pass the time, and were never expected to. They both held various jobs over the years, and those jobs all carried serious salaries. Both daughters drew in the neighborhood of $200,000 a year in salary from Barneys, says a source from the store's finance department. What their jobs didn't carry, however, were serious responsibilities.

Liz, the older one, kept a low profile, like her brother Bob, and made only a slight impression around the store. Nancy, the younger one, more than compensated for her sister's gentrified style, however. Nancy was the problem child, but tons of fun. She had Fred's face— an unfortunate resemblance she noted in her eulogy for her father— Barney's foul mouth, and the gas-guzzling appetites of her brother Gene, whom she worshiped. Nancy lived hard. Every once in a while, an employee would spot her unsteadily negotiating the store's escalator, and when the Pressmans made a large charitable donation to St. Vincent's Hospital nearby, the staff jokingly took to calling it the Nancy Pressman Memorial Wing. St. Vincent's has a well-known alcohol and drug rehab facility.

The staff could always tell when Nancy had launched a new romance, because she inevitably brought her new beau to the store to be outfitted. "It was sweet, and it was sad," remembers a former employee. "She came in and just bought them clothes and clothes and clothes and clothes and clothes. It seemed like every two weeks there was some new guy that she was bringing in there, and they were just piling up the clothes."

Nancy also showed up like clockwork at the store's money room, where they kept the cash. The family had the right to draw on this cash when they were caught short, after signing the proper forms, of course. "Money for the cleaning lady," Nancy might mumble, drawing $500 and scrawling her name on the side of a paper coffee cup to leave with the bemused bursar. A few days later, another hasty emergency would arise, and a quick squiggle on a napkin would register a similar transaction. Finally, even Fred had had enough, and instructed the money room to stop cashing Nancy's cups and napkins. For a time, anyway.

She was well liked, though. Down-to-earth, unpretentious, never one to put on airs, that was our Nancy. She had a mouth like a truck driver, more than one of them said, but they said that to her face, too, and she would open her wide mouth and roar with laughter—ahhh haaaah! At Marino's office, they had a nickname for her: the straight lesbian. "Oooh, hard-core, that Nancy," says another employee. "She was hard-core. I liked her, and she liked me."

And then, lo and behold, on June 19, 1988, "Nancy Ann Pressman, a daughter of Mr. and Mrs. Fred Pressman of Harrison, N.Y., and Dr. Kenneth Alex Dressler, the son of Cary C. Dressler of Montreal and the late Ruth Hecht Dressler, were married last evening at the Pressman home." The day after, Liz's palpable consternation was the buzz of the women's store. Score one for our Nancy. It took another year for Liz to bag Dr. Seth Neubardt.

The sisters' rivalry had nothing on the brothers'. The disparity in the pecking order between Gene and Bob, four years younger, conformed to the mythic model so classically it might have been etched in hieroglyphs on a pharaoh's tomb: Gene, stiff and straight with upraised scepter and the Egyptian jackal-god's head; Bob, small and wide, a lowly clerk scratching away at his clay tablet. The Jewish mythotype is more succinct: "Bob was the fat kid," says a former executive.

In a 1993 *Vanity Fair* article, Phyllis Pressman proudly recounted an early example of the brothers' nascent business relationship: "Gene played guitar in a band, and he asked me if he could have the sophomore dance at our house and if his band could play. When I agreed, he decided he should get paid. That night, he set nine-year-old Bobby up with a table, a chair, and a cashbox, and Bobby collected the money and stamped the kids' hands." It's hard to know what to find more unnerving: this early onset of lifelong second-fiddlehood, or the apparent cluelessness of the parent who promotes it.

Each son dutifully continued to play his assigned role. Gene spent his school years throwing spitballs and honing his unruly persona. He was never much of a student, and didn't try to be. In college at Syracuse, he bumped uncomfortably from one field of study to another. He started out in the business curriculum, but lasted less than a semester. The liberal arts faculty reminded him of high school and bored him witless. He liked the art school, the next stop in his academic wanderings, but found it too structured for his restless spirit.

The school of television and radio beckoned next, mostly because it looked easy, but before too long, Gene found himself "hooked on cinema," as he told an interviewer. And so he graduated from Syracuse a cinema major. That love affair lasted for two months in Hollywood, where Gene discovered that cinema wasn't exactly hooked on him. In the end, of course, he landed back at the store. "He knew he could always fall back on his family business," says his boyhood friend Jeff Klein.

Bob's progress to the store sidestepped any detours for fun or self-delusion. He trooped off to Boston College, where he studied business, and later, to Pace University, where he collected a master's in business administration. Bob himself likes to recount that he was the only student in his business school class who came from retailing and planned to go back.

At the store, the brothers eased effortlessly into the old garment-district stereotypes that any clothing man would recognize instantly: Mr. Outside and Mr. Inside. Bob had been groomed to oversee the financial workings of the store, but he was also expected to take on all the other unglamorous tasks that traditionally fall to Mr. Inside. "He was assigned to worry about the air-conditioning, worry about the telephones, worry about the overtime—the typical job of an inside man," says a former executive. Did he ever complain that he didn't want to worry about the air-conditioning (because, in point of fact, he didn't)? Not that anyone heard.

Mr. Inside kept his deepest resentments to himself, but every once in a while things would slip out that suggested Bob Pressman really didn't care for the retail business one bit. "Bobby didn't like being involved with customers," says a former salesman. "He would come on the floor, and if you wanted to get rid of him, you'd say, Bobby, I got a customer over here. You want to come walk with me while . . . and he's gone, boom!"

Every so often, Bob couldn't avoid getting involved with a customer, although never face-to-face. And when he did, it was clear that the soul of Barneys was changing. You can't be a great retailer if you don't love your customers in some kind of way, even from afar. There is a basic truth here: No one wants to buy from people who don't like them. There was the time in the middle 1980s, for instance, when Bob noticed a credit to a customer for $1,600. Five suits had been returned and the customer got his full money back. That was a sizable credit and Bob wanted to know what happened. The customer had made clear when he bought the suits that he cared about one thing and one thing only—cuffs on the pants. The pants he got were too short, and they had no cuffs, so the salesman, after apologizing profusely, had refunded the money and offered to remake the suits. Couldn't you manage to push the suits on him anyway? Bob demanded gruffly. The salesman was a Fred man, and he spoke in heat. Only an asshole would try to shove the suits on this guy, he shot back. It took Fred's intercession to keep the salesman from being fired straightaway, but Fred took the salesman aside and pleaded with him. Do me a favor, said Fred, and don't ever do that again.

But Bob had a vexing problem of his own, and that problem would only get more pressing as the years wore on. By the time Barneys had reached its apex in the fashion world, the problem just wouldn't go away. Bob had to find money. In reality, Mr. Inside's job came down to propping up Mr. Outside, and he resented this part most deeply of all. The women's store wasn't making any money. "It was merchandised like a boutique, but it was a full store," says a former executive high up in the Barneys organization. "Volume was always less than anticipated, and it was always hard to make the numbers in the plan. Gene's response was always that the plan was too high, the people in the store are lousy, somebody's screwing things up." Adds another executive, "People look at the years from 1985 to 1992 as the golden years at Barneys, but the scoreboard says you're bleeding money and you're not going to get to play anymore."

The family's way of life was lavish. The family collectively took around $5 million a year out of the store in salaries but still the bills piled up. There were houses to maintain, and like the store, they required continual redecoration by Peter Marino. In 1983, Gene and Bonnie bought a rambling, twenty-five-thousand-square-foot Tudor house at 209 Hommocks Road, in the leafy Westchester bedroom community of Larchmont.

"I remember being dragged through the site, with Gene going, 'Look what we're putting in here,'" says Neil Kraft. "We were renovating our kitchen about the same time they were renovating theirs, and Gene was always giving me advice that for me, on my thirty-thousand-dollar salary at the time, was ludicrous. But the details and the stuff that he did, you know, were amazing—just amazing. And the kitchen was all white cabinets, state-of-the-art. It's sad, but I think Gene's strongest aesthetic was not for clothing, but for living. It's spectacularly beautiful."

The house lies off a long, horseshoe-shaped driveway on a bluff overlooking Long Island Sound, with dormer windows snugly set in a shingled mansard roof and a high semicircular sunroom in the back. It has a distinct 1920s feel, the period whose decorative style Gene liked best. You can almost imagine some bootlegger waiting offshore until he spied the winking lights from Hommocks Road signaling him that it was safe to deliver his load of hooch to the famous gangster Bugsy Siegel.

That is exactly what Gene did imagine and his imagination caught fire with the romantic picture, which combined macho derring-do with smoky nostalgia. The house appears in almost every magazine article written about Gene and Barneys, always with its pedigree as Bugsy Siegel's onetime residence. The only problem with this being that Siegel never owned the place. The closest most locals can come to the origins of the claim is a vague local legend of some bootlegger's tunnel under the house, which Gene embellished into his naughty version of "George Washington slept here."

Larchmont is a quiet, decorous kind of town known for its discreet, old-world charm. It has a largish international community, many of whom work for the United Nations, and its residents can get a bit sniffy about the more raucous, newer-money suburbs to the west, like Harrison, where Gene grew up. Gene didn't make much of an effort to endear himself to his new neighbors, either. Parading around with your shirt off, or even in a string bikini as Gene liked to do in the heat of summer, might pass muster in Harrison, which one neighbor likened to a "banana republic," but it is simply not done in Larchmont.

The neighbors found Gene's posturing droll. "Why would you want to live in a house that Bugsy Siegel lived in? Bugsy Siegel was dreadful," says a former resident of the Hommocks Road house. "Gene incorporated that into his persona, like pasting hairs on your chest. I know other people who have done this."

Sometimes the neighbors found Gene's posturing not so droll. Abutting Gene's property on Hommocks Road is a strip of land, known as the reserve property and owned collectively by the neighborhood for the benefit of those landowners without frontage on Long Island Sound. The reserve runs to the Sound, with a dock at the end of it. "The first thing we knew when Gene had begun the renovations on his house was he decided to close off the front entrance to the reserve," recalls a former neighbor. "And I'm sure he knew he didn't own it, but I get the feeling he was somebody who just sort of thought you could do things and then see what happened and do the fixing up after. And when the people on the street copped to the fact that he was basically using reserve property, they made a great huge fuss and he basically had to undo what had been a great deal of work."

Despite the unpleasantness on Hommocks Road, life inside Casa Bugsy was gay. There were constant parties, and the expensive wine from the fourteen thousand bottles Gene kept in his cellar flowed freely. "We would have these wine tastings, and Gene absolutely could not tell one wine from another, but he was sort of impressed with the cost of it," says Neil Kraft. " 'This is a hundred-dollar bottle of wine,' he would tell you, which even then was extraordinary. This happened dozens and dozens of times. And I was thinking, I don't want to know this. There was just something about the way he talked about it. You know, you would sit down in a chair and he'd tell you how much the chair cost."

Behind the house was the dock where Gene moored the Cigarette speedboat he had christened *Bonnie*. If Gene's guests enjoyed his fine wines and his fancy cigars, they positively dreaded an invitation to ride in the boat. The odds were high that some misadventure on the high seas would befall them as Gene opened the throttle up full on this powerful plaything. "It was always a disaster," says Kraft. "You'd be hitting the water at forty miles an hour, and inevitably the boat would break. Every time I went out, I swore I was not going to go out with him again." Occasionally it caught fire. "He didn't know anything about it or how to really take care of it and use it," says Kraft. "It was just kind of this loud toy."

A very expensive loud toy, at that. Prices for a new Cigarette can easily top $100,000. Gene also owned a 1952 Gullwing Mercedes-Benz and a 1962 Aston Martin, worth perhaps $300,000 together. Gene's enthusiasms, however brief, were never cheap.

Gene was the family's most conspicuous consumer, but he was hardly the only Pressman with a taste for the high life. Nancy spent $1.2 million to redecorate her home, Peter Marino once again applying his high-priced touch. The Pressman women also helped themselves to the store's overpriced merchandise with a free hand. Inventory shortage is the term applied to discrepancies between the inventory recorded as sold and the actual depletion of the stock on hand. It is computed as a percentage of the store's retail dollar sales over a set time period. Shortage covers merchandise theft, but it is also a handy catchall for sloppy bookkeeping and other paper errors that creep into the records. Like, for instance, goods taken by Pressman family members that the family might forget to pay for.

Barneys listed its inventory shortage as 2 percent, but that number was only for public consumption on one of the many sets of books the store prepared for various internal and external audiences. It was a fluid number that could be manipulated at will. "Shortly after I arrived at the store, they said to me, 'What do you want to book as the shortage percent?' " says a former senior executive. "And I said, 'What do you mean, what do I want to book? What was the shortage?' And they didn't want to tell me."

In fact, the real inventory shortage came closer to 9 percent of sales—the industry average is around 2 percent. Woefully inadequate inventory control played a part and was always a big problem at Barneys. As sales grew at double-digit annual rates, Barneys never imposed the structure necessary to manage a $100 million enterprise, either technologically or managerially. Fred continued to run things with the thumb-and-forefinger feel of his father, and neither Gene nor Bob took the slightest interest in such banalities as computer systems or organizational charts.

But ineptitude doesn't nearly account for all of that inventory shortage. "He pulled out of his pocket some tickets, some stubs from merchandise tickets," recalls the former senior executive of a meeting she had with a senior Barneys accountant. "And he said what happens is when the family need clothes, they just walk in and take them, and they usually just leave me with the stubs. But it's never recorded that way. The transaction is never recorded. So the logic of the whole thing would be that some portion between the two percent shortage and the nine percent shortage was this great amount of clothing that had disappeared. It was a lot of money."

That wasn't all Barneys paid for, either. Barneys workmen routinely worked on the Pressman residences; and a host of other services, from Gene's boxing trainer to Nancy's psychiatrist, were charged to the store. A painter on the store's payroll never showed up at the store at all, and lived at the Rye Town Hilton in Westchester while he worked on the Pressman residences. Did the Pressmans pay the store back for these services, as they were legally required to do if they didn't declare them as income on their tax returns? It is difficult to find a record of it anywhere if they did. "If you were to audit Barneys' books, you would never find entries for the boxing trainer or work on the house," says a former accounting executive. "No one paid any attention to this."

Except Bob, of course, and Bob wasn't telling. Bob kept all the secrets. There were always several sets of financial statements, depending on who was supposed to be looking at them. This isn't against the law, but it is misleading, which indeed was the whole point. The buyers for the women's store, for instance, lived in blissful ignorance of the financial hemorrhage seeping through the minimalist frocks they purchased. Knowing might cramp their style, it was feared. "The statements were never as good as the buyers were led to believe," says the accounting executive. "The women's store wasn't making money, but no one wanted them to know so they wouldn't cut back." Yet another set of financial statements was "adjusted to comply with the bank's expectations," says the accountant.

The hard truth of the matter was camouflaged by running all manner of expenses through a complex web of affiliate companies Bob had established. Those companies, which oversaw such activities as local real estate investments, credit card operations, or licensing activities, served as convenient vehicles to make the store look considerably healthier than it really was. "If you didn't charge rent to your accounting operations, let's say, because you owned the building, how fair a picture of the business is that?" explains the former accountant. "The Pressmans were very good at that kind of thing."

Bob would grumble halfheartedly at his brother's heedless spending. Occasionally, he would plead for a little restraint. Fred preferred not to ask, or pretended not to hear. "They don't tell me what's going on," he would say with a resigned shrug. Inside, Fred was already starting to shrink. He knew in his heart that things were already starting to go badly wrong, but reining Gene in just wasn't something he could bring himself to do.

Gene was more direct. "Go find the money someplace else," an executive remembers Gene telling Bob in one meeting when Bob suggested cutting back Barneys' spending on advertising or the lavish buying caravans Gene regularly led across Europe. "I'm going to do what I'm going to do," declared Gene.

So Bob went back outside and stared hard at the same cashbox he had watched over when he was nine years old and started thinking of clever ways to fill it. It must have felt very familiar and very painful. But if Bob didn't like running the store, he did like making deals, and luckily for the family, he was pretty good at it.

At about the same time the women's store was first being built, Bob and Irwin Rosenthal, a brilliant Harvard-trained lawyer who would later become Barneys' chief financial officer, made a series of real estate investments in the Chelsea area through a wholly owned affiliate called Preen. With financing from France's Crédit Agricole and the Greater New York Savings Banks, Barneys invested roughly $18 million in three loft buildings: 230, 245, and 249 West Seventeenth Street. Bob and Irv Rosenthal got the buildings at rock-bottom prices at a time when rents in midtown Manhattan were skyrocketing. When Bob releveraged the buildings soon after, pulling out all the equity up front, he had netted a tidy $10 million to $15 million profit on his investment. That was a good beginning, but it was only a beginning. Bob hadn't finished playing around with Preen and its potential for hiding, monetizing, and leveraging the funds that Barneys would come to need desperately.

Meanwhile, on the men's side of the business, Fred was flogging his buyers to cut better and better deals, thereby pushing Barneys' ingoing margins even higher and trying to make up for losses in the women's store with higher profits in menswear. "Fred was recognizing that the needs of the business were being strained by his expenses," says Peter Rizzo. "The first way he reacted was to generate high ingoing margins, reducing your markdowns and coming up with the cash value." There was a limit to how hard the Fred men could push their suppliers on price, however, and they were reaching it.

Here is where Bob made another important discovery that was to become a hallmark of the new Barneys management style in the years ahead. Bob discovered that you didn't have to pay people even close to on time, and some people you didn't have to pay at all. Given the attitudes that had governed the way Barney and Fred Pressman conducted business for sixty-five years, this was a startling departure.

"Barneys was always a very good payer when Freddy was there," says Sheldon Beil, whose company, Beil Electronics, did almost all the electrical contracting work for Barneys for thirty years. "They paid their contractors. If I went up there and said, Freddy, you got ten thousand dollars? I need the money today. He would arrange to make the check in two hours.

"Bobby, through his experience, found out that the general contractors never paid their subcontractors for thirty, sixty, ninety days. So he started that whole plan of holding back money. He felt, why should we pay subcontractors? Nobody else does. Instead of paying them in five days or ten days or thirty days, he'll pay them in ninety days, one hundred twenty days. That's when a number of the old-time contractors just stopped doing business with Barneys. Because Bobby would cut the bills down. He would pay late. And then pay them and tell the bank to hold the check." Beil stopped working for Barneys in the late 1980s.

Did the Pressman family thank Bobby for playing the heavy? Not then and not ever, and what he saw as their ingratitude tortured him. "In the family's eyes, Gene could do no wrong, and Bob could do no right," says someone who worked closely with the family. "Bob was always the official scapegoat."

7

"WHY USE FAUX GOATSKIN WHEN YOU CAN USE REAL GOATSKIN?"

None of the financial turmoil beneath the surface of Seventeenth Street did anything to shake the Pressmans' firm conviction that Barneys must keep growing. Quite the opposite: The turmoil itself made expansion look even more appealing. The Pressmans never liked to solve problems by rolling up their sleeves and just fixing them. Mere tradesmen could do that. They preferred solutions that required "vision," a favorite word that argued for taking the heart-stopping swan dive into the unknown.

There is ample precedent for this in the annals of business. Barneys

wouldn't be the first business that opted to redress an imbalance between revenue and expense by looking for clever new ways of making
money rather than cutting costs. "You couldn't just sit still," a former
senior Barneys executive said. "You would see your margins erode. You
couldn't raise prices freely, and there was an awful lot of pressure on
costs."

In theory, at least, this assessment wasn't altogether unsound. Barneys had managed to make its name known around the world as the
ultimate purveyor of the superb. Just walking around carrying a Barneys
shopping bag—black, of course, with the name embossed in silver—
identified the bearer as a shopper of substance and discernment. And
in fact, many shoppers took to carrying a spare Barneys bag just to
ennoble their workaday purchases. With one store downtown as its
sole business, Barneys wasn't cashing in on this reputation to nearly
the extent that it might. Even before it opened, the women's store was
viewed as a vehicle for doing that. The men's store alone was a much
better business, but it wasn't a better business opportunity. So while
the women's store may have been killing Barneys on the cost side, it
gave the company options it hadn't had before.

As early as 1986, the family had started looking for a partner with
deep pockets who would grasp hold of their hands, ask no questions,
and leap alongside them. Bob engaged the gilt-edged investment banking firm of Goldman, Sachs and Company to help identify suitable
candidates. An early walk around Wall Street yielded nothing. Word
had gotten around that the Pressman boys could be a little erratic.
That they were also too enamored of themselves anyone could see at
first meeting.

Everyone agreed that the most desirable match would be a so-
called "strategic" partner—in other words, a partner whose long-term
business interests stood to gain by its association with Barneys. A
partner who viewed Barneys as purely a financial investment would
look only to the dollars it would reap, and would expect Barneys to
produce those dollars more promptly than the Pressmans knew it could.
And when those dollars didn't appear, it was bound to ask uncom-

fortable questions that the Pressmans didn't like to contemplate—even among themselves. That scuttled the idea of a public offering, too. But a partner bedazzled by Barneys' taste and hooked on its sparkling "vision," ah, now that was a partner you could do business with.

Japan was the likeliest place to look for such a partner for several reasons. It seems laughable now, but back in the late 1980s, many astute businessmen believed the world stood on the threshold of what some called "the Japanese century." The Japanese had nothing but money, a condition due to the frothy real estate lending that drove what is now referred to as Japan's "bubble economy." They were spending that money with reckless abandon on anything with a fancy Occidental brand name. This meant not just your typical Barneys shopping list of Armani, Chanel, and Calvin Klein, but show-stopper acquisitions like Rockefeller Center, the Pebble Beach golf course, and Columbia Pictures.

In 1989, a watershed year for Barneys as it happened, a Japanese industrialist named Ryoei Saito shelled out $82.5 million at Christie's for Vincent Van Gogh's *Portrait of Dr. Gachet*. The price still stands as the record for a single painting sold at auction, although today the painting wouldn't bring anywhere near what the late Mr. Saito paid for it. The same holds true for many of Japan's gassier investments in the West—Barneys being just one of them.

But there were reasons beyond high spirits for Japanese retailers in particular to gaze longingly at Barneys. Japanese retailing had never shaken off the cumbersome regulations and tangled relationships with suppliers that had plagued it since the Meiji Restoration of 1868. That's when the kimono retailers of Edo, as Tokyo was then called, first created the Byzantine distribution system that left them at the mercy of their suppliers and a host of unnecessary middlemen. Despite its inefficiency—or even because of it; one of every five Japanese makes a living on the endless distribution chain—the system stuck.

Manufacturers set prices for both the retailer and the many tiers of wholesalers who served him in a system known as *tatane*. The paltry retail margins under the *tatane* system commonly fell below 30 percent. In return, however, the manufacturer would buy back any goods the retailer didn't manage to sell at full price, and pay rebates for the goods the retailer did sell. The manufacturer also picked up the retailer's expenses for promotion, financed the retailer's inventory, and even supplied its own workers to offer "guidance" in the stores.

Basically, *tatane* reduced the retailer to a passive landlord who did little more than lease space to the manufacturers whose wares he sold. Margins were low, but in return the retailer led a cushy life free of almost all risk. Enterprising retailers might chafe, but they had little choice in the matter. Any retailer who had the gumption to strike out on his own would quickly find himself subjected to a boycott that left him with virtually nothing to sell.

This stultifying arrangement had already started to break down when Goldman, Sachs began dangling the prospect of a Barneys alliance before the margin-starved Japanese. Goldman turned up three prospects: Mitsukoshi, an old-line department store; Seibu, which became the first store to import French fashion to Japan in 1961; and a company called Isetan.

Isetan had deep roots. In 1886, a draper named Tanji Kosuge—he took the surname from his wife's wealthy family—opened a kimono shop called Iseya Tanji Drapery in Tokyo's Kanda district. The shop thrived. Tanji Kosuge had more than a little Barney Pressman in him, and some of Fred, too. He created original designs that he had his manufacturers execute and sent his salesmen out with samples to the homes of his best customers. He stayed open all night, and he ran seasonal bargain sales. Before long he began buying out other kimono stores in the neighborhood, and in 1899, he enlarged the Kanda shop. By the turn of the century, Iseya Tanji Drapery ranked among the five leading dry goods stores in Japan.

In the years leading up to their bruising encounter with the Pressmans, Tanji Kosuge's descendants succeeded in transforming his kimono business into one of Japan's most formidable fashion merchants, now called Isetan. A year after Barney Pressman started hawking suits, Isetan opened its first department store in Tokyo. When Kuniyasu Kosuge, the fourth-generation scion, took over as head of the company from his ailing father, Tanji Kosuge III, in 1984, Isetan had sales of around $4 billion—$1.6 billion from its main store in Tokyo's Shinjuku district alone. Kosuge was thirty-eight years old, and considered very much a hothead in a country run by old men.

The striking parallels between the two young-men-in-a-hurry who ran their family businesses spread a benevolent aura of faith and goodwill over the initial meetings between Barneys and Isetan. For Kosuge, vision was everything. He had spent seven years abroad while he learned the business, and dreamed of making Isetan a global force. He pushed Isetan into new markets—Taiwan, Shanghai, even London. He wore stylishly baggy green suits, which only made the blue-suited elders on the Isetan board even warier of him. His wife was comely and well-groomed.

Barneys had several things Kosuge wanted badly. Chiefly, it had margins approaching 50 percent. Isetan struggled to reach 35 percent. It also had a network of manufacturers Fred had developed in the late 1970s and early '80s, mostly Italian, that produced goods directly for Barneys' private label. The private label merchandise, which accounted for 25 percent of its sales, was arguably the best deal in the store. Fred's demanding standards and his persnickety choice of manufacturers ensured private label goods of the highest quality. Meanwhile, Fred's hard-bitten negotiating tactics with suppliers meant that Barneys could charge very reasonable prices for its private label goods and still make a handsome profit. Kosuge drooled when he saw the kind of merchandise Barneys could source directly, bypassing the armies of middlemen blocking his own path.

Beyond that, blood and history inspired a level of trust Kosuge would never have felt in dealing with a large U.S. public company. Both companies still carried their family names. For the descendants of the founders to dishonor those names would be unthinkable. Here was a guarantee more ironclad than any contract: The ancestors, living and dead, were watching.

The first meetings in New York and Tokyo in late 1988 went swimmingly. Gene and Kosuge recognized each other as kindred spirits immediately. You mean, you're a visionary?—you can imagine one saying to the other. Isn't that remarkable. I'm a visionary, too! "Leaving Kosuge and Gene alone in a room for too long was dangerous," says a Barneys executive. "They both saw the world through similarly tinted glasses."

"We were on a high, they were on a high," Gene told *New York* magazine in the only extensive interview Gene and Bob gave after the bankruptcy, when they retreated behind a silk curtain of silence. "It felt like family from day one. They were very worldly, very international. They made decisions quickly. It's very unusual to have a third-generation family and a fourth-generation family with the same vision and trust. It was almost a dream come true."

The auspicious occasion was celebrated over drinks at a swank Tokyo club, with B-girls standing in for angel choirs. The tab came to $2,500 a person. Kosuge picked it up.

In March 1989, Barneys and Isetan met again, this time on the Manele golf course in Hawaii. Accounts of the game differ: One puts Bob's score for nine holes at 90, while a later version raised this abominable total to 120. By all accounts, the Japanese were highly amused and may have even taken this as a testament to Bob's seriousness as a businessman, harmoniously balancing Gene's flair and his fluid golf strokes.

This only shows the pitfalls of judging a man by his golf game. Bob was neither as bad a golfer as he appeared, nor half so serious about the business of running Barneys. And Gene, while undoubtedly devoted to the game, wasn't nearly as good as his 17 golf handicap suggested. "Don't ever play him for money," a Barneys executive remembers being warned by a caddy at the exclusive Westchester Country Club, where Gene played regularly. Was he that formidable a player? the executive wondered. "No," replied the caddy. "It's just that he sort of doesn't know how to keep score." Adds another golfing buddy: "He just can't bear to lose."

He didn't on this occasion. The Pressmans came back from Hawaii with an astonishingly good deal. The first part of the deal, which had been negotiated the previous January, established a joint venture between Barneys and Isetan to build a chain of Barneys stores around the country. The plan called for twenty-five to thirty Barneys outposts of around sixty-five hundred square feet, each selling mostly women's clothing. The idea, as Gene saw it, was that America's women wanted the kind of daring fashions they saw in the fashion magazines but couldn't find in their local stores. Gene and Bob buoyantly predicted sales of $100 million for the Barneys America stores within several years.

It was pointed out to Gene that America had too many stores already, and that the current sales climate was chilly. Gene did not find this the slightest bit daunting. "It might be overstored, but it's not over-good-stored," he patiently explained to a *Women's Wear Daily* reporter. "We're going in with something that isn't there now."

According to the terms of the deal for Barneys America, as the new Barneys, Inc., unit was called, Isetan would buy $12 million in preferred stock, convertible into between 25 and 35 percent of Barneys America common stock. The employees of Barneys America would get 10 percent of the common stock, with the Pressman family getting the rest. At full dilution, the Pressmans would end up holding 51 percent of the equity in Barneys America, Isetan 42 percent, and the employees 7 percent, but each Pressman share carried three votes, giving the family an overwhelming dominance of the company.

Bob and Nobuo Nakanishi, the Kosuge confidant who served as the chief negotiator on the Japanese side, formed a warm relationship of their own. Bob called Nakanishi "Panda" in view of his round face. Nakanishi in turn fondly called Bob "counter-Panda" in their communiqués. The two later socialized together and later took a skiing vacation with their families in Deer Valley, Utah.

"Panda," Bob asked Nakanishi on the slopes, "why didn't you negotiate harder?"

"Understand, Bob," said Panda, "twelve million dollars is less than the sales in our Shinjuku store for one morning. If we lose everything, it's a morning's work." It turned out to be much more than a morning's work when the full damage was tallied, and along the way, Panda lost his job over it.

The second element of the deal, contained in a March 1989 "General Letter of Intent" between the two companies, established a joint venture called Barneys Japan. Under this agreement, Isetan would have the license to use the Barneys trademark throughout Asia, with the Pressmans holding a 20 percent stake in the enterprise. As its first project under the agreement, Isetan would build a thirty-thousand-square-foot store in Tokyo's Shinjuku neighborhood to open in November 1990. Isetan committed to building three stores in Japan as a start, and planned a second, much larger store in Tokyo to follow Shinjuku in short order.

In return, Isetan would pay Barneys a minimum royalty of 2.75 percent of merchandise revenues annually, with the royalty to increase each year over the twenty-year term of the agreement. That didn't quite match the 5 percent royalty Barneys had wanted, but Kosuge and Nakanishi, who advised on the negotiations, doubted that Barneys Japan could generate gross margins substantially over 40 percent, as the Pressmans swore it could.

Here, Isetan held out a plum. Barneys would provide technical assistance to Isetan to teach the Japanese how to achieve the kinds of margins Barneys boasted in New York. To the extent that Barneys Japan exceeded gross profit margins of 37 percent—in other words, sales minus the cost of goods sold—Isetan would pay the Pressmans half of the excess. A kind of exchange program was set up, in which young Isetan employees were dispatched to New York to study at Pressman U., while Barneys executives worked closely with Isetan in Japan.

What Isetan really hoped to do was apply these lessons to its Isetan stores, which is where many of the young people they called the "Isetan kids" would be sent after they returned. If Isetan could manage to pick up just an extra 7 percent in margin on even half its sales—not a fantastical expectation—it would boost its bottom line by $140 million a year. A windfall of that magnitude could justify the whole deal, whatever else happened. "You know, it all could have worked!" says one executive who watched everything fall apart from the inside.

The Isetan kids were amazed at what they encountered in this Land of Oz. They sat in awe at Gene's feet while he preached about something called the "magic mix," a term more evocative than descriptive. "Magic mix, it's a Barneys word," recalls Hiroshi Higuchi, one of the Isetan kids who went back to work in the Isetan store and served for a time as a liaison to Isetan's law firm in its ensuing litigation with the Pressmans. "It could apply to anything. Gene Pressman used it a lot."

Everything was new and captivating. The strange colors that Barneys would juxtapose—red and black, for instance. At Isetan, all employees carried a little chart that laid down strict laws about how to match colors according to its rigid rainbow. At Barneys, the Isetan kids learned to toss that tired rainbow out the window. It was heady stuff. Higuchi worked closely with Simon Doonan on displays, both in New York and in Japan. "Doonan picks up garbage, puts it in window, and makes great window," marvels Higuchi. And everywhere, the curious phrase, "that's *fabulous*," echoed through the store. What can this mean—that's *fabulous*?, the Isetan kids wondered. But they caught on fast. All together now: "That's . . . *fabulous*." Soon enough, the Isetan kids were saying it, too.

The real crux of the deal, however, centered on a joint venture to build big stores in the United States, although that had not been discussed in the earliest meetings. Gene had it in mind all along, however, and the other aspects of the deal, however important to Isetan, were just sweetmeats to the main meal for him. The Pressmans had already considered the possibility of expanding the downtown store yet again by building on the parking lot across the street. It was an unappealing option, particularly after the Pressmans saw the salutary effect of having its women's store adjacent to its men's business. If the women's store moved across the street, good-bye to all those men's ties and shirts that women bought as they passed through that department en route to the little black dresses.

Moreover, trouble loomed not too many years off with Barneys' sweetheart lease on the main men's store due to expire in March 1996. The lease for sixty thousand square feet was a laughable $200,000 a year. Comparable leases in the neighborhood suggest that Barneys' new lease would rise to somewhere around $1.2 million. The Pressmans tried several times to buy the space from the landlord, Treger Realty, but every time the two parties got close to a deal, the price suddenly doubled. Treger figured it had the Pressmans over a barrel, since the family had already sunk a fortune on the women's store next door.

The proposed partnership with Isetan got the Pressmans out of their big-store bind in spectacular fashion. Kosuge wanted this, too, and people close to the negotiations say it was never Kosuge's aim to serve as a landlord, collecting monthly rent checks from the Pressmans forever. That was already the outdated role of the Japanese retailer—precisely what Kosuge wanted to escape through his alliance with Barneys.

"There is no question whether the structure was to develop real estate in partnership with Barneys. It was," says a former senior executive. "In fact, Isetan wanted even more of a stake in a U.S. retailing venture from the outset, and the Pressmans didn't want that." It is one of the many ironies of the blood feud between the two companies that each side ended up claiming to be exactly what it said it wasn't at the time: All through the bankruptcy Isetan played the aggrieved landlord saddled with a recalcitrant tenant, while Barneys portrayed itself as one of two equal partners in a joint enterprise gone sour. It was the opposite in 1989. Isetan wanted an active partner and Barneys wanted a silent landlord.

The capstone of their relationship would be three stores in New York, Beverly Hills, and Chicago. Isetan would put up 95 percent of the money, the Pressmans the remaining 5 percent up to a cap: $147 million for New York, $65 million for Beverly Hills, and $35 million for Chicago. In return, Isetan would get all the cash flow from the stores until the return topped 14 percent with Barneys paying rent, operating expenses, and real estate taxes out of the money thrown off by the stores themselves. For every $100 Isetan invested in the stores up to the cap, it would get the first $14 in cash after operating expenses were met. The Pressmans and Isetan would split each dollar after that down the middle.

It was a truly wonderful prospect for the Pressmans. Isetan was handing the family a free empire and couldn't take it back for 499 years—the full term of their agreement. "Freddie went to Japan the first time, he asked me to come and have lunch, and we went to have lunch, and he said to me, how come you never go to Japan?" says Martin Greenfield. "You cannot believe how nice these people are, Freddie tells me. He tells me of an incident where he ate lunch and he left a tip. Those tips are not accepted, they are included, and he tells me how the woman ran after him, to give back the money. And then he told me about these people he was going to do business with. To me, he said, it was like a marriage made in heaven. Later, he called it the marriage made in hell—you know, afterwards. I said, you know, I never went to Japan because I have no desire."

Bob was considerably more blunt about the true outcome of the negotiations. "We fucked the Japanese," he crowed. And in a way, it was true. He had indeed, if you were inclined to analyze the deal copulationally. "I think Bob was only happy when the other person in a deal was unhappy," says an executive who worked closely with him.

The Pressmans started erecting their new empire almost immediately, and all at once. On its own, Barneys had already opened a small satellite store in New York's World Financial Center, a gleaming series of office towers near the tip of Manhattan, in 1988. Three more stores would now follow in short order in the wealthy suburbs of Manhasset, Long Island; Short Hills, New Jersey; and Chestnut Hill, Massachusetts. Within the next several years, Barneys had a total of fourteen full-price stores and six outlet stores in eleven states, from Washington to Florida.

For the most part, those stores in such far-flung locales as Troy, Michigan, Houston, and Seattle never really fired the Pressmans' imagination. To the Pressmans, it was like they never really existed at all, and hardly anyone noticed as, one by one, most of them closed. As with all true New Yorkers, their heart's desire found its deepest longings on the island of Manhattan, and it was there that the Pressmans focused their frantic energy.

Barneys found sites in Beverly Hills and Chicago relatively quickly. At least it thought it did. Arthur Gilbert, an eccentric real estate magnate who conducted meetings in tennis whites, owned a five-story building on Wilshire Boulevard at the corner of Camden Drive. He also owned 60 percent of the blockfront, with Saks owning the rest, plus some land behind the boulevard. Gilbert, who is a trustee of the Los Angeles County Museum, happens to have one of the world's leading collections of what are called "micromosaics," tiny pictures made up of thousands upon thousands of stone specks. He is a very detail-oriented guy.

Saks had its Beverly Hills store on the next block—a ramshackle affair that had gone up in the 1920s. Saks desperately wanted to move, so it proposed a tax-free swap: the site of its store for Gilbert's land adjacent to the Saks parking lot. Its only stipulation was that Gilbert not relet the old Saks store to Nordstrom, the high-priced department store chain from Seattle. Saks had gotten wind that Nordstrom had set its sights on Beverly Hills, and it didn't want to facilitate the invasion. Arthur Gilbert and Mel Jacobs, then chairman of Saks, settled the deal with a handshake.

As soon as the Pressmans came through town, they realized the old Saks site would serve perfectly. The Pressmans and Gilbert came to terms quickly on the old Saks store that Gilbert was shortly to take over. "That's when Mel Jacobs said, 'Whoops—that's not exactly what I meant,' and backed out of the deal," recalls one of the Barneys team. Arthur Gilbert was livid, but there was nothing to be done. In the end, Gilbert offered the Pressmans a five-story office building and a small bank building he owned on the Wilshire and Camden corner. In return, Gilbert would get $1.4 million a year from Barneys.

What this did, however, was once again to pit Barneys against a suspicious local populace. The citizens of Beverly Hills, never timid and always ready to stand their ground on matters of principle, have two overriding concerns in all questions of land use: commercial encroachment—stopping the spread of commerce into a neighborhood that a Barneys negotiator described as looking "like Queens but with one-million-dollar houses"—and parking. At the same time, Saks was filing to expand its parking lot into the residential zone adjacent to Barneys' site. Suddenly, the two stores found themselves unlikely allies in a firefight with an enraged local citizenry.

"All hell broke loose," remembers a Barneys executive. "Mel Jacobs was threatening to pull Saks out of Beverly Hills altogether if he didn't get approval, and that created a huge amount of ill-will. At one meeting, he packed the audience with Saks employees, which came very close to provoking a fistfight with the Beverly Hills residents."

Barneys wanted its site badly, and realized that the only way to win approval from the city council was in the coin of highest value in Beverly Hills, namely, parking. Barneys would expand the existing underground garage to five levels, which would require the complete demolition of the building on top of it. Beverly Hills would get its car palace, and ultimately gave its approval to the Barneys proposal, but the cost of that one concession doomed the $65 million cap Isetan had set for the Beverly Hills store. The garage alone would end up costing $12 million. It's a very beautiful underground garage.

Back in New York, the search for a suitable site proved considerably more difficult. Isetan and Barneys had left vague the question of how grand a space Barneys would acquire for its flagship. It was assumed that the store would occupy somewhere in the neighborhood of 200,000 square feet. Finding a suitable site of that size in the cramped corridors of midtown Manhattan, however, was no easy matter.

There was a deserted Alexander's department store on Fifty-ninth

Street and Lexington Avenue, a block away from Bloomingdale's, but Fred and Gene both despised the location. Real estate cachet on the Upper East Side of Manhattan is measured directly in feet from Fifth Avenue, and slips away fast with each step one takes toward the East River. By the time you've crossed Park Avenue heading toward Lexington, you've already squandered most of the snootiness value you sought from that neighborhood in the first place.

The old Manhattan Savings Bank building at Forty-seventh Street and Madison Avenue was considered briefly and rejected. The Pressmans looked more closely at several buildings on Park Avenue in the low Fifties, but the suburban railroad track from Grand Central Station ran directly beneath them.

Then, bingo! Jonathan Miller and Henry Hart Rice, Barneys' agents at the real estate firm of Grubb and Ellis, hit on the Met Life building at 660 Madison Avenue, between Sixty-first and Sixty-second streets. It would be difficult to find a lusher spot—just at the headwaters of two golden shopping tributaries, where the tide from Madison Avenue's precious boutiques to the north empties into the overflow from Fifth Avenue's grand department stores to the south.

The 660 Madison Avenue building had some drawbacks, to be sure. The architecture firm of Emery Roth built it in 1955 as the original headquarters of J. Paul Getty's Getty Oil, but Getty could have made its dimensions more commodious. The ceiling, at eleven feet, might have extended up another two or three feet. The columns might have been broader and better spaced. The building's condition was not good. Even worse, it was covered in a cheap aluminum wrapper like an embarrassing Christmas present from the kind of store you wouldn't shop in. Overall, Barneys had a second-rate building at a first-rate location, but the Pressmans figured that Japanese money could correct any shortcomings, or at least disguise them.

The Pressmans worked out a novel proposition, since it hardly needed to buy an entire twenty-three-story office tower to house a store. It proposed to split the building into two condominium units. The first, which Barneys would purchase, would consist of floors one through nine of the building—around 240,000 square feet—plus a proportionate share of the building's common space for air-conditioning, loading docks, and the like. The common space would add another 60,000 square feet. Met Life would take the second condominium unit comprising floors 10 to 23, plus its share of common space.

The proposed price for the Barneys unit was $70 million, or $233 per square foot. That in itself would not be exorbitant, but in the blink of an eye, the New York store had somehow ballooned 50 percent beyond the size Isetan and the Pressmans had foreseen. "There wasn't any discussion about this with Isetan," says a Barneys executive. "It seems strange, doesn't it?"

The Pressman team approached Metropolitan Life with this offer under a cloak of deepest secrecy, although in retrospect it's not exactly clear why the family took such elaborate precautions to conceal its identity. One argument went that if Barneys' rivals got wind the Pressmans were coming, they would make damn sure to nail down any designer who might defect. But that doesn't really make much sense, since Bergdorf, Saks, and Bloomingdale's would still have ample time to shore up their defenses once Barneys started construction on any site it planned to occupy.

It was really always more a matter of saving face. The Pressmans took it as an article of faith that the world shared the same kingly expectations of the family that the family had for itself. Were they to fail to secure the site they had chosen, they feared, it would make them a laughingstock. In truth, no one cared about this half as much as they did. "I'm not sure it made any sense at all," says one of the few Barneys executives who knew about the plans.

The skullduggery had a slightly burlesque quality to it. Barneys wouldn't tell Met Life whom it was negotiating with, but it worried that Met Life would hesitate to sell half its building to an anonymous buyer. So it pretended it wanted to explore the idea of a long-term lease, with a purchase option down the road. In reality, the Pressmans had a positive horror of leasing, what with its lease on Seventeenth Street coming to an end and causing Barneys no end of trouble.

The negotiations dragged on, often in separate conference rooms simultaneously so that various Pressmans could come and go without being recognized. Code names were employed. In a kind of Ian Fleming flourish, they called the uptown store Project X, which must have delighted Gene. Met Life didn't learn whom it was haggling with for the first six months. It had come up with its own estimate for the cost of refitting the building's aluminum shell, but the actual cost looked like it would run considerably higher. Eventually, Barneys brought back Goldman, Sachs to hammer out the details with the higher-ups at Met Life, and still the deal came within a hairsbreadth of falling through.

Design work started simultaneously on the New York and Beverly Hills stores in early 1991, and it was clear from the start that Peter Marino's office would be overburdened. Marino's practice specialized in big-money residential work and fancy boutiques. It simply wasn't equipped for two projects this size at the same time. The crush of work meant that Marino would often submit plans for subcontractors to bid on when those plans were only three-quarters complete. As in the women's store downtown, the subcontractors would find themselves working from a different set of drawings than the ones they had bid on originally.

The scale of the project was massive. *Interior Design* magazine later called it "one of the most ambitious retailing ventures the city has seen in decades," adding that "the audacity of the Barneys scheme still confounds many." Over one thousand shop drawings were submitted for the first six floors of the store, each of which needed approval by Marino's staff. If laid end to end, the store's shelving would have stretched seven miles.

"Submissions came in at one hundred drawings a week at times," says Ralf Dremel, one of the overburdened architects. "People just couldn't take it. I was working until three o'clock in the morning just trying to keep up with that stuff. Because as soon as you hold up the contractors, that's it. It means extra charges and change orders and that's how you would get a lot of run-ups on the overtime."

Each floor of the uptown store got its own designer from Marino's staff, which was an unusual arrangement. It was one way to give each floor a distinct, boutiquelike character, which the Pressmans wanted, instead of making it homogeneous, like a department store. It also served a political function. It gave the Pressman responsible for each department his or her own architect, which saved that Pressman the headache of trying to pry a single architect from the grasp of another Pressman.

This arrangement also made the architects easier to dispose of. Sometimes several architects worked on one floor; but not at the same time, rather serially. "You got eaten up and spit out," says one of the project managers. "People came and went constantly. You had to suppress your own ego; otherwise you didn't stand a chance, because they would swallow you up whole."

Phyllis Pressman chewed through four architects on Chelsea Passage alone, which established a store record for architect casualties. "I would go back to the office crying, like, three days out of four," remembers one of them. "She could say the meanest, horriblest things, and just deflate you to nothing, until you felt completely useless. I promised when I walked out of that office that I would never again let a client make me cry."

One thing none of the architects had to worry about was budgets. "We never spoke about the budget, that's for sure," says another architect. "Budget was never an issue. That's not unusual for a Marino project, but I've never seen anything like it at any other firm I worked for."

The centerpiece of the main floor is an elaborate inlaid mosaic of white and gray Carrara marble. The pattern was worked out at the corners in negative images of itself, so that if one corner realized the pattern in white and gray, the opposite corner would mirror that geometry in gray and white. These positive and negative patterns interlocked as they worked their way toward the center of the mosaic. The intricacy of the pattern required the artisans employed by Franz Mayer of Munich to lay the floor out by hand, tile by tile, as they went along to make sure it fit together seamlessly.

The Marino designers were kept apprised of the progress by photographs that were sent regularly to New York from Munich. The trick was not just to get the pattern right in the corners, but to "solve" the pattern where it met in the middle, obscuring the spot where positive and negative came together. It was dizzying work, and hideously expensive. This floor alone cost $100 per square foot—$600,000 in all.

The uptown store's less noticeable features got the same Versailles treatment. Marino found a small workshop in Indonesia that would apply a crackled mother-of-pearl finish to wooden shelving. The mill workers at Chantiers-Baudet in France would carve the wood shapes, ship them to Indonesia, where the pattern would get its mother-of-pearl overlay. The Indonesian artisans would then send their work back to Chantiers-Baudet for final assembly. The bill for this kind of treatment came to roughly $300 a square foot. "We didn't think twice about it," says an architect.

Out in Beverly Hills, another set of workmen was applying the same opulent standards to the western palazzo. The custom-built fish tank, for instance, couldn't follow the fish tank norms, because that would give you a glass fish tank with an unsightly silicone bead in one corner to make a waterproof seal. Barneys used mitred, three-quarter-inch Plexiglas, but instead of sealing the tank at the corner with silicone, it poured in molten acrylic. This method hides the telltale sealing line at the corner of the tank. It is minimalism at its most minimal.

"The Pressmans kept saying they wanted this to be the most beautiful store in the world," says one of the top architects on the project. "They wanted it to be the most beautiful store in the world, and they weren't concerned about cutting corners. On Madison Avenue, we did a whole boutique with goatskin—the whole boutique was lined with goatskin! It looks almost like parchment paper, but it's actually goatskin. How many people in New York City know how to lay goatskin on woodwork? I was arguing that you could do this in a faux finish, and you might spend an eighth of the price. The response was, like, why use faux goatskin when you could use real goatskin?

"So I'd call up Peter and say, Do you have a specification for this goatskin? Can you tell me anything about it? He said, Goatskin is goatskin. That was his response. Goatskin is goatskin. What he meant by that was he didn't have the slightest idea either about how to do it, because there is no specification for goatskin. Peter's major business was doing very, very, very high-end residential work where the client wanted the best of everything, and wanted to be able to say they had Peter Marino as their designer. He's used to dealing that way. So a lot of what he did was he'd go out and he'd find the finest craftsmen in any field and he would describe to them in sketch form or verbal form very loosely what he wanted. They would go implement it and send him the bill. And then he would tack on his own markup.

"The Bloomingdale's people thought the Pressmans were out of their minds to spend that kind of money. Who's going to say, 'Hey, why did they paint on that goatskin finish—they should have bought real goatskin. I'm not going to buy my stockings here, because who wants to look at faux goatskin'? It was just beyond the realm of reality."

At the same time, Barneys America was constructing and opening its seventy-five-hundred-square-foot branch outlets at a breakneck pace. Nor did the family's preoccupation with the New York and Beverly Hills stores prevent it from lavishing the same no-holds-barred treatment on these provincial outposts. Several of the out-of-town stores installed floors made of anigre, a light-colored Brazilian hardwood. Anigre contracts and expands significantly, depending on the moisture content in the surrounding air. As a result, a contractor must let the anigre flooring sit on the site for a good month before it is installed, so it can adjust to the local weather. Of course, the schedule didn't allow for that kind of delay, so the floors were installed as soon as they arrived. You could see the quarter-inch gaps in the floor where the wood contracted after it had been laid down.

Marino also specified mahogany storefronts. Now, mahogany is a beautiful wood, but it doesn't weather well. In the Houston and Dallas stores, it didn't take long for the hot Texas sun to bleach the rich brown right out of it.

"They did a lot of stupid things like that," says Michael Ratner, whose firm, Richter and Ratner, did most of the interiors for the Barneys America stores. "They would order all these exquisite things, and you would come back six months later and it would look like shit. Peter Marino has exquisite taste, and so does Gene, and they each fed on that. Peter would show Gene something that would cost an outrageous amount of money, and Gene would love it, so they would go ahead and just do it.

"They often used curved glass on the showcases, for instance. Making curved glass is not a precise science: You make a bed of sand in the shape you want and then you heat the glass and let it fall into the bed. The glass then takes up the shape of the sand. But it's hard to get exact measurements this way. So you'll make one curved glass case, install it, and find that it doesn't fit quite right. Sometimes, you have to have it made three or four times until it's precisely the right size."

And yet, you had only to see Fred laboring alone and late at night over a shoe display to see that all this was not just a matter of pride run riot; it was also a sincere form of worship. In his reverence and humility, Fred might have been a Levite dedicated to a life of religious service in the days before the temple in Jerusalem was destroyed.

One of the workmen at the new Houston store happened upon Fred at his devotions one night. "It was like an artist at work, like a brilliant sculptor. Just a cherry wood table with men's shoes, no less than three hours at night by himself. He manipulated them and moved them—the different forms and the shapes and the styles that he just put together in different ways, and then the groupings contrasted to each other. It was like watching somebody do a calculus problem, just building upon itself until it was complete—this sculpture of shoes. By the time it got done, this table was magnificent. And all over the place were men's shoes. The table just spoke to me; I don't know, maybe it was the hour—this heavenly essence of it."

On August 26, 1991, Barney Pressman died. He was ninety-six years old. Barney had retired from the store in 1975, and for many years he had lived in Miami Beach with his second wife, Isabel. The family didn't take too well to Isabel and there was bad blood, so there wasn't much socializing between them. Barney stayed robust until very shortly before he died, a blessing he attributed to the ministrations of his Chinese doctor. But the store was never far from his mind. Every day, he called collect from Miami to ask, "What's selling? What's new? What's old?" They never told him the truth, of course.

When Barney died, work on the Houston store was plunging ahead. No one hung black bunting on any of the stores to mark the founder's passing. In the minds of the family, he had passed long ago, and continuity was apparently not a virtue any of them prized. It's hard to tell from the outside what people may be suffering on the inside, but to the workmen on the Houston store, it looked as if the Pressmans felt more at ease contemplating footwear than memory.

"Not a tear, not a look of depression. They wouldn't have been there if it wasn't for him, and they just went about their business," recalls the same workman who witnessed the ritual of the shoes. "Maybe it's what he would have wanted them to do—you know, the show-must-go-on kind of attitude, but it just didn't seem to faze them. I think what drove them was the time frame—the store had to get open for business, there could be no delays. They weren't going to let anybody see any emotion, because the clock had to keep ticking. Maybe at night they all came together."

There were more pressing matters to worry about, namely, money. It soon became clear that work on the core and shell of 660 Madison Avenue would far exceed Metropolitan Life's original estimate. Part of the reason was Peter Marino's decision to swaddle the building in cream-colored French Luget limestone. With its cherry red awnings shading oversized windows and delicate wrought-iron railings, the new design looks like a soigné transplant from the Avenue Montaigne in Paris. It's an airy counterpoint to the grim office towers around it and it works stunningly well. But somebody still had to pay for all that Luget limestone, and it certainly wasn't going to be the Pressmans.

There were nightmarish complications belowground as well. Lehrer McGovern Bovis, the construction company on the job, had to demolish an existing parking garage in the basement and burrow through another six feet of rock. The extra space would house a truck turntable and loading dock to service the entire building through its one freight elevator.

The granite proved unexpectedly stubborn, but Lehrer McGovern couldn't just blast away at it. Barneys' two classy neighbors—the Pierre Hotel and the Metropolitan Club—were both landmark buildings. To make sure they remained upright during the job, the New York City Landmarks Preservation Commission set strict limits on the explosive firepower Barneys could employ and installed sophisticated seismographs in both buildings to ensure that it complied. Nonetheless, Lehrer McGovern exceeded its limit on a number of occasions. "We'd get a report the next day that we had to change what we were doing to make sure that we didn't drop any chandeliers on anybody's head," says one of the architects.

If that wasn't bad enough, the Metropolitan Transit Authority was fretting about the subway tunnel that ran below Sixtieth Street just feet from where Barneys was blasting. To keep it from caving in, Lehrer McGovern drilled a series of holes over the top of the tunnel and installed rock anchorages that literally tied the rock to the foundation wall of the building. A series of bolts kept the tunnel from moving during the excavation. A minor mishap occurred when Lehrer McGovern accidentally overtightened the bolts and ended up dragging the entire subway tunnel about three eighths of an inch toward the store. That did not please the Metropolitan Transit Authority.

Met Life swooned, but not over the aesthetic grandeur of its building—over the cost. By the middle of 1992, the whole project was coming close to unraveling as Met Life made ominous noises that it might walk away from the whole deal. Met Life's architects, Kohn Pedersen Fox, originally estimated that it would take between $40 million and $50 million to replace the aluminum shell of the building and redo the core—half of which Met Life would pay for under the condominium arrangement it had worked out with the Pressmans. It now appeared that the final bill could run over twice as high.

Until then, Isetan had allowed the Pressmans to operate with a shockingly free hand. Barneys would send over requisitions against specific invoices, and Isetan paid. "They didn't appear to be looking at the bills too closely," says a Barneys executive. The accounting firm of Coopers and Lybrand had been hired to do the construction audit, and Isetan was presumably getting their reports. But oddly, Isetan did not see fit to station an employee anywhere near the site to monitor the progress of its sizable investment. "If it was my money, I'd be sure that I had somebody watching, but that never happened," says one of the chief architects.

It might have been because Isetan was fighting for its life at the time. In a pop heard round the world, Japan's overinflated bubble economy finally burst, leaving a thin film of soap scum where Kuniyasu Kosuge's global vision once floated. In 1990, the Japanese stock market fell by more than half. The overvalued real estate market collapsed, and Japan's banks stopped lending. Very quickly, Japanese banks found themselves with over $600 billion worth of bad loans. In 1992, Isetan's sales fell for the first time since 1961, and profits plunged 64.5 percent. The money Isetan was blithely signing over to Barneys' goatskin suppliers would help send its total debt over $1 billion by 1993.

Isetan soon found itself with a nauseating decision to make—pull the plug on Barneys or keep spending to prop up a project that had spiraled out of control. "The choices weren't too pretty," remembers an insider. "For months and months, Isetan wouldn't talk about it, and then when they did, they kept saying, 'You ask too much.' We told them they had no choice."

Isetan glumly realized how right the Pressmans were. Isetan's thirty-thousand-square-foot Barneys store in Tokyo, opened November 1990, was doing everything Isetan had wanted, although it was not yet in the black. Isetan had picked up the rudiments of Barneys' style remarkably quickly, while it steered clear of the vaporous excesses that made its New York model such a mess. If Isetan pulled out, it not only jettisoned the huge investment it had made in the United States, it also cut Barneys Japan loose from the institution that anchored it. The sickening truth of Bob Pressman's crude bluster had been borne out: The Japanese were indeed fucked.

Toward the end of 1992, Metropolitan Life called it quits. After threatening to sue, Barneys reached an agreement with Metropolitan Life to take the rest of the building off its hands for the nominal sum of around $6 million. That left Isetan with an office building it didn't want, plus the daunting expense of finishing work on the building's exterior with no financial help from Met Life. In the end, Isetan reluctantly signed another check for $120 million to keep the Madison Avenue project going.

It was among the last decisions Kosuge and Nakanishi would make. "We knew Panda was under pressure, but we didn't know how much pressure," says a Barneys insider. The sales losses, the mounting Barneys debt, and a $70 million gamble in foreign currency that went bad had exposed Isetan to attack. A stock and property speculator called Shuwa Corporation had been buying up Isetan shares since the late 1980s. In 1993, Shuwa was poised to unload its 29 percent stake to Ito-Yokado, a national supermarket chain that could use them to engulf Isetan itself. Isetan only managed to cling to its independence by enlisting the giant Mitsubishi Bank, its leading creditor, to buy the Shuwa shares instead.

The price of Mitsubishi's rescue, however, was virtual control of the company. Kosuge was ousted as president in the summer of 1993, and took the ceremonial title of honorary chairman. Panda exited with him. In Kosuge's place, Mitsubishi installed Kazumasa Koshiba, a blue-suited Isetan veteran with thirty-five years' experience in the mundane tasks of administration and sales. Kuniyasu Kosuge resigned from the board in 1996, leaving his family with nothing but a .43 percent stake in the kimono company that the Kosuges had run for over a century.

The mad year leading up to the unalterable opening date of the Madison Avenue store—September 8, 1993—was marked by chaos, exhaustion, and rancor. The Pressmans were constantly at each other's throats. Any semblance of family harmony was shredded. Gene needled his wife, Bonnie, mercilessly over the layout of the ground floor, which Bonnie nominally oversaw. She had been named senior vice president in 1991, and she wanted hosiery in the back. Gene insisted it be in the front. What the fuck did Bonnie know, anyway? She was just a model, with no education. Gene would berate her publicly in this fashion at design meetings. And then, just before leaving the room, he would turn and fart loudly to underscore his authority.

Meek as she was, even Bonnie walked out of several meetings after she had absorbed more pummeling from Gene than she could bear. The Marino architects used to call Bonnie's heavy-footed trudge down the corridor her "death row" walk. For the most part, though, Bonnie took it. Most people thought her talented and capable, but it was her long-suffering stoicism that defined her persona in this Yiddish Theater Euripides.

The marriage had all but broken down by then. Husband and wife were living on separate floors of the Larchmont house. Everybody knew that Gene was having a liaison with a girl from the publicity department and borrowing apartments from friends around town for afternoon trysts. "Couldn't he at least afford his own apartment?" one of them wondered. The girl rose rapidly in the executive ranks, as did another reputed girlfriend in the advertising department. In 1995, Bonnie Pressman was diagnosed with breast cancer and underwent a successful operation.

Unlike Bonnie, Bob raged at Gene—just not directly. He raged at a proxy Gene, who was his secretary Rose Fedorchak. Rose had the unlucky job of also serving as a proxy Fred, a proxy Phyllis, and a proxy Isetan as well. As things worsened, Bob took it all out on Rose. "That's where he would focus all the hostility and frustration for which he had no other outlet," says an executive. "You could tell by the level of harassment of Rose how Bob was feeling: The ebb and flow of abuse served as a pretty good barometer."

Even the most straightforward matters between the two brothers degenerated into a comical contest of wills. Despite the fact that Gene and Bob had offices next door to each another, their doors were situated in such a way that there was no easy access between them. So it was decided to cut a door between Gene's office and Bob's office.

"The guy who got the unfortunate assignment almost had a nervous breakdown over this," says one of the top executives. "Getting them to agree on where the door should go, how it should swing, whether it should be locked or unlocked, and what color it should be painted was a major undertaking. Finally, I gave up and said, just put it in. I couldn't get them to agree on this door. This took months. To do a simple door."

By now, Bob and his wife, Holly, had been ostracized by the rest of the family. No one had ever really liked Holly, a former money manager at Morgan Stanley whose strident manner rubbed many people the wrong way. Holly bitterly resented her husband's second-class status within the family, and she wasn't shy about sticking up for him.

And Fred? Fred was torn between longing and unease. Against his better judgment, he had succumbed to Gene's fantasy. He would sometimes drive his beat-up BMW up Madison Avenue and park across the street from the site on a Saturday afternoon and just sit there gazing up at it. Bergdorf's was down the block, Bloomingdale's a few blocks east. Almost seventy years after his father had scrounged his first suit to sell, Barneys would join what they called the B-line: the elite coterie of uptown department stores whose names all began with the letter B. He had finally arrived—but where, exactly?

Fred had a lurking fear that Barneys was getting in much too far over its head, but he couldn't get to the bottom of it, no matter how doggedly he tried. Bob kept the details of the mounting crisis to himself and resisted all of Fred's entreaties to tell him what in hell was really going on. "It will be taken care of," he assured Fred and Gene. Bob saw himself as the lone mechanic who kept the Pressman illusion machine from breaking apart at the seams, and he wondered to colleagues why his family never thanked him for it. "Don't they know what I've done for them?" he would complain bitterly.

The final months unfolded in a haze of cement dust and misery. By now it was clear that only superhuman efforts and vast amounts of cash would get the store ready to open on September 8. Over one thousand workers manned the construction site at the end. They worked virtually around the clock, seven days a week, holidays included. That meant double- and triple-time pay. The hardier among them volunteered for three shifts back to back—no one was turned away, and the money was just too tempting to resist. A union man could rake in $5,000 in a week with all the overtime, and many of them did, living on coffee and amphetamines and trying not to walk off a beam seven stories up and enter history as a martyr to fashion.

In the end, fashion claimed two victims. One fell off a scaffolding and the other "walked" into an empty elevator shaft. Fatigue may have contributed to the first death, but the second looked to many like foul play. Construction sites generate huge piles of scrap metal that are collected from the site and sold. Barneys might have been throwing off as much as $30,000 worth of scrap metal a week. The construction workers establish a pecking order, and woe betide anyone who jumps the line to grab someone else's share of scrap. One story goes that they warned the guy first. He didn't listen.

The workmen kept slogging ahead, often too exhausted to see where they were drilling a hole. "They'd double and triple prices for a job that was inferior by anyone's standards," says one of the architects. In some places, sockets and walls run two inches out of plumb over six feet. Often, workmen with the right skills couldn't be found at any price. "You couldn't even throw money at the problem," says an architect. "People just couldn't do it. You can't say yes when you have everybody working double shifts."

Ultimately, Lehrer McGovern instructed its workmen simply to ignore the architects, who were still scrambling to incorporate the daily design changes mandated by the Pressmans. A week before the store opened, Liz Pressman informed "her architect" that she had made a small boo-boo: Liz had specified 250 square feet for the size of her baby clothes department; she really meant 500 square feet. The architect remembers it well.

"One week before it's due! And I said it was impossible. Lehrer

McGovern instructed everyone in the field that they were to disregard us in every way, that we were not to have any say-so whatsoever. But Liz got her way. She called her mother. She called her brother. And all of a sudden, I got orders that within one week I was to have the capacity fabricated that she wanted. We found somebody in Brooklyn and basically said, you'll never work for us again if you don't come up with the pieces we need. They forced us to treat people like crap. But at that point, it was a question of, it's my job, you know?"

Nick Scarpone, the project manager for Peter Marino, finally cracked under all the pressure. Scarpone had a nervous breakdown and left Marino's firm not long after the store opened to study theology somewhere in the Midwest. "He personalized it," remembers one of the architects who worked with him. "He just couldn't adapt to the constant changes, and he was faced with changes all the time."

The bill for the final three months of construction came to $75 million—$10 million of that in overtime expenses alone. Lehrer McGovern Bovis is one of the larger construction firms in the New York area, and it has many years' experience building the craggy monuments for which New York is known. No one can remember when one of its clients had even come close to spending so much so fast.

The store did manage to open on September 8, 1993, but minutes before the guests arrived for the gala opening the night before, workmen were frantically stowing dropcloths in the empty dressing rooms and stashing buckets in empty cabinets. While the guests took in all the opulence around them, the paint was still drying in parts of the store.

Several hours before, Fred suddenly took it into his head to reverse the direction of all the escalators. He didn't like the way the traffic would flow through the store. Changing the direction of the escalators means a lot more than flipping a switch. For one thing, every "up" and "down" sign throughout the store must be changed, too. It took considerable persuading by several Barneys executives to get Fred to accept the hard fact that the store was finally finished.

The heartbreaking travail of building the Brooklyn Bridge has passed into legend, but when the Roeblings had finished it, a New Yorker could walk from Manhattan to Brooklyn for the first time. The best you could say here was that a particular kind of New York woman could ride from Alaïa to Yamamoto. "At the end of the day, it is still a store," says one of the top architects on the project. "No matter how good it is, it's not St. Peter's. And keep this in mind, too. The Medicis spent their own money."

8

HONOR

Well before the Madison Avenue store opened, the Pressmans had to admit to themselves that the business they were anticipating for the new store could never justify the money they kept pouring into it. The obvious solution: Raise the projections. That they did with a vengeance. In their more expansive moments, the brothers dreamed that sales per square foot on Madison Avenue might even top $800. "By the time I left, they were talking about the company doing well over three hundred million dollars the first year after Madison Avenue opened," remembers an executive who participated in the planning sessions.

It took some doing to manufacture the clouds on which these air castles were to be built. At one point, Barneys hired the market research firm of Walter K. Levy to estimate how many of the downtown store's customers would continue to shop at the old Seventeenth Street Barneys. The Pressmans insisted that both stores would thrive and argued with anyone who pointed out that no store had managed to pull off the two-store stunt since Gimbel's, and Gimbel's had gone out of business. Nonsense, said the boys. You had two completely separate groups of customers.

You couldn't prove it by Levy, however. The Levy firm's estimates, based on a sample of four hundred people, simply didn't support the rosy projections the Pressmans had concocted. Gene blew up. Clearly, the low number came about because Levy had used too small a sample. Gene insisted that Levy redo its study using a much larger sample. Bob didn't think that would alter the outcome much, but Gene wouldn't budge.

"That's what I want," he huffed. "These results are crazy, and I need a bigger sample, and they're not going to get paid until we get it."

"What are you *talking* about, Gene?" said Bob. "We don't pay *any-body*."

Everybody in the meeting laughed heartily at this. Nothing's funnier than the wicked truth. You only had to walk around the unfinished Madison Avenue site to know how true. During construction, the walls of the store were often covered with hateful graffiti.

That wasn't the worst of it, either. "Death threats against the Pressmans. Threats of violence. Oh, yeah," says a former security man for the store, "these people wanted their money." There was no point investigating every single death threat, since nothing could be done about it, and besides, there were simply too many people to investigate. The only thing Barneys security could do was keep a close eye on the doors so that when a wild-eyed creditor stormed into the offices to collect—and many of them did—he couldn't get anywhere near the boys.

The deadbeat stories started filtering out shortly after the Madison Avenue store opened, but the practice had been going on for years and only worsened as the financial vise tightened. Bob Pressman could joke so brazenly about not paying the bills because he had turned what started as an expedient shuffle into a systematic ballet a long time before. By the time the Madison Avenue store opened, Barneys had grown financially dependent on juggling a "float" of unpaid bills that hovered between $30 million and $40 million at any one time. After Amy Spindler, *The New York Times*' fashion reporter, pried the lid open in late 1993, all the lurid tales started spilling out. Characteristically, the Pressmans initially responded by trying to get Spindler fired.

Michael Ratner, head of Richter and Ratner, was owed $900,000 for all the work he did on the interiors of the Barneys America stores and the Chicago Barneys New York store on Oak Street. He finally sued the Pressmans for the $146,000 he still hadn't collected seven months and almost a hundred unanswered phone calls later.

"I ran into Gene by chance one day and told him I couldn't get his chief financial officer to return my phone calls," says Ratner. "He looked through me like I wasn't even there. One of the reasons I feel so bitter about what happened is that I lost my relationship with my bank over this. I actually had to go out and find an asset-based lender to continue running my business, and that probably cost me anywhere from three hundred thousand to five hundred thousand dollars in added interest as a result."

There were many others like Ratner—designers, artisans, subcontractors—each with a similar story to tell. Bills went unpaid for months, often causing immense strain on the small businessmen who built the Pressmans' stores and homes and stocked them with finely wrought things. Sometimes the bills wouldn't get paid at all, leaving creditors no options besides a costly, debilitating lawsuit or a settlement for a fraction of the money owed. The smart ones knew Barneys' reputation beforehand and took what steps they could. Bill Olson withheld a shipment of his custom-built furniture a week before the store was due to open and refused to release a single chaise longue until he had been paid in full. He got his money.

Most of them didn't have this kind of leverage. For young designers, the chance to showcase their talent in Barneys could propel an entire career. The opportunity was too rich to pass up, so they threw the dice. It was often a life-and-death gamble. Barneys always demanded an exclusive on the merchandise it carried, meaning the designer couldn't sell to any other store. Barneys had made its reputation on such exclusives. The more its clout increased, the more unyielding became its posture toward vendors who begged for the right to sell to other stores as well.

In the case of a fledgling designer, Barneys could usually make its

demands stick. So when the checks never came, many of these designers had no other source of income to see them through. First came the
polite requests, then the desperate entreaties, and finally the impotent
outbursts. Barneys did not even pay them the courtesy of bullshit; just
silence. "People were getting stiffed right and left," says an executive
from the human resources department. "I was getting calls from vendors saying, 'Can't you help me?' You say to yourself, it's got to be
pretty bad when there's no one else to take their calls besides the
people who are doing the hiring."

Ties to the family meant nothing anymore. Harvey Weinstein's
father had made tuxedos for Barney Pressman. Harvey and Fred had
weathered the struggle for autonomy, inseam to inseam, as a new generation of clothing men took over their fathers' businesses after the
war. Now Harvey couldn't get a check cut, either. "So I ended up
writing a letter to Fred saying I feel so bad that there's this four-
thousand-dollar credit you're probably not using on other garments,
since the ones you have are five months old and we can't get anybody
on the phone. Nobody will talk to us. We've sent six duplicate bills.
And I'm sure we got a check very quickly thereafter, but I think Fred
was very hurt that I had to write to him at all. I closed out the Barneys
account; it just wasn't worth it."

Designers like John Bartlett and Todd Oldham stopped shipping
to Barneys for a time. Nicole Miller, another leading designer, came
close to crossing Barneys off. In the apparel business, small designers
who can't afford to wait for payment often do business through people
called factors. Those factors will advance payment—for a fee—and
assume the burden of collecting the designer's accounts receivable.
Many of the factors stopped doing business with Barneys, or put them
under close watch.

Under a barrage of hostile publicity, Barneys finally released an
official statement. It was not conciliatory, nor was it even remotely
true. "Our current reported vendor payment issues are unfortunate and
genuinely reflect poor communication on our part," read the statement. "We are diligently working to remedy this communications is-

sue. As we are a private company, we have no obligation to publicly report our results but we will report that our business is incredibly healthy." And that, more or less, was that.

The statement didn't mention the big box of checks stashed underneath a desk in the accounting department. The checks had been made out to the appropriate vendors, and signed. They had even been entered into the accounts payable ledger. They just hadn't been mailed, and they wouldn't be mailed until the outcry got shrill enough or until the threats carried more real menace than bombast. "If you really wanted a check for one of your suppliers, or it looked like the product really wasn't going to come, then they would handpick the check for you," says one former executive. "They didn't have the money to pay. The cash flow wasn't there."

The spirit of brigandage infected Barneys' employees, too. Chaos ruled, both before and after the Madison Avenue store opened. The staff pilfered gleefully, like looters in a riot zone. Employee theft at Barneys had always run higher than average, but it grew to epidemic proportions after Barneys started expanding. Barneys helped the larceny along by declining to use those clunky plastic sensor tags that impede shoplifting—"Image, sweetie, image," says a former public relations staffer. Instead, it relied on its security staff to surveil likely suspects, both among the shoppers and among the employees. But if you've got the old triangle working against you, there's not a whole lot even a platoon of store dicks can do.

The triangle, as they call it in the security trade, means the need, desire, and motivation to steal. "If an employee has all three of those, he or she is going to steal from you, regardless," says a former Barneys security officer. Need was the weakest leg of the triangle, since Barneys tended to pay people at all levels well above industry standards, but desire and motivation got reinforced every day. Implanting immoderate desire was Barneys' whole raison d'être, and as far as motivation went, a sense of easy entitlement leached down directly from the top.

"They'd like that pair of alligator shoes that Barneys sells for nine hundred dollars, and they felt that Barneys didn't pay them enough money for the amount of work they did, so you're going to have employees with a propensity to steal," says the security man. "When I was with Barneys, we caught everyone from stock boys to store management stealing; some were paid very well, some were paid very poorly. There were a significant number of internal thefts with large dollar values associated with them, and we made a great deal of arrests."

At the Barneys satellite in the World Financial Center, a porter made off with over $100,000 worth of suits. At the Madison Avenue store, many of the cabinets weren't fitted with locks until several months after the store opened. A particular Baccarat crystal figurine of a leopard that sold for around $1,500 walked out of Chelsea Passage four separate times; every time Barneys restocked him, he walked off again. "The place was a zoo," says a Chelsea Passage employee, aptly.

The Pressmans saw the financial crisis looming by the summer of 1993, or at least Bob did. Barneys needed a lot more cash than it could squeeze from a few cabinetmakers and dress designers. It finally dawned on Bob Pressman that Barneys had found the bottom of Isetan's deep pockets, and there was nothing left but loose change. That just wouldn't do. Not only were the stores running massively over budget, but the constant delays kept adding to the imputed interest that Barneys already owed Isetan.

The $247 million that Isetan had originally pledged to the New York, Beverly Hills, and Chicago stores comprised a smaller cash portion and imputed interest on that cash. The imputed interest reflected what it would have cost the Pressmans to borrow that money from, say, a bank. Isetan had already sunk $225 million into the stores, but Barneys couldn't begin paying the interest on it through its $26 million rent until the new stores opened for business and started generating some cash. The longer the clock kept running on construction, the longer the imputed interest kept accruing.

Barneys had started dipping into its own working capital to keep construction going. Within months, it had sunk $36 million of the money it used to run its stores into Madison Avenue and Beverly Hills. The Pressmans tried getting Isetan to focus on the disaster dead ahead, but Isetan had its own crises closer at hand to attend to. Nakanishi had gone; Kosuge too; and the losses from Kosuge's unhedged currency trades preoccupied the newly arrived bankers from Mitsubishi.

To keep everything from coming undone, Barneys took out its first outside loan—a private placement among several large insurance companies for $60 million. In December of 1993, Bob Pressman went to Japan again with a request for more money that, he icily informed the Japanese, Isetan couldn't turn down. They simply had no choice, he told them bluntly. No money, no store; no store . . . well, the last thing Isetan needed was to see its Barneys investment go up in a blaze of goatskin.

Isetan unhappily agreed with Bob's cold-blooded analysis, but required Bob and Gene to pledge their personal fortunes as a guarantee against new loans. Here is where the cultural gulf between the two partners yawned widest. The brothers' personal guarantees didn't mean much in financial terms, and the Japanese knew it. As best anyone could tell, Bob's and Gene's fortunes consisted almost entirely of their Barneys ownership stakes. Isetan has since said that Bob and Gene made some vague reference to some outside real estate investments, but no one took this very seriously. Barneys was pretty much it, and it gave them a nominal worth of around $50 million apiece.

The brothers' Barneys ownership had been established through a series of trust agreements Fred had drawn up in 1982. The trusts gave Gene and Bob about 20 percent each of the equity in Barneys, Inc. Fred had half, and the sisters had about 5 percent each. The trusts also restricted ownership of Barneys stock to Pressman family members. In the event that Isetan had no recourse but to seize the brothers' assets, the stock was off limits. This rendered the personal guarantees largely symbolic, but that symbolism nonetheless counted heavily to the Japanese, who saw in it a bedrock of family honor.

Honor means different things to different people. Bob and Gene obviously didn't see it quite the same way at all. Gene didn't like the setup one bit, and complained bitterly to Bob. Bob calmed Gene down by explaining why the guarantees were largely meaningless, and as far as the bedrock of family honor stuff, hey, you can't put bedrock in the bank.

"Ice in winter." That's how Bob referred to the value to Isetan of the personal guarantees, and got Gene to sign. "Isetan knew about the restricted stock," says a top executive who was there at the time. "But what they didn't know is that Bob and Gene never really had any intentions of honoring that agreement."

Thus was launched a series of short-term loans to the Pressman family's wholly owned Preen Realty, Inc., affiliate—known collectively as the Preen loans. Like a child who runs through his weekly allowance by Monday, the Pressmans kept coming back for more. December 1993: $36 million, which replaced the $36 million of working capital Barneys had already spent; February 1994: $19.99 million; March 11: $6.96 million; March 31: $35.96 million; March 31, again: $18 million; April: $4.91 million; June: $11.37 million; July 25: $5.1 million; two days later: $2.17 million. In all, Isetan loaned Preen $140.46 million— $88.35 million of which went into Madison Avenue, and $52.11 million into Beverly Hills.

In addition, Preen assumed two loans for $18.25 million and $19 million made to BNY Licensing Corporation, the vehicle for overseeing the Asian licenses and technical assistance fees. That brought the Preen loans to a total of $177.71 million.

Nor was this the last of the borrowing binge. In April 1994, Chemical Bank, Barneys' longtime banker, arranged a second private placement for $40 million. The notes carried an interest rate of 8.32 percent and were to come due in June 2000. This proved a bit trickier to pull off. Late in 1993, Chemical informed Barneys that its accounts payable were still running 13 percent past due. That would queer a second round of borrowing. On December 16, 1993, Barneys cut $32 million worth of overdue checks, and recorded them paid. Chemical never knew that Barneys had never mailed those checks out when it syndicated the debt.

None of the customers who flocked to the new store on September 9, 1993, could discern the depth of Barneys' distress, and there was really no reason why they should have. For the last two years of its life before it filed for bankruptcy, Barneys worked heroically at keeping up appearances, and in the main, it succeeded. No one knew—not Barneys' customers, not its creditors, not its employees, not its executives outside of a select few, not even Fred—how much trouble Barneys had gotten itself into so damn fast. If there was a principle that guided all public utterances, it was this: No one must know.

The Madison Avenue store produced its desired effect of amazement and awe on the public. When the doors opened at 10:00 A.M., a crowd of two hundred was already waiting to get in. An hour later, the crush of shoppers jostling past the checkerboard-patterned cosmetics counter on the first floor could barely move. By lunchtime, the wait for a quick bite at the Mad 61 restaurant downstairs took close to an hour. At day's end, some thirty thousand people had taken in the spectacle and spent $1.3 million. In its first five days, Barneys reported that it sold $6 million worth of merchandise.

"It was like the floodgates had opened up," says Patrick Gates, who managed sportswear in the men's store. "I remember the first five days. I've never seen any sort of response like that in any retail environment I worked in. I mean people were coming in and just buying, buying, buying, and it was full. It was incredible."

The ground floor, like that in most department stores, held mostly cosmetics, perfumes, and accessories—little things like $155 knit gloves by Jodie Arden that extended past the elbow and all the way up to the armpit. Tiny luxuries such as these carry the highest markup—up to 75 percent—in any department store and make the main floor a store's most valuable real estate. Thus it puzzled many why Barneys left a six-hundred-square-foot hole just inside the Madison Avenue entrance that opened to the restaurant below.

No one denied, though, that the open gallery enhanced the unmistakable grandeur of the first impression. So did the exotic fish in the custom-built fish tanks, including a sand shark named Sinatra who later had to be removed for behaving toward his tank-mates in a manner all too characteristic of the family that employed him.

Byzantine faces in gold-backed glass mosaic, recalling the church of San Vitale at Ravenna, stared implacably from the wall behind the apothecary. The message was clear: This is not a store, this is a shrine. Or maybe that wasn't the message at all. Maybe the real message was that style existed apart from any context, sanctified by taste alone. Early Christian martyrs above the cosmetics counter? Why not, provided they're sufficiently fabulous.

If this was a fashion shrine, however, the price of worship excluded most parishioners. On the third floor, Hubert de Givenchy, an old family friend from the days when Fred first commissioned him to design menswear, sold replicas of his greatest designs from the past forty years for $2,500 to $5,600.

At a press conference the day before the store opened, Gene Pressman faced down a crowd of reporters primed to point out the incongruities of opening a business like this in the middle of an economic recession. A $5,000 dress can be considered a good value if it's one-of-a-kind and you can afford it, argued Gene in a perfect encapsulation of Pressman economics. "We only know how to be Barneys," he added, overlooking the fact that no other retail institution had ever undergone such a wrenching redefinition of what it was and what it stood for over the years. This was only the latest incarnation.

You could see just how much Barneys had changed by the room Gene chose for his press conference on opening day, which was the room where they sold those deadly Manolo Blahnik spike heels. Barneys Madison Avenue, not to mention all the other Barneys large and small, was first and foremost a women's specialty store now. At a minimum, 60 percent of the floor space was devoted to women's clothing. On Seventeenth Street, 65 percent of the store volume came from menswear and another 5 percent from Chelsea Passage; only 30 percent came from women's wear.

You had to look hard to find the entrance to the menswear section of the Madison Avenue store. It was around the corner on Sixtieth Street. The only way to reach it through the main entrance took a man past the jewelry and cosmetics sections to an unceremonial opening at the back end of the main floor. On the upper floors, the two sexes didn't connect at all. Gene and Bob maintained that men and women preferred to shop separately, but the store's architecture made the shift in priorities palpable.

The six thousand square feet that Barneys devoted to Giorgio Armani on the second floor made it the largest Armani boutique in the world outside of Armani's own stores. But every one of Barney Pressman's hokey verities had been discarded—"select don't settle" chief among them. The banner outside the men's store on Sixtieth Street proclaimed, "Calling all men since 1923," but that was more than a little disingenuous.

The new Barneys wasn't calling all men at all. It was calling the men who could pay $395 for Poulsen Skone English shoes, or $2,500 for Calvin Klein suits, but it wasn't calling the men who drove downtown to talk gabardine with the clothing men of Barney's day, or even Fred's. It wasn't calling the 56 cadet portlies and it wasn't calling the 36 extra longs. To be honest, the banner should have read, "Calling a few rich men to Barneys."

"You know, what killed all of us is something we never thought would happen to the business—that Barneys would ever be such an insignificant player in menswear," says one of the store's top merchandising executives. "One of the stupid decisions this company made was to chase the men's designer business to the point of turning off the classic business. There had always been a large portion of our moderate European clothing business that was heavily classic—San Remo, Linea Rossi. That's what we had been selling, and by the carload. Most guys who are really corporate are not going to walk around in Donna Karan or Calvin Klein suits in a meeting."

You could still find superb workmanship at appealing prices—particularly Barneys' private label goods. Fred's old Italian boy network saw to that. A company called Liba produced Barneys' private label shirt, which sold for $120, and virtually the same shirt for Giorgio Armani, which sold for $195. Barneys bought that shirt for $40. But private label goods made up only around a quarter of Barneys' sales, even though the gross margin on private label ran a full six points higher than the gross margin on branded goods.

Merchandise aside, something burly and warm had gone out of the old men's store, and the steady customer who had shopped downtown for years could feel it, even if he couldn't put his finger on it. "I had shopped at Barneys for eight or nine years, and it wasn't one specific incident that did it," says a young investment banker at Merrill, Lynch and Company. "It was just that all around the store, things started deteriorating. The shirts often fell apart or were the wrong size. The quality of the tailoring decreased. It makes a difference if the sleeves are supposed to touch your wrists and they don't. You notice, and if there are options, you take them. The uptown store isn't as conducive for shopping—all the designers are on different floors—so I switched to buying my suits at Saks and Bergdorf's and a lot of my coworkers did the same."

In 1995, a desperate Gene went looking for an outside advertising agency for the first time in fifteen years. The advertising Barneys had been running for the previous two years certainly got noticed, but it came across as fey; instead of offering men the rib roast of their wardrobe, it seemed to be serving them an escargot.

In early 1993, Barneys had been all set to shoot a new ad campaign in Ireland, but pulled out at the last minute. The money just wasn't there. Instead, one of its talent scouts had come across a young French illustrator named Jean-Philippe Delhomme, whose wispy, noseless cartoons had a half-formed kind of charm. No one in fashion had used drawings instead of photographs before, and God knows, they were a lot cheaper. True, you couldn't really see the clothes, but fashion photographs don't give much of a sense of what clothes *really* look like either, and besides, when it comes to menswear, one suit looks pretty much like another.

It was a perfect Barneys gesture, all arched eyebrow and terribly smart. Copywriter Glenn O'Brien penned his insouciant epigrams over the drawings—no one wrote wittier copy—and Barneys had the startling new "Sometimes" ad campaign. It created an instantaneous buzz in fashion circles. "Sometimes your tie starts a conversation" appeared over a Delhomme drawing of a black man in a black and brown suit. "Sometimes the devil makes you do it" ran above Delhomme's pinstriped yuppie holding what appears to be a perfume spritzer.

You either loved it or you hated it, and it wasn't hard to tell who would come down where. If you had to ask what any of this had to do with haberdashery, you clearly didn't get it. Into this camp fell all the old customers of the clothing men. Maybe you couldn't stake the future of the store on these customers anymore, but it was an act of heedless bravado to dismiss them so offhandedly.

When Gene hired the Goldsmith Jeffrey ad agency in the summer of 1995, Barneys' own research had already confirmed the worst. "That advertising apparently just continued to reinforce this elitist, extremely sophisticated image," says Goldsmith Jeffrey president Bob Jeffrey. "And that really alienated people. Barneys found out in its own research that the average person was really, really intimidated. They did not want to go into that store because they were afraid that they were not cool enough, not hip enough.

"One of the objectives of what we were going to try to do with our advertising was to lighten up the image of Barneys and kind of go back to earlier aspects of the brand personality—you know, warmer. Barneys had gotten so obsessed with sophistication and uptown and being chic and all that, that they basically turned off all their historical franchise, especially the men. Men don't want to deal with that. A chairman of the board may be making a million dollars a year, but he doesn't want someone to make him feel like he's not fashion forward.

"To me, it's a classic marketing one-oh-one mistake. You are who you are, and even if you want to upgrade and move uptown, well, take that concept with you. That's what's worked for you. Why would you change that? The only reason why it did change was hubris and ego. That's where the tragic element comes in, although I hate to say 'tragic,' because it presupposes a certain level of nobility. I don't think the Pressman lineage is that high."

The abdication of the men's business might have proved less damaging had Barneys truly managed to transform itself into a broader women's store. But again, its you're-not-nearly-cool-enough-or-svelte-enough-or-rich-enough-to-shop-here posture undid it. "Barneys did take a very strict definition of its women's clothing customer," says Marvin Traub, who was watching Barneys closely from his office at Bloomingdale's, where he was chairman. "She was petite, took a small size, was interested in forward fashion, and liked almost any color as long as it was black. There was a very strong definition that came from the management as to who they were seeking, to the extent of excluding other customers, which was somewhat different from the Bloomingdale approach."

Bloomingdale's had once defined a shopping culture and a certain type of customer itself, back in the 1970s, and Gene consciously emulated the Bloomingdale's that had once held the position of head merchant to the zeitgeist. But even at Bloomingdale's peak, Traub never forgot who bought his goods. "Remember," says Traub, "Bloomingdale's was a one-point-two-billion-dollar business. That meant recognizing that there are a lot more than thin size-sixes who live on the Upper East Side and have a lot of money. It means you are perfectly happy to have a large-size department, and you recognize that there are businesses below the designer and bridge price points."

It wasn't just the unforgiving merchandise that put many people off; it was the undisguised sneering from the sales help that went with it. The hip kids in the black T-shirts on the floor distilled all Gene's disdain and channeled it directly at the very people whose hard-earned money Barneys needed so badly. This reputation had dogged Barneys since the women's store opened in 1986. It often felt as if the sales-people were hired to judge rather than to help. As the business collapsed, the high-handedness got even more flagrant. "It got to the point where *we* would get shade from the salespeople, and we *worked* there," says a former Barneys public relations staffer.

This, too, represented a radical shift in the store's character. The Barneys of Barney and Fred's day believed in smothering its customers with helpfulness, whether they wanted to be helped or not. In the early 1980s, Barneys had briefly tried handing out "Just looking" lapel buttons to shield browsers from Barneys' overly ingratiating salesmen. It never really worked. The Barneys salesman of the good old days was a shopper-seeking missile.

In ten years, Barneys had gone from hard-sell to why-sell? Many shoppers braved the frosty climate anyway, because Barneys still managed to unearth fashions they couldn't find elsewhere. But they knew what the weather would be like when they got there. "I always dressed before I went shopping at Barneys," says John Greyson, a regular for years. "They had *their* attitude; I had *my* attitude."

Ultimately, though, the attitude took its toll. A customer at the World Financial Center store brought back a silk blouse to exchange because her sweat had left large black blotches at the armpits after one wearing. The salesperson, a young woman in her thirties with a foreign accent and a black T-shirt, gave a Gallic shrug. There was simply *nussing* she could do. The customer most likely had a glandular problem better attended to by a physician, she suggested helpfully.

"There was an attitude that you were doing the customer a favor," says a former manager of the store. "You're not waiting on idiots—these people are spending large sums of money!" Not at the World Financial Center store, however. In the early 1990s, the ten-thousand-square-foot store was selling just $2.5 million worth of merchandise a year and barely made a profit.

Not that Barneys couldn't ingratiate itself to the right people when it wanted to. On March 5, 1994, Barneys opened its Beverly Hills store on Wilshire Boulevard. The store ended up costing around $120 million, almost twice as much as the $65 million originally budgeted for it. In many ways, the Beverly Hills store remains the most aesthetically pleasing store Barneys built. The elliptical staircase that winds in a syncopated spiral to the skylight; the mosaics designed by fashion illustrator Reuben Toledo; the generous windows that give onto views of swaying jacaranda trees—it all adds up to a jewel of a store that impresses without looking like it's straining for effect.

Twenty years after his first disappointing encounter with cinema, Gene had finally made it back to Hollywood. In the Barneys cosmology, Hollywood still reigned supreme. If you were one of the close celebrity friends of Barneys, like Jack Nicholson, the store's largesse could be staggering. It could even be staggering when you weren't. Barbra Streisand's assistant once spent $500 on a bracelet as a gift from Barbra to her secretary, but Streisand herself wasn't one of the store's steadier shoppers. Nonetheless, an assistant manager who worshiped Streisand continually sent her gifts as a token of his love. Lest Streisand overlook the sentiment behind it, the merchandise always arrived with a signed note, "Love from Michael." Guillermo Rios, who ran the store, cultivated the Hollywood party circuit so tirelessly that he landed in rehab and ultimately had to be brought back to New York.

In Barneys' 1995 fiscal year, which ended July 31, 1995, the Madison Avenue store's sales were $140 million, or $655 per square foot, according to a study done after the bankruptcy filing by Deloitte and Touche Consulting Group. That fell well below projections, not to mention far below the despised "Burger King" down the block, which is what Gene called Bergdorf Goodman. Bergdorf Goodman's sales per square foot ran between $1,000 and $1,200. Almost a year and a half after it opened, the 124,000-square-foot Beverly Hills store had sales of $51,240,000—or about $415 per square foot. Good, but not good enough to keep Beverly Hills from losing close to $2 million that year.

Shoppers simply weren't spending enough, while Barneys was spending far too much. "When I first met him, Bob Pressman said to me, gross margin is not my problem. I'm running regularly fifty-two percent in gross margin. My problem is my expenses are well over that," recalls a former planning executive. "So if your margin is fifty-two percent, and let's say your expenses are running at sixty percent, it doesn't take a mathematical genius to know that you're in the hole. And that truly was the situation."

The grand expansion was an unmitigated disaster, although you couldn't tell that from the books. According to the Deloitte and Touche study, in fiscal year 1993, Barneys recorded earnings before interest and taxes—EBIT—of $11,260,000 on sales of $175,074,000. In fiscal 1994, bolstered by the opening of the Madison Avenue store the previous September, it logged EBIT of $22,797,000 on sales of $291,548,000.

In both years, operating expenses outweighed gross margin—the difference between revenue and the cost of goods sold: by $10 million in fiscal 1993, and $2 million in fiscal 1994. And that's before figuring in any rent payments to Isetan, or to any of Barneys' other landlords. It also doesn't include $3 million of equipment-leasing charges in fiscal '93, or $10.5 million in fiscal '94.

So how did Barneys manage to show a healthy cash flow in both years? Here's how: In a series of transactions that began on July 15, 1992, Barneys' Preen affiliate "purchased" from Barneys, Inc., a 100 percent interest in the money due from Isetan under the Technical Assistance Agreement. It put a price of $94.5 million on the present value of the income it expected to receive from Isetan over the forty-nine-year life of the technical agreement. Preen also "purchased" licensing royalties from BNY Licensing for $30.9 million. Finally, Preen agreed to reimburse Barneys $5 million for certain costs it had previously incurred.

Barneys had wide latitude in assigning a value to the rights Preen "bought." Consequently, the $130 million number kept wriggling around as Barneys changed assumptions on the discount factor used to make its present value calculation, and the exchange rate for the yen.

When the transaction showed up in Deloitte and Touche's presentation to the creditors committee in March 1996, it turned out Barneys had booked $55,725,000 in income for fiscal 1993, and $88,086,000 for fiscal 1994, all from the "sale" of the Asian royalties and technical agreements to Preen. Remove that "income" and the statements told a much grimmer tale: a loss of $44,465,000 for fiscal 1993, and a loss of $65,289,000 in fiscal 1994. That part, at least, does represent real money.

Barneys was no longer just a chic specialty store for Manhattanites at this point. It had managed to realize the disgraced Kosuge's vision for a string of Barneys across the land—the cornerstone of the original agreement between Barneys and Isetan. By 1994, when the last of its out-of-town outlets opened, Barneys comprised fourteen full-price stores and six outlet stores in eleven states. It was projecting total revenues of $400 million by the end of its 1996 fiscal year on July 31, and unfortunately, that projection seemed well within reach.

Unfortunately, because the more stores Barneys opened, the more money it lost. Madison Avenue raised the question whether Barneys' severe style might even be too New Yorky for most New Yorkers. Barneys America carried that drab Manhattan palette deep into the multihued heart of the country. The stores were doomed before they even opened. In its presentation to Barneys' creditors in March 1996, Deloitte and Touche concluded that only three stores in the entire chain were more than marginally profitable: Madison Avenue, Manhasset— the one glittering success in the expansion—and Seventeenth Street.

Not that Bob and Gene had the slightest doubt about their impending triumph in the provinces. It went without saying that a style-starved nation would swoon when Barneys came to town. At the height of the Barneys America expansion, Bob was chatting with Lou Frankfurt, the head of Coach Leather, at a cocktail party. Frankfurt later recounted the meeting to a friend.

"I hear you're building stores all over the country," said Frankfurt, whose own company had expanded with great success. "What kind of market studies did you do?"

"Market studies?" replied Bob. "Why do we have to do market studies? We're Barneys!"

And so they were. "You were not allowing people to dictate your business, and that is where I was coming from," remembers Patrick Gates, a former divisional manager for men's sportswear. "I had done the Neiman thing, and they are successful at it, but here was the first opportunity to say no. I wanted to create an environment where you could walk in and say, this does not look like Bloomingdale's. This does not look like Saks. It does not look like Neiman. I have a point of view which is great for New York. But when you stepped outside of New York, it failed miserably. The Barneys America scenario is that it was too New York."

In 1994, Barneys opened a store in Tower City Center in downtown Cleveland. The women of Cleveland flocked to it, and they flocked away from it just as fast. "Cleveland is not black country," recalls a woman who worked on the marketing of the store for the shopping center. "These people are sophisticated, but they don't wear their dresses cut most of the way up the thigh. You walked into Barneys and you wondered: Is there anything here besides black? Is there anything besides short? The salespeople didn't smile and they gave customers this haughty look, like they're better than you are."

Cleveland was the first of the out-of-town stores to go. Sales in fiscal 1995 came to just over $1 million, and they put it out of its misery quickly. "It could have worked," says the marketing consultant. "Some of the merchandise was really phenomenal—they had everything it took, but to make it work, you need to listen, and they didn't listen to people who had lived in Cleveland all their lives."

Nor did they listen in Houston. The menfolk of Houston, for instance, wore floral shirts, four-pleat pants, and two-button jackets that buttoned somewhere in the neighborhood of the navel. Barneys was pushing flat-front pants and four-button jackets that buttoned somewhere up around the nipple. Ironically, the items that sold best were some of the kitschy throwbacks to the 1950s—things like cardigan sweaters with vertical stripes, Banlon shirts, and skinny stovepipe pants. Barneys brought them back saturated in postmodern irony and cleansed of their original dorkiness.

In Houston, the fashion-backward geezers liked these relics just fine for their own hokey sake—no irony today, thank you. They had been waiting for this stuff to come back since 1957. "Somebody finally catered to their taste level, because these guys had never forgotten. Of course, they argued about the prices—like, my God, I used to be able to buy this Banlon shirt for sixteen dollars. It was weird," says Gates.

The store managers, many of whom had been hired away from local rivals like Neiman Marcus, begged Barneys for the kinds of clothes the locals liked to wear. "It was a constant struggle," says Gates. "My branch managers are calling me, saying, Patrick, I need four-pleat pants! I'm like, I would not put a four-pleat pant in there if it was the last pant in the world. It is not who we are. We were into dry, resilient crepe-type fabrics, and they are asking me for, like, luxurious rayon blends that draped. Hey guys, you don't get it! We are not into drape here! We are into structure! We did not believe in that soft look, so we didn't give a damn, and it cost us. The attitude was, build it and they will come.

"It was just people being so insular in New York that they didn't realize that in Houston, it is one hundred twenty degrees until December. They opened the store with the French blanket suit as a statement. In Houston, oh my God, you couldn't imagine. I mean even the finest-gauge merino wool seemed heavy-weight for people down there. So you'd get this incredible rush when you opened and then you'd just fall off the face of the earth."

Of course, Barneys often managed to shoot itself right in the Manolo Blahniks the moment it pulled into town. It didn't just ignore the prevailing customs; it mocked them publicly. In Dallas, Barneys took out an ad in the local newspaper to promote the hair salon that would operate on the premises. "We don't do big hair," read the ad in a backhanded swipe at every woman in Texas with teased-out tresses. What on earth were they thinking? "The last thing you want to do is insult the Texas people the way they did," says Gates.

All Gene's most pugnacious instincts came out in Texas, since Texas belonged to Neiman Marcus, whose parent, Harcourt General, also owned Bergdorf Goodman. Neiman Marcus holds a special place in the retail history of this country. Barney Pressman was still pressing pants when Al and Carrie Neiman, and Herbert Marcus, Carrie's brother, carved out a special niche catering to Texas's new oil and cotton money. Neiman Marcus opened in Dallas in 1907, and within a few years, Carrie Neiman was carting back Paris couturiers like Lanvin and Reveillon. By 1929, it had sales of $3.6 million and a reputation for shameless ostentation that it never lost. Neiman Marcus most certainly *did* do big hair.

Gene had nothing but contempt for Neiman Marcus and determined to show Dallas how true, laid-back cool is done. It must have galled him when Barneys failed to make even a teensy dent in the Texas consciousness. The Houston store opened in 1991. By the 1995 fiscal year, it had sales of $4,613,000 in a substantial space of 20,646 square feet. That's a miserable $223 a square foot. Dallas was a similar disaster: sales of $4,303,000 in 17,373 square feet, or $248 a square foot. Both stores operated solidly in the red.

Gene had other reasons for his special animus toward Neiman Marcus. Upon hearing that Barneys was planning to invade its turf, Neiman took a particularly hard line with designers who sold both stores. A store cannot drop a vendor because that vendor starts selling to a competitor, nor can it even threaten to do so directly. That would be considered in restraint of trade and patently illegal. Which doesn't mean it doesn't happen all the time.

The retail trade has its time-honored linguistic formulas for communicating this message with a wink and a nod, but the meaning still comes through as clear as the Ten Commandments. At Neiman Marcus, the formula that was taught to managers went something like this: "We really enjoy doing business with your company, but we are seriously reviewing the number of stores that you have right now in distribution. If you were to increase those stores, it would seriously hamper our expansion plans with your company." Nothing too concrete, nothing too evidentiary—"an eloquent way of putting it," says a former Neiman employee.

Neiman Marcus wasn't the only store to strong-arm Barneys when Barneys started challenging retailing's entrenched elite. Before Madison Avenue opened, just about every store on the B-line took a whack at Barneys and tried to jar its designers loose. Many designers sympathized with them, too, and looked at the new Barneys as a mixed blessing at best.

Every swanky fashion designer maintains his cachet by playing a little hard to get. High fashion stands on rickety stilts and is easily upended. A designer must not appear overly accessible to the common folk or encourage price cutting by allowing too many stores in the same neighborhood to sell his frocks. On the other hand, he can't play peekaboo too successfully either, or he won't generate enough business. Distribution is a precarious balance, and designers take great pains to ensure that they hover somewhere between the untouchable and the tarty.

The new Barneys was clearly upsetting that balance, and Gene didn't give a damn if designers didn't like it. He must have felt Barney Pressman's bile gurgling within him, remembering tales of how Hickey-Freeman and Greif did to Barney what Ralph Lauren, Chanel, and Alaïa were doing now to him. They wanted no part of the Madison Avenue store.

So when Azzedine Alaïa called Gene from Paris to inform him that he wouldn't sell Barneys uptown, just downtown, a little bit of Barney Pressman must have sputtered through Gene's voice when he exploded, "You fucking asshole! If you don't sell me uptown, I'm throwing you out of every fucking store in the country!" and slammed down the receiver.

Alaïa had a good point, however. "The argument was that we didn't need more distribution of the high-end labels in that particular area," says Gates. "You know the big designers all had their own stores, plus they sold to Bergdorf's, plus they sold to Bloomingdale's. Why do they need another outlet? It is a good argument, and it was really unsettling. I felt for the vendors, because what were they supposed to do?" Gene cowed Alaïa into staying, but before the melee ended, Ralph Lauren, Chanel, Yves Saint Laurent, and Karl Lagerfeld had all pulled out.

The most important designer of all, Giorgio Armani, only sells his most expensive goods in Barneys Madison Avenue under duress. Armani never lost his abiding respect for Fred, but he fought like hell to stay out of Barneys uptown and Beverly Hills. Particularly with Armani's own Peter Marino–designed store opening a few blocks north, Madison Avenue was beginning to look like some kind of Armani mall. Worse, Armani took a public poke at his old pals, which sent Gene around the bend. "We don't think they've done such a good job with women's wear," an Armani executive was quoted as saying in *Women's Wear Daily*. "And we're not that impressed with the branches they've opened."

Armani had boxed himself in years ago, however, as he soon learned. In April 1993, an arbitration tribunal in Geneva reaffirmed Barneys' right to carry Armani's top-of-the-line Borgonuovo label in both stores. Armani had given Barneys that right when he bought back the rights to distribute his lower-priced White Label line in 1979. Now he had to live with the consequences. The Geneva tribunal did uphold Armani's right to withhold the Borgonuovo line from the Barneys branch stores, and as soon as he heard the news, Armani plucked it from Barneys in Houston and Dallas.

But the ruling continued to rankle. On a subsequent tour of New York, Armani discovered that Gene had moved his White Label merchandise from the second to the third floor of the men's store, installing Prada in his place. Armani left the store screaming, cut short his tour, and flew back to Milan in a fury. In some ways, Barneys was the store that Giorgio built. He owed Barneys a lot, but Barneys owed him even more. The highly public split boded ill.

* * *

All the forces conspiring to pull down the house of Barneys came together in 1995. Bob Pressman had just about run out of fig leaves from the Asian royalty sales and had no other way to hide Barneys' skinny red income statement. Sales had climbed to $337,385,000, but the company showed a loss of $48,529,000. That was only around $10 million less than the actual loss, which was slightly cushioned by a remaining $9,769,000 from the Asian royalties.

Moreover, Isetan was carrying the Preen loans on its books as current assets, meaning they had to be paid back in a year. Bob must have known he didn't have a prayer of doing this, and had known this when he took the loans out in the first place. A reckoning was coming, and the means to forestall it were fast slipping away.

There was a bright spot in all this, however. For the first time in three years, gross margin came in ahead of operating expenses, which meant that the stores as a whole were making money if you didn't take the rent and equipment leases into account. How much does that mean? Not all that much—a good many money-losing businesses would show a profit if they didn't have to pay rent—but it was something, anyway. It represented a real reduction in operating expenses of about 5.5 percent and a jump in same-store sales of close to 13 percent. Gene, who had been spending less and less time in the store, perked up and started dreaming of the day, maybe five years off, he figured, when Barneys would finally start making money. Five years! Barneys didn't have one.

Inside Barneys, turmoil had been raging since the great expansion commenced, and it now threatened to tear the institution apart from within. The company had split into warring factions—"Bob's people" and "Gene's people," as they were known. Gene hired the merchants he wanted, often paying them as much as 25 percent above the industry norm and inspiring in them his general contempt for rules of any kind. That pretty much made it impossible for Barneys to transform itself from a one-store family business into a national retail chain. Gene's

"Barneys, *c'est moi*" attitude defeated all attempts to impose any kind of corporate structure.

"Gene operated from a bizarre frame of reference relative to the merchandising side," recalls a former human resources executive. "There was no particular attention paid to organizational planning. Who was going to be hired? How many people did we need to have, and what was the compensation structure? What were competitive industry salaries?"

Employees who had joined Barneys from the great corporate retail academies watched open-mouthed as Gene's wilder caprices took on a certain Caligula quality. The public relations staff knew, for instance, that failure to keep the jelly-bean bowl on Gene's desk filled would trigger an obscenity-laced outburst. Among their other occasional duties was holding Gene's feet while he did situps in the gym upstairs.

Gene commandeered the store manager at Madison Avenue to accompany him on his daily two-hour run—Gene ran the marathon in just over four hours. When it was politely suggested that the store manager might have more pressing duties during a companywide crisis, Gene ran with the woman who had been hired to manage the spa Gene envisioned for the new store. The spa never opened, but the woman remained on the payroll so Gene wouldn't have to run alone.

Personnel policy was similarly whimsical. "If Gene didn't like somebody one day, didn't like how they looked, or if they gained weight, or if they were a certain color, or if their ass was too big, I would be told to fire them," says the former human resources executive. "I would do what I felt any professional should do. I would say, wait a minute, we could have a potential liability here, I don't have any rationale, I have no documentation, it isn't based on performance. I put those things on the table befitting my job, and it wouldn't matter."

Not surprisingly, the executive turnover in the early 1990s was enormous, although generous severance packages usually ensured a docile exit. Of the one hundred or so people this human resources executive hired, maybe twenty remain. "There is a bond among all of us, you know, just sort of a wink you give one another that you've had that similar experience of that family's company," she says. "And although we may have made good money there and had discounts on beautiful clothing, and appreciated everything that their merchandising savvy has contributed to retailing and certainly to New York City, it was the most dysfunctional employment experience I've ever gone through."

The last straw for this executive came when Gene demanded she dismiss a mailroom employee who had drawn the line at fetching the Pressman family's dirty linen. "I went to Gene and I said, we could have some major union issues relative to you dispatching this young gentleman up to your sister's house to go get her laundry.

"Gene was up in his boxing ring upstairs working with his trainer, and he said, put on the boxing gloves and go a round with me on this. And I just did not want to do that. A few days later, Bob fired me and said, this has nothing to do with your ability, your performance, or your intellect. And I thought, that's very interesting. Then what does it have to do with?"

The stress was taking a huge toll on the family, too. Through all of this, the family took great hunks of flesh out of each other verbally, even while they applied the poultice of unswerving loyalty at the same time. It's a vision out of Dante's hell: the Pressman clan, eight bleeding men and women chewing on one another's limbs, wounding one another one day, healing the next, only to commence the wounding again. What manner of unfortunates are these, Dante might have asked Virgil, and what sin have they committed that they merit such misery? *Ecco la sfortunata famiglia Pressman di Nuovo York,* Virgil might have explained. They built the most wondrous clothing store on the great isle of Manhattan, but they sacrificed their humanity for it.

"They were each other's worst enemies and best friends at the same time," says the human resources executive. "They were trapped—they only had each other. No one reached out to them in friendship because they reached out to no one else." Barney Pressman's whispered counsel to Fred had turned into a self-fulfilling prophecy. It had come back to haunt the whole clan: "Remember," Barney had said, "the Pressmans have no friends."

For all their wrangling, everyone always ended up deferring to Gene—Phyllis through blind mother-worship of her firstborn, and Fred through some kind of fear that family chaos would prove more destructive than his anxious, reluctant support. Only once publicly, at a meeting of senior executives, did Fred reach the limits of his endurance. Something had sent Gene around the bend, and he was spewing invective at anyone within range. "Gene!" said Fred with uncustomary firmness, slamming his hand down on the table. "That is enough!" The executive who witnessed this scene had never seen Fred challenge Gene so openly before, and never saw it again.

Fred wasn't altogether supine. In 1992, Bob Pressman, at Fred's urging, hired Coopers and Lybrand to help whip Barneys into some kind of corporate shape. Coopers didn't make much headway. "It was the most amazing thing for me," says one of the Coopers consultants. "I walked into a company as a consultant where they wouldn't share the numbers with the consultants. When we looked at it, we only saw the dollar-per-square-foot volume, and we thought this is terrific. Because no one could have imagined where all that money could go."

Charles Bunstine III was also on the Coopers team, and in November of 1992, he joined Barneys as a senior vice president, charged with overseeing operations that nobody had much bothered with before. In 1995, Fred pushed to have Bunstine made president and chief operating officer, with the boys as cochairmen and chief executives above him. Fred took the title of chairman of the executive committee. Bunstine had come out of Leslie Wexner's The Limited chain, and clearly knew more about the nuts and bolts of retailing than any of the Pressmans. He was also a fine athlete, and could beat Gene handily at golf, which went further than his corporate know-how in commanding Gene's respect.

It was during Bunstine's tenure that the cast of characters who had personified Barneys changed dramatically. Connie Darrow, the raccoon-eyed head of women's merchandising, left in a huff in December 1993, and Bunstine had a hand in ushering her out. Mallory Andrews, the Pearl Mesta of Barneys' most successful soirees, left as head of public relations. Simon Doonan took over her duties, along with advertising, and again, Bunstine's hand was evident. A showdown between Doonan and Glenn O'Brien led to O'Brien's departure.

Many of the freewheeling sprites who plied the breezes of fashion at Gene's bidding folded their bright wings, and many of them blame Bunstine for poisoning the air. Bunstine was the arch-suit, the way they saw it, not to mention an intensely political animal with sharp teeth behind his affable smile.

Bunstine sees things differently: "You walked into an organization where they thought they were winning, and they were getting their brains beat in." Bunstine did manage to go a long way toward cleaning out some of the rot in the timbers of the operation. Inventory was computerized and brought under some control; the accounts payable lag shrank to a manageable 13 percent overdue. As important, he managed to restore some semblance of harmony between "Bob's people" and "Gene's people," even though some of the key figures departed along the way.

Among Bunstine's principal missions—and this was very much in the back of Fred's mind—was to insulate Barneys from Gene. This was the trickiest maneuver of all to pull off, and Bunstine didn't quite manage it in the end. It required Fred's staunch, if quiet, support, but Fred's strength was ebbing. Like Fred with Barney, the boys now fled their father's approach in the store. What power he hadn't ceded, they had seized, following time-honored Pressman tradition. "Don't say that's a testimony to great parenting," Fred had admitted in an authorized 1993 article in *Vanity Fair*. "Some of it has to be a way of abdicating responsibility and then being a second-guesser."

As chief operating officer, Bunstine had all fifteen of Barneys' division heads reporting to him—twice the number of reporting assignments in the average retail organization. Bunstine had threatened to leave if he didn't get control over merchandising and marketing, but while his promotion did officially grant him that authority, Gene was not so easily shouldered aside. He had looked on impassively while several of his closest confidants lost their heads—Mallory Andrews was godmother to his son—but he was damned if he would let Charles Bunstine clip his manhood, no matter how good a golfer he was.

"In his gut, Gene couldn't handle it," says a former top executive. "To Gene, Barneys was Gene and Gene was Barneys. It was more than he could stand. Gene kept insinuating himself into situations where the new organization was designed precisely to keep him from insinuating himself. Charles bitched about it constantly."

Fred did second-guess from the sidelines, but his second guesses told him as little as his first. He would call Bunstine in Bunstine's car while Madison Avenue was being built. You've got to get somebody over to Peter Marino's office right away to watch what they're doing, Fred would say in an alarmed whisper. It's totally out of control!

He would badger Bob for the numbers—the numbers that Bob wouldn't tell him. He would sit late into the night in the controller's office, trying to make some sense of the haphazard, uncomputerized inventory and figure out what Barneys' seventy-eight hundred vendors were really owed. And later, he would worry incessantly that his family would end up losing the store he had built and handed over to them. "What's the outcome for the company?" he would ask Bunstine constantly. "What's the future for the family?"

9

"THE CROWN JEWEL OF THE RETAIL WORLD"

Fred Pressman was looking more haggard than usual during the summer of 1995. He never masked the strain of his constant worrying very well, and the two years since Madison Avenue opened had given him plenty to agonize about. But he was obviously laboring now under a special kind of curse. His eyes had sunk even deeper into his head, and his frame, normally slight, was shedding pounds perilously close to the bone. That summer, they discovered the cancer that was certain to kill him—cancer of the pancreas, it was, which tends to do its work in a spectacular hurry.

The Fred men had their metaphor ready-made, and it even came as a mental relief to some who found in it a way through their painful confusion over what had gone wrong. Now, at least, there was some cause and effect: Barneys killed Fred—Barneys being a euphemism for what some of them still can't bring themselves to say. Even today, there seems little reason to look further than the simple facts at hand. The life of the store *was* the life of the man—that is the way he had chosen to live—so why not his death, too? The surface of things is begging you to believe it. You may tug at the threads all you want, trying to find a subtler pattern in the weave. Try not to. It would only dishonor the lifelong devotion of Fred's misplaced heart. "The thing about the end—I don't like talking about it, because I saw what he went through after years when he was so full of life: He was dead before he got ill," says one of Fred's closest protégés.

Fred stayed Fred, however, with a vigor that astonished everyone who saw him shriveling daily. Fred's radiologist, a young man at the outset of his career, came in to the store. Fred had left instructions to give him anything he wanted. Even Armani? asked the wide-eyed young doctor. Even Armani, he was told. He picked up two suits, a sport coat, and a pair of slacks. What about an overcoat? asked the doctor, easing into the rhythm of Fred's largesse. Don't do this to me, moaned the salesman to himself, but he steeled himself and called Fred. He wants an overcoat, too, the salesman tells Fred. Oh, all right, sighs Fred, by now deathly sick—but please, not an expensive one.

Fred never stopped coming to the store until just weeks before he died. He never stopped looking for a new way to fold a shirt using fewer pins, so the customer would risk fewer pinpricks when removing them. And he never stopped worrying about where the money was coming from and what it would all mean to his family. The worry probably kept him alive much longer than the few months pancreatic cancer normally allots its victims. Long enough, unfortunately, to see his worst nightmare unfold in the last months of his life.

Bob Pressman never had any doubts that things would work out for the best, since he calculated—rightly—that it would have been in everyone's best interest for things to fall out as he expected. Bob planned that Barneys would exchange its ruinous burden of debt and give Isetan an ownership stake in Barneys, Inc., in return. That stake would have to be negotiated, but it would free Barneys from the strangulation of payments that had mounted to $40 million to $50 million a year by 1995—payments the Pressmans knew full well they could never hope to make.

Barneys maintains that some kind of global retailing partnership was what everybody—including Isetan—intended from the outset. It probably was. Could Kuniyasu Kosuge have meant to inscribe his name on the illustrious roster of his ancestors as the Pressmans' landlord and chief creditor? That seems unlikely; it would be a pretty puny vision for a fellow who dreamed very big. If anything, it was the Pressmans who originally had no intentions of making good on the airy prospects of ownership they dangled in front of the Japanese. It was Bob's negotiating triumph to have returned from Tokyo with unlimited cash secured only by empty promises, and he said as much when he crowed about it.

Now, however, the tables had turned and there was no other way out. By their own hands, the Pressmans had brought themselves to the point of giving up what they had never meant to relinquish. But instead of facing the lovesick Kosuge, Barneys now confronted a dour bunch of suits who had seen Kosuge's vision come close to destroying his dynasty, and Isetan along with it. To put it mildly, they were dubious. Although the Japanese were prepared to discuss what came to be called the "global solution," they wanted to know exactly what their money was buying. The way Gene saw it, the answer was simple: You're buying a piece of me. But that just wasn't good enough anymore. The question in early 1994 was, were the Pressmans ready to give up enough equity to conclude a deal?

Fred knew the Japanese would demand a significant stake in the business, and the implications for his family's future made him crazy with anxiety. "Fred and I always wished we had just stayed on Seventeenth Street," Phyllis confided to a Barneys executive when the three of them were riding downtown in Fred's car. That's not altogether true: Fred loved the new store with all his heart, but the prospect of losing everything had poisoned that love. Not Gene, though. Gene still lived in a dream world. "He couldn't imagine how anybody could not want to be part of his creation," says a former executive, describing Gene's attitude. "Gene viewed Isetan as a bunch of dumb bankers— and dumb Japanese bankers at that. This was not exactly a recipe for getting along." As always, it fell to Bob to fix what no one admitted was broken.

One of the first documented mentions of a formula for the global solution appears in a loan agreement dated March 31, 1994. The agreement, drafted by Isetan, speaks vaguely of future negotiations concerning Isetan's "desire to acquire up to a 49% equity interest in Barneys, Inc. . . . in the context of a so-called 'global' or 'permanent' refinancing, restructuring, payment or other resolution of the . . . short term loans extended by [Isetan of America] since October 28, 1993 . . . together with the resolution of issues related to various agreements between [IOA] and its affiliates and [Barneys, the Pressmans, and their affiliates] (the 'Global Solution')." The tedious legalese is quoted here only because the Pressmans brandished it as proof positive that Isetan acknowledged its intent to swap debt for equity all along. This it seems to fall well short of doing, however suggestive the language in the document may be.

Barneys responded in August 1994 with a proposal to wipe out all loans and take over the new stores in return for giving Isetan 42 percent of the company. At the same time, Barneys offered to modify and extend the royalty arrangement for Asia—that protean creature whose monetary value seemed capable of stretching to fit any financial framework demanded of it at the time. Isetan scoffed.

"We sent a letter back saying this was the most one-sided thing," Yasuo Okamoto, an Isetan lawyer with the firm of Hughes, Hubbard and Reed, told *American Lawyer* magazine. "We wanted maybe to make the $180 million in short-term loans [the Preen loans] into a longer-term loan. Debt for equity was a consideration—we always wanted to see if they could survive—so we said, 'We can restructure the loans, but you've *got* to tell us what Barneys is worth.'"

That Bob could not bring himself to do. He had lived uncandidly all his life, and he wasn't about to let the current crisis provoke him into straight talk. During the bankruptcy proceedings, Barneys always claimed that it had furnished Isetan with all the information it needed. That simply was not true, but Isetan undoubtedly bears the responsibility for not probing hard enough. In retrospect, both Isetan and the Pressmans were culpable. You could say that Bob didn't want to tell, and Isetan didn't want to know. Isetan always points to the trust it had placed in the Pressman family to justify its languor, but it held fast to that trust long past the point of prudence or good sense. Somewhere along the way, unwavering trust turns to credulousness.

On the other hand, Bob's smoke screens certainly didn't make it any easier for Isetan to see the carnage going on, even had the Japanese approached Bob with the healthy skepticism he warranted. A catch-22 situation developed: Bob didn't want to divulge the hard—and, as only he knew, damaging—information Isetan wanted until Isetan got "in gear" with the global solution, as Bob put it. Michio Jomuri, a former senior executive at Mitsubishi Bank, and Kazumasa Koshiba, the thirty-five-year Isetan veteran who had been bumped to president after Kosuge's ouster, gave every appearance of wanting to make an equity deal. But they weren't going to get "in gear" until Bob first provided them with a credible set of numbers.

In this way, critical months slipped by. The only thing that didn't stand still was the interest on the debt, which kept creeping higher while the two sides stared each other down across the Pacific. By 1995, neither side could make the deal they could have made in 1994. "The problem—like the interest—just kept compounding," says a former executive. Bob suspected that Isetan's intransigence was just a negotiating tactic, since he knew that a global solution offered the only mechanism for Isetan to get its money back. Isetan wouldn't be crazy enough to turn its back on the only game in town. Right? No fucking way, Bob convinced himself. So Bob played poker: He cajoled, he barked, he cajoled, and he barked some more—going so far as to threaten to stop paying rent, not a very credible bluff, since everyone knew that Isetan would simply seize all the properties if he did. But he never doubted that, in the end, the two parties would somehow arrive at the "global solution" and it would set everything right.

So much so that the Pressman kids kept dipping into the Barneys till for spending money more liberally than ever, even while the company was careening toward bankruptcy. In 1994 and 1995, according to top Barneys executives, the Pressmans took at least $13 million to $15 million out of Barneys, and possibly much more. "In the end, they assumed everything would be okay," says a former executive.

One of the many things the Japanese didn't know about—and Bob never did tell them—was how much money the Pressman family had siphoned from the business for their own use over the years. They did this through a complex web of affiliate companies, primarily for tax reasons but also for discretion's sake. Preen Realty, Inc., was the largest and most active of these affiliates, but there were plenty of others. Fener was another, Gadiston a third—the list went on. For the most part, Preen, its subsidiaries, and other Barneys affiliates oversaw the family's real estate holdings, like the parking lot across the street from the old store on Seventeenth Street, a string of restaurant investments, and the building at 106 Seventh Avenue where Barneys had its offices and warehouse space.

The affiliates served as the conduit for sluicing funds from the store for the family's investments, such as Basco and Williwear, not to mention the large sums the Pressmans drew upon for their costly personal upkeep. Salaries, as high as they were, were never meant to serve as the family's sole means of support. In this, the Pressmans differed only in degree from many family business owners, who often make no meaningful distinction between their business and household accounts. Barneys even employed a bookkeeper whose sole job was to take care of the Pressmans' personal bills—from psychoanalysts to *Sports Illustrated* subscriptions.

The degree, however, was considerable. In 1995, for instance, Barneys' total rent expense relating to leases with Pressman affiliates came to $38.6 million. Not all of that money went to the family—$30 million of it went to Isetan; but the $8.6 million left over was paid by Pressman entities to other Pressman entities at a level that reflected the needs of the Pressman family. Moreover, the rental payments to Pressman-owned properties represented only one kind of affiliate transaction; there were numerous loans over the years between Barneys and the affiliates, and between the affiliates and each other, used not only to support the Pressmans' lifestyle, but also to fund the local real estate and other investments. This was Bob's real artistry, and his passion. In this secret domain, Bob was the master. While Gene basked in the approval of others, Bob retreated to his chemistry lab in the basement and made . . . money.

At the beginning of 1995, the various affiliates owed Barneys upward of $58 million for funds they had withdrawn over time. With the need to formalize a global solution growing more pressing, Bob tried to remove a large chunk of this negative overhang. Reed Elsevier was the largest tenant in 245 West Seventeenth Street, which the Pressman family owned through its Fener real estate partnership. Bob figured out a way to utilize Reed Elsevier's superior credit to obtain sharply lower financing on the property, the benefit to be split between Reed and Barneys. Reed would net-lease the entire building, financing 100 percent of the rental cash flow instead of just a portion, as it had done before. Barneys would then sublease its warehouse space in the building from Reed. This transaction gave the Pressmans a $24.5 million windfall, which they plowed back into Barneys to make good on money the family had already taken out.

At the close of the fiscal 1995 year on July 29, that still left the affiliates owing Barneys $34.3 million. When Barneys' creditors learned just how much money Bob had been squirreling away in the affiliates—money that was now gone forever while they waited to see what paltry fraction of their debts they would collect in the bankruptcy—there were howls of rage. "The big difference between the Pressmans and other family business people is that the Pressmans' core business was losing money and they were *still* taking money out of it—money that came from Isetan's pocket," says a member of the creditors' committee. "Bob was the guy running around trying to sweep up after the elephant in a way that was not exactly moral."

At least part of the money Gene took out of the store in 1995 went to pay for what the local Westchester newspapers called a million-dollar renovation on his Larchmont home. It looked to the neighbors like Gene was preparing to hunker down for a siege. The walls around the front of the property ran four feet high—the legal limit imposed by the town of Mamaroneck. Gene wanted to raise them to eight feet. Around the side of the property, Gene wanted to replace a four-foot wire mesh screen atop his three-foot wall with sturdier cement buttressing.

Gene filed for permission to extend the wall, arguing strenuously that he needed very high walls to protect him and ensure his privacy. Nonsense, replied the neighbors, who complained bitterly that the wall would block their view of the Long Island Sound. No one else in their peaceable hamlet felt the need for such fortifications, freedom from siege being one of the many benefits of living in Larchmont. The town's Zoning Board of Appeals concurred.

Gene, as usual, wasn't about to back down. His lawyer, Albert Pirro, Jr.—married, as some of the neighbors insinuatingly pointed out, to the county district attorney (do we need to draw you a diagram?)—propounded the ingenious argument that the walls out front were really *retaining* walls, and, hence, exempt from the town's height restrictions, although it remains unclear what the walls were retaining. And as far as the side walls went, replacing the existing wire mesh with concrete falls more under the heading of *repair* than new construction. Pirro was pressing this line of attack vigorously in State Supreme Court.

Things got ugly in town. Did Gene's unleashed golden retriever bite Peggy Miralia on the arm? That's what Miralia, Gene's truculent neighbor across the street, told police. Gene's workmen on the house said it didn't happen that way at all; the way they told it, Peggy Miralia "kicked, punched, and dragged the dog across the street onto her property," according to police chief Richard Rivera. What could possibly provoke a suburban housewife to slug a golden retriever? This, too, remains unexplained. "Get away from me, you fat fuck," Gene would scream at Peggy Miralia when she harangued him on the road.

* * *

As 1995 wore on, the mirage of the global solution would shimmer just over the next sand dune, only to evaporate as the two parties trudged toward it. In February, Isetan executive Michio Jomori said he was "fully committed to going ahead with the global solution," or at least that's what one Barneys top executive recalls hearing him say. Isetan even hired Merrill, Lynch and Company while Barneys hired Salomon Brothers to help structure the global solution. But by May, Barneys had discovered that Merrill, Lynch didn't have the authority to negotiate the global solution after all.

That same month, Barneys and Isetan met again in the Four Seasons Hotel in Tokyo. The tone was civil, but decidedly frosty. Barneys suggested a means by which Isetan could save $3 million a year in taxes: If the $26 million rent was structured as a preferred stock dividend on Isetan's equity, it wouldn't be considered taxable. The maneuver would save Isetan $3 million a year in taxes. "Isetan said, okay, but we want our money back; they just didn't get it," says a Barneys executive present at the meeting.

Oh, they got it all right. What, asked Isetan, would be the PCH implications of Barneys' brainstorm? The PCH case provides the critical legal precedent for recharacterizing a lease in bankruptcy. According to the ruling in PCH, if a lease looks like a loan and acts like a loan, a judge can declare it a loan in bankruptcy, stripping the real estate's owner of its asset and lumping the landlords with all the other creditors on line to get paid. The real estate would thus move onto the company's balance sheet, along with all its other assets. By accepting Barneys' money-saving proposal, Isetan wanted to know, would Isetan open itself up to the recharacterization of its leases in bankruptcy?

It was for this reason that Isetan ultimately rejected the proposal Barneys put forward at the February meeting in the Four Seasons Hotel. But the question Isetan had raised planted a pernicious seed. In the spring of 1995, Barneys had hired a young partner at the firm of Le-Boeuf, Lamb, Greene and MacRae as bankruptcy counsel. The Pressmans had met John Campo in 1988, when he was the trustee for a bankrupt estate from which Barneys was looking to buy some assets. Campo had learned the bankruptcy trade as an assistant United States trustee in the New York Southern District office, but he had never shepherded any big clients through a bankruptcy himself. That wasn't why Bob and Gene hired him anyway. Campo projects a menacing air, with a hard stare that looks well practiced and a prizefighter's mug. His short, sharp beard makes him look like he's wearing a black Astroturf muffler around his acne-scarred cheeks. The Pressmans hired Campo to cow Isetan, and there's no question they got the right face for the job. "Campo had this *mean streets* persona," says a Barneys executive. "Bob figured Campo would strong-arm Isetan. Unfortunately, Campo had no stature."

Campo thought about Isetan's PCH question, and then he thought about it some more. Why couldn't you apply the PCH reasoning to the *existing* Barneys financial structure? Campo wondered. After all, you could make the case that the $26 million Barneys owed Isetan annually already looked a lot more like a preferred return on a joint equity investment than simple rent. Viewing it that way, the leases on the Barneys stores owned by Isetan aren't really "true leases" at all; for one thing, they're above market rates, and they have built into them a provision for splitting profits once Barneys' payments to Isetan exceed the 14 percent return on Isetan's original capital investment. In other words, the leases are nothing more than a stopgap financing mechanism pending the working out of a global solution. So reasoned Campo, and wrote a memo outlining his approach that somehow found its way to Isetan's lawyers at Hughes Hubbard. This was Bob's idea of hardball, the intent being to jolt Isetan to the negotiating table. Isetan didn't miss the point. "The tone was, 'Isetan, you better do what we tell you or we're going to punish you badly. You will be the only one who suffers and you will suffer badly,'" David LeMay, a Hughes Hubbard bankruptcy partner was quoted as saying. It only emerged just how self-defeating a tactic this was when Barneys made good on the Campo threat after the bankruptcy.

Isetan didn't take kindly to Campo's saber rattling, and the Japanese conceived an immediate and intense dislike for the bad cop in this good cop–bad cop routine. Isetan didn't like the good cop— Charles Bunstine—much better. Bunstine, now president and chief operating officer, was desperately trying to steer a cheerful course through these increasingly angry waters. It wasn't easy. First, he needed to placate Bob and Gene, who could barely tolerate each other by this point. In truth, Bunstine didn't like them much, either. Then he had to put the best face on the Pressmans' conduct to Isetan, who had begun to suspect that the Pressmans were systematically deceiving them. Isetan put less and less stock in Bunstine's sunny portrayal of Bob and Gene's antics. "They learned to hate him—a lot," says a former executive.

In July 1995, just before the end of fiscal year on the thirty-first, Joseph Ceccarelli, Barneys' treasurer, made another entry in the books. He entered an extra $75 million as income for Barneys in that year. Because these were pro forma financial statements, there is no footnote explaining where this money came from, however. As it turned out, the $75 million was just spending a little time on the books. At the end of November, Ceccarelli wiped out the $75 million with an entry that read: "debit royalty receivable, credit cash."

There is some dispute over the source of this $75 million. In its subsequent investigation into possible fraud leading up to the bankruptcy, the Manhattan district attorney probed particularly hard for its origins. Ceccarelli told a top Barneys lieutenant that he removed the $75 million on his own authority, without getting a go-ahead from Bob Pressman first. Barneys has maintained that the $75 million simply comprises the final installment of the total $265 million it recorded as the present value of 50 years of royalty payments due from Isetan. It insists that it removed the $75 million in late November 1995 to comply with Isetan's demand that Barneys separate all the licensing "income" from the operating expenses.

Whatever the circumstances of its removal, the $75 million had an anaesthetizing effect while it remained on the preliminary books. Isetan said it had wrangled with the Pressmans over the terms of a global solution using those numbers. Chemical Bank also worked from financial statements that still included the $75 million bump when it arranged for a $150 million syndicated loan to Barneys in September 1995.

Barneys says it turned off the anaesthesia at the meeting in late November at its accountants' office in New Jersey, with Coopers & Lybrand looking on. What Isetan saw in the cold November light dismayed them. They had no idea that the business they had funded so openhandedly—to the tune of almost $600 million—was lying bleeding and close to death. It was even unclear to some of the executives within Barneys whether they could reach a global solution before running out of cash to operate. At its last meetings with Bob, Isetan finally peeked behind the mirror at the way the the Asian royalties had been accounted for. Hundreds of millions of dollars of supposed "income" that they had assumed—reasonably or unreasonably—had come from the sale of Prada bags and Jil Sander black dresses and Armani suits and all the other indispensable trappings of a tasteful life—those millions and millions of dollars just vanished before their eyes. They had never existed, except as an accounting assumption that Barneys continues to defend as reasonable and candid.

An enterprise that Isetan had assumed to be a "good business with a bad balance sheet," turned out to be a "bad business with a bad balance sheet," as one later Barneys bidder described the upshot of the November revelations. "Barneys was a really bad business with a bad balance sheet—a fundamentally dysfunctional bad business. When they filed for bankruptcy, what I think surprised everyone was that it was a bad company. I think it surprised Isetan. It surprised the creditors, for sure. Chemical was making loans to the company four months earlier. A brand-new unsecured loan for one hundred fifty million! What the fuck were they thinking?"

An independent audit of the company's financial statements carried out by Ernst and Young in 1996 gives the best picture to date of what was really going on. After cleaning up the treatment of the Asian royalties, the sale of rights to operate Barneys' credit card, and various diversions to and from a tangle of Barneys' affiliated companies, Ernst and Young restated the results through the fiscal year ended July 31, 1995. Net income for fiscal 1994 had been reduced by $77.5 million, turning a profit of $9.5 million into a net loss of $68 million. This contributed to an overall reduction in retained earnings for the 1995 fiscal of $249 million. The retained earnings deficit—in other words, loss—by July 31, 1995, was restated $334.8 million. Based on what it found in six months of digging through Barneys' tortured affairs, Ernst and Young concluded, in part, that "the recurring losses from operations and the substantial deficiency in shareholders' equity raise substantial doubt about the company's ability to continue as a going concern."

As the Japanese looked at some of this evidence for the first time in October, they realized that they faced a sickening new reality. It changed the way they saw the Pressmans and their own prospects, not just financially but emotionally. It is this latter dimension that Bob had failed to calculate as he endlessly spun his "if they do this, we'll do that" scenarios to convince himself that Isetan simply had to make a deal. In the harsh light of these latest revelations, all Isetan's suppositions about family and honor and the ways they impel human beings to behave suddenly vaporized; the ground on which Isetan felt it might rebuild Barneys with the Pressmans fell away. Where Isetan and the Pressman family had had something called a relationship, however unhealthy, a void had opened and into it tumbled the future. "They were *very* upset at what they saw," says a Barneys executive present at many of these meetings. "They realized they had a partner they could not trust."

Bob and Gene traveled to Tokyo twice in November for what would turn out to be among the final meetings with Isetan, and were shocked to find that Isetan had begun treating them like nonpersons.

One day, Bob was left to contemplate his misdeeds from nine o'clock in the morning until nine at night. On another day, Bob and Gene were shown to an airless cubicle, ten feet by ten feet, in Isetan's corporate headquarters building in Tokyo. Gene described it as a "dentist's waiting room" to *New York* magazine. Six years before, Kosuge had toasted their common future, then so bright, with $2,500-a-head cocktails. On this occasion, Gene and Bob got soda and crackers. When they met briefly, the Japanese subjected the boys to a stern lecture on morality and proper codes of conduct. "We *trusted* you," Michio Jomuri kept saying over and over. "It was like parents yelling at their children," is how Gene later described the novel experience to *New York*.

Bob still clung to the hope that Isetan would yield to a global solution after it had spanked the Pressmans sufficiently. By now, the Pressmans were saying they were willing to give up 80 percent of Barneys to Isetan and negotiate some form of shared control. The events of the past few months had seemed to take a lot of the fight out of Bob, although it had hardly made either of the brothers any humbler. A simple apology might have helped, but none came. Isetan's stated position was that it wanted nothing less than full control, but it had hinted through a back channel that it was prepared to discuss this point. So Bob and Gene waited, and then they waited some more. Gene still didn't seem to appreciate what all the fuss was about, and even the current crisis didn't bolster his meager patience. "I'm outta here," he declared, and left to go window-shopping. Finally, the word came down and it was no word at all: "We have come to an undecided position," Bob was informed.

The indecision of the Japanese was partly genuine, although some on the Isetan board had apparently determined that they just couldn't stomach any further business dealings with the Pressmans, no matter what the consequences. The consequences, however, were as grave as they could be. It would mean writing off the short-term Preen loans and otherwise recording in a most public and humiliating way the grave misjudgment that underlay this whole funky adventure in retailing. "At some point, they made a decision to take a huge write-down rather than roll everything over into a global solution," says a Barneys executive. "In the end, they didn't want their assets in the hands of people they considered scum."

Back in New York, the Pressmans were making a last desperate stab at pulling off a global solution and salvaging the store. They hired the Blackstone Group, a small and extraordinarily well connected investment banking boutique with ties to Mitsubishi. Over at the Barneys corporate offices, Isetan installed a team of lawyers and accountants to pore over Barneys' books. At the same time, however, Barneys' top brass had finally started thinking the unthinkable: There just might be no global solution after all; the whole thing could come crashing down around them, goatskin, gold-leaf mosaics, and all.

Suddenly, Campo's bankruptcy scare tactic turned into a full-blown bankruptcy strategy. Normally, it takes three to four months to prepare a company to file bankruptcy. The Pressmans had a month, the way they saw it. So while Isetan camped out full-time at Barneys, Barneys executives camped out full-time at Blackstone. Isetan, of course, couldn't know about the bankruptcy preparations, since that could easily scuttle whatever slim chance of a global solution remained. "It was pretty difficult to keep the two lines from crossing," says one of the shuttle diplomats.

Then, toward the end of December, Isetan delivered yet another crushing nondecision—all the while leaving its team of analysts in place at Barneys. This proved the event that triggered a bankruptcy filing as the likeliest course of action, even though Barneys never stopped hoping that Isetan would relent at the last minute. The cash was running out, and Barneys couldn't weather another month while Isetan prevaricated. Moreover, most retail bankruptcies tend to get filed the first week in January, just after the Christmas season has left the coffers full of cash.

From then on, Bob and Gene couldn't be found at either Barneys or Blackstone. They both skipped town—Bob to the Caribbean isle of

Nevis; Gene first to the ski slopes of Aspen, and then straight to Hawaii. "There was a lot of black humor among the troops," recalls one executive. "If there's a paradigm for the Pressmans' leadership style, that was it. People were just astonished and pissed off that here the Pressmans were, vacationing in the playgrounds of the rich while we were all spending our winter vacations at Blackstone. On the other hand, it's difficult to determine whether the brothers' being away was the lousiest thing for morale, or the best thing." In Hawaii, Gene played golf as if the most nettlesome thing on his mind was whether to use a three or a four iron. And he happened to be playing with Tomio Taki, one of Barneys' most important suppliers. "They think I was fiddling while Rome burned," Gene sputtered in his apologia to New York. "What was I supposed to do? Tell everybody we were about to declare bankruptcy?"

There was one big thing Bob and Gene did need to take care of personally—it probably accounts for a good part of the thousands of dollars in cellular phone charges Bob racked up on Nevis that winter—and that was making sure they had enough to live on comfortably after bankruptcy dismantled the corporate cash machine. In the final weeks before the bankruptcy filing, the Pressman brothers doubled the $450,000 salaries they drew from Barneys. (That wasn't their only salary; they drew similar amounts from the Pressmans' Fener affiliate as well.) Then they made those salary increases retroactive for a year and took them out a second time. In addition, they gave themselves one-time nontaxable advances of between $1.2 million and $1.5 million.

Bob also took care of the other family members with retroactive pay increases. Nancy needed a special bequest, since she was laying out around $1.2 million to have Peter Marino redo her house at the time. So they made her an officer of the family company that rented the downtown parking lot to Barneys, raised the rent Barneys paid for the lot, and backdated the lease. The lump sum went directly to the parking lot affiliate's newest executive officer—Nancy Pressman. All told, well over $5 million in cash got sucked out of the cash-strapped company in the final weeks before the filing, according to an executive who lived through the experience.

When Barneys filed for bankruptcy, it had $937,000 left in the till. Dozens of small artisans who had mortgaged their professional futures to the Pressman demand for exclusive distribution were left gasping for air. Several charities whose splashy benefit parties the Pressmans had recently hosted never got the checks they were due. This apparently was an oversight.

"Over the years, the 'Barneys' name has come to mean the highest quality, service, dependability and continuity in the men's and women's fine clothing retail industry. In fact, it is considered by many retail industry executives to be the 'crown jewel' of the retail world. The Barneys Debtors' customers are extremely loyal, in part because of the dedicated employees whose service reputation is unequalled."

Robert L. Pressman and Eugene Pressman swore to that statement as part of their petition for protection under Chapter 11 of the U.S. Bankruptcy Code. On the night of January 10, with a fresh blanket of snow covering the ground from a blizzard the day before, John Campo raced to the home of Cecilia Morris, the bankruptcy court's chief clerk, in the New York suburb of Pleasantville, about half an hour's drive north of the city. Isetan had the right to start foreclosure proceedings the next day if it hadn't gotten its rent check. Campo officially filed the bankruptcy petition at 10:56 P.M. Bob and Gene had just lost the family store.

10

GREETERS AT THE FAMILY STORE

All bankruptcies proceed along a path known in the bankruptcy trade as DADA. The letters form an acronym that plots the emotional phases of the participants as they sift through the rubble of a broken business. First comes denial, then anger, then depression, and finally, acceptance— DADA. In Pressman poetics, however, it is to be read not as a spondee—both syllables stressed equally—but as a trochee, with the metrical stress falling heavily on the first syllable: DAda. Any poet knows, you never end a line on a trochee. It breaks the rhythm. This whole poem ends on a trochee.

Denial and anger resounded throughout most of the needlessly long Barneys bankruptcy proceedings in a relentless bleat: DA! DA! DA! As part of the materials it had prepared shortly after the filing, Blackstone fielded what is known as a 100-cents-on-the-dollar reorganization plan, in which all creditors would get their debts paid in full—all except Isetan, against whom Barneys filed suit for breaching its agreement to restructure the loans. As part of the suit, Barneys also demanded $50 million in back rent. This was denial at its most operatic. "The reorganization plan was so hedged as to be meaningless," one top Barneys executive recalls. "That's like saying you can win the Tchaikovsky piano competition if everyone else drops out. No one focused seriously on how you would accomplish this."

DA! At a bankruptcy filing all "discrepant" letters of credit—in other words, letters of credit issued before the filing but not drawn upon—are considered to be debt from before the bankruptcy. Barneys had between $40 million and $50 million in letters of credit to its suppliers outstanding. Three days before the filing, one of the bankruptcy advisers warned Martin Lewis, one of the two Blackstone Group bankers handling Barneys, that those letters of credit would start bouncing soon after the bankruptcy began—cutting off the lifeblood merchandise Barneys needed to stay in business. Oh no they won't, Lewis shot back breezily. Bounce they did, all over New York. "The vendors were going apeshit," recalls the adviser. "Armani was threatening to pull all his stuff and send it elsewhere." It took several frantic months to take the spring out of the letters of credit.

DA! In February, a hearing was held for Barneys' creditors to air their grievances—it's called a 341 meeting after the section of the bankruptcy code that authorizes it. A certain amount of rancor can be expected at these affairs, but even battle-hardened bankruptcy veterans feared violence this time. "It was like a lynch mob—I've never seen anything like it," says a bankruptcy lawyer in the case who has lived through innumerable 341 meetings. "I literally had this image from the old Frankenstein movie when the townspeople go to burn down the castle. I have rarely witnessed such enmity. Finally, the U.S. trustee asked if I would take the microphone and try to restore order."

DA! Not long after, Isetan took a $320 million write-down for the fiscal year ended March 31 due to the Barneys debacle. Once it had officially said farewell to its money, it cast off any reason to make the best of things and resolve matters speedily. From this point on, blind hatred for the Pressmans pushed it forward. "Bunstine tried to tell all of us what was in store, but it surprised me anyway," says a Barneys lieutenant. "I expected anger from Isetan, sure, but no one expected quite so much venom."

Isetan now wanted to hit back and hurt the Pressmans badly. "Bob always said that the Japanese were fucked. Well, they weren't fucked now; they were dead. Isetan fell on its sword, so it had no incentive to yield. It had bled already," says a top Barneys executive. "You could see on their faces that they had taken the hit." A mediator was called in to get the two sides to at least start talking civilly. It was a disaster. The Isetan executives could barely bring themselves to look at Bob and Gene. "It was just painful—like Chinese water torture," recalls a participant in the meetings.

The courts eventually ruled that Isetan could enforce Bob and Gene's personal guarantees for the money they borrowed—now close to $200 million with interest. Isetan did nothing dramatic, but it took a wicked glee in garnishing a Porsche here, a boat there, pinprick-style. A lawyer with no allegiance to either side cringed as he looked on. "It's sick—this is a blood feud," he said. "It's like pulling the wings off flies."

Up in Larchmont, State Supreme Court judge Nicholas Colabella ruled that Gene couldn't build his eight-foot walls after all. Nor could he hoist up the three high gates he intended for his new high gateposts, which were already standing. Gene had hurriedly raised those gateposts the previous September before an amended town ordinance took effect subjecting gateposts to the same height restrictions as walls and gates. Colabella's Solomonic ruling permitted Gene to keep his new gateposts, since they predated the amended ban. So there they stood, eleven feet tall, looking foolish and out of place next to Gene's regulation four-foot walls. That was where Gene's maneuvering had gotten him, but that wasn't the end of it. The Miralias fought on—Peggy Miralia was the neighbor across the street who allegedly mugged Gene's golden retriever. Tear down the gateposts! they shouted, or they might have if they had lived someplace less civilized than Larchmont. What they did do was go back to court.

The press reveled in the whole spectacle of Barneys' comeuppance.

Here was a story where they could legitimately deposit all the ill will accumulated toward Barneys over the years. "I had always been a little intimidated by Barneys' imperious manner," wrote Maureen Dowd, the acerbic columnist for *The New York Times,* on January 18.

> But emboldened by the news that it handles money with less skill than I do, I headed to Madison Avenue to gloat. I no longer needed to pretend that I wasn't appalled by the $1,345 Comme des Garçons brown jackets covered in black netting that doesn't make you look at all Comme des Jeunes Filles, $95 beaded pin curlers or a $45 nylon replica of a Barneys shopping bag. . . . Now Barneys is bankrupt, so we don't have to be. I can understand deficit spending. But at least the Government had the decency to shut down.

This little matter didn't end there, either. Barneys jousted with Dowd, sending her a ten-dollar gift certificate to mock her contention that there's nothing at Barneys to buy for that risible sum. Anyone who knows anything about how the press works knows that this is just begging for another sock in the eye. Dowd complied with another column a few days later, going down the computerized list of items under ten dollars Barneys had sent along: "The selection was bleak: eye lash groomer, Clinique scruffing lotion, yo-yo, Filofax map of Philadelphia. I decided to mail the certificate back to the bankrupt Barneys. They need every dollar they can get," wrote Dowd.

A month later, someone leaked a nasty tidbit to the gossip column of the *New York Post* claiming that Dowd had once tried to pry a discount on a Prada handbag out of Barneys. When the saleswoman declined, Dowd reportedly threw a tantrum. Dowd wasn't about to let this pass, and another stinging column soon appeared. She wasn't even in New York on the day she was supposed to have thrown her tantrum in Barneys, she maintained. Another editor had told Dowd that Barneys was peddling this tale around town to make her look bad. Once again, Barneys had managed to bean itself with its own hardball.

"You'd think the *soigné* emporium would be busy with important things, like that little matter of the $600 million it 'borrowed' from the poor Japanese and spent the way its own customers would," wrote Dowd. "But, no-o-o-o, there's still plenty of time for recreational vengeance." Barneys denied the charge, but wisely, if belatedly, chose not to present its backside for another public thwacking.

The bankruptcy started off badly. Before long, it was clear that Campo's reliance on the precedent of the PCH case wasn't going to work, and it had never made a lot of sense in the first place. Maybe it could have worked as a scare tactic, but its scorched-earth severity made it practically useless as the actual blueprint for a bankruptcy. Nothing would have remained for either party after the $550 million debt held by creditors got repaid, even had bankruptcy judge James Garrity, Jr., recharacterized the original Isetan deal. Equity gets paid out last in a bankruptcy. "Isetan walks away with dick, and the Pressmans walk away with dick, and all the Pressmans end up doing is antagonizing the thousand-pound gorilla—which is the way they operate," says a bankruptcy lawyer in the case. "This is their tragic flaw—the Pressmans think their shit doesn't stink."

The Manhattan District Attorney's Office thought maybe it did. Sometime not long after the bankruptcy began, it started investigating whether Barneys had in fact committed criminal fraud. According to former executives who were questioned, the DA wanted to find out when Barneys first started planning to file for bankruptcy and whether it borrowed money knowing that it would soon be seeking the protective shelter of the bankruptcy code. Barneys was already brandishing the threat of bankruptcy when Chemical Bank arranged the $150 million syndicated loan in September 1995, although it insists it never contemplated acting on that threat until December. The DA also delved into the phantom $75 million from the summer of 1995—where did it come from, where did it go, and what cosmetic purpose might it have served in between? Nothing appears to have come from the investigation, but it remains anybody's guess whether the district attorney is finished with Barneys for good.

Under the strain of the bankruptcy, the vaunted Pressman family solidarity started breaking down. Whether by design or inattention, one of the debts that didn't get paid out before the bankruptcy froze it was a bill for several hundred thousand dollars to a company called Nanelle Associates. Nanelle was owned by Liz and Nancy Pressman and held the license for Kilgour, French and Stanbury. Suddenly, Liz and Nancy had no choice but to stand in line like any other creditor, which they didn't appreciate one bit. On the creditors committee, this became known as the "fuck the sisters transaction." Liz and Nancy held Bob responsible, and even talked briefly of suing him, which was not the kind of thing one Pressman was supposed to do to another, whatever mutual contempt they may have felt privately.

The sisters also felt that Bob should never have used the $24.5 million realized through the real estate transaction with Reed Elsevier to pay Barneys back for money advanced to the family. Their reasoning went like this: Since Bob and Gene had grabbed more in advances from the store than they had, using the $24.5 million to repay the debt gave the brothers a disproportionate share of the real estate windfall. They felt cheated. "This was money they had never earned in the first place," says a Barneys executive. "The family's sense of entitlement is staggering."

Those were dark days for Bob, who bore the blame within the family for the whole debacle. Bob was supposed to have fixed it, and now look where all his legerdemain had gotten them! For expiatory purposes, it was satisfying to have Bob to kick around as the empire collapsed. Still, there were occasional moments when Gene's discomfiture managed to bring a fleeting smile to Bob's face. At one meeting, Gene was upbraiding a smartly dressed young woman who served as a financial adviser in the bankruptcy. "How can you advise us when you know *nothing* about our business—*nothing*!" Gene snapped.

"Oh yeah?" replied the chic adviser. "It so happens I am your primary target customer, and I happen to be wearing a full set of clothes that Barneys carries. Why don't you tell me what they are?"

Gene mumbles awkwardly; he hems and haws, but not a single

designer name comes out of his mouth. A nervous titter breaks the uncomfortable silence and builds to a gale of laughter. He really doesn't have any idea. Cruelly—perhaps unwisely—Charles Bunstine ticks off every item without skipping a beat: Donna Karan suit, Richard Tyler shirt, Manolo Blahnik shoes—all distinctive designs that any half-decent merchant should recognize as quickly as a wartime plane spotter picks out the silhouette of an incoming enemy bomber. Bob hasn't had this much fun in a long time. He's not about to let go of this one, and he needles Gene with it constantly. "I wouldn't give her a hard time today, Gene," he might say at a meeting a few weeks later. "She's wearing stuff from our store."

On May 22, 1996, Fred made a new will. He did not have long to live. The last two lines of the will read: "I make no provision hereunder for my son Robert L. Pressman, for good and sufficient reason." What could have prompted Fred to take up the paternal rod now when he had spoiled his children throughout his life? Some surmise that it was the "fuck the sisters transaction," which committed the unpardonable sin of disloyalty to family, but that's just a guess. Bob still held his ownership stake in Barneys through an earlier trust agreement, which remained unchanged, but this sudden, ferocious rebuke must have stung him hard.

On July 14, 1996, Fred Pressman died at the age of seventy-three at his home in Harrison, New York. He had held tight to life for its own strange sake, long after so much of what had given it meaning for him had rotted away. He was already sick when he applied for membership to the exclusive Westchester Country Club, and he only withdrew his application eight weeks before he died. "I wondered why he did it," says Carl Portale, a magazine publisher and close friend of the family who sponsored Fred for membership. "His attitude was, I wanted to do it because it was there."

Many of the world's foremost designers and retailers turned out for the funeral among a crowd of maybe a thousand mourners at New York's Central Synagogue. Isetan sent no representative. Anyone who sought either meaning or feeling in the faces of Bob, Gene, Phyllis,

Nancy, or Liz instead found nothing. It had been much the same when Barney Pressman died five years earlier, this disconcerting blankness that left onlookers wondering where the grief had gone. Let some other family rend their garments; the Pressmans wouldn't give the world that satisfaction. "It was eerie. At Fred's funeral, they were just too perfectly dressed, too perfectly composed," says someone who had worked closely with the family for over ten years.

At the store, things went on exactly as before, but Fred did receive a posthumous *homage* of sorts. In October, the downstairs restaurant Mad 61—the recent subject of a violent dispute with its owner Pino Luongo, an old investment partner of the Pressmans—was renamed Fred's. The menu added a new signature dish called Fred's Salad, made with the same Italian tuna Fred ate every day. "He did it at a time when the rest of us were eating Bumble Bee," marveled the new chef.

Fred's death did nothing to knit the fractious clan together. The creditors didn't much care if the Pressmans took potshots at one another, but they did need the family to pull in the same direction to get the bankruptcy resolved. The committee recommended hiring a turn-around expert named John Brincko to serve as Barneys' senior Chapter 11 restructuring officer for precisely this reason. Brincko didn't have much background in the retail business, but he had recently steered a small, family-owned California company through a nasty crisis. His success hinged on maneuvering a guy not unlike Bob Pressman into a corner, and in this the creditors committee felt he had done a masterful job. Brincko's appointment marked the beginning of the end for president Charles Bunstine. Bunstine had already alienated Isetan, the creditors, and many Barneys' employees by aligning himself with the Pressmans' disingenuous "who, us?" posture. Gene and Bob didn't lift a finger when Brincko pushed Bunstine out and took over as president and chief operating officer.

The U.S. bankruptcy industry takes very good care of its own. In any bankruptcy, a small band of specialists—lawyers, accountants, advisers, and the like—swoops in to minister to the stricken company. Whoever ends up wheeling the patient home ultimately pays the bill.

Since no one knows who that will turn out to be, no one squawks too loudly at the lavish fees. Moreover, Barneys was a cripple in a designer cast. Everybody wanted in for the sheer glamour of it.

"Every day, everyone is calling you up and becoming your best friend," recalls one astonished Barneys creditor who sat briefly on the committee. "Inviting you for dinners. Giving you tickets to a show, to a Knicks game. 'Oh, yeah, and I know your brother-in-law.' 'You know, I'm familiar with your sister company.' Everybody is lobbying. You know, it's the same situation as taking out an appendix. The hospital requires five surgeons to be at the operating table, hey, you need to pay five surgeons to watch that five-minute appendix removal. Why is all this necessary? I don't know."

Two years in, the bankruptcy had generated some $25 million in assorted professional fees, and the meter was still running. "I call the bankruptcy code the lawyers' full employment act," says a disgusted Barneys executive. "All bankruptcy means is, you stop paying interest and you start paying lawyers, and it seems to come out to just about the same thing." Even some of the advisers got a little sheepish when they talked about it. "We've drawn all these professional fees, and we're all going to end up looking like schmucks," said one of them—and the bankruptcy was barely a year old at the time; it had another two years to run. "There's nothing to show for it."

Brincko's contract called for him to draw $65,000 a month in salary, plus another $7,500 in commuting and living expenses, which paid for his apartment at the swanky Ritz Towers. The initial one-year contract, which started running March 1, 1996, also made Brincko eligible for $195,000 severance pay, plus a performance bonus. But if the creditors expected Brincko to earn this paycheck by introducing the Pressmans to the novel concept of fiscal austerity and puncturing their denial, they were soon disabused. Instead of derailing the gravy train, Brincko hopped aboard with gusto.

Before long, Brincko was jetting regularly to Europe and nibbling caviar and blini with Gene at the Principe di Savoia Hotel in Milan during the fashion shows. He also managed to overspend his $35,000-a-year clothing allowance from Barneys—"and that was at a thirty percent *discount*," griped one of the creditors. "He started dressing incredibly well and decided he wanted to stick around for a while." Brincko favored Brioni, a small Italian tailor in the Abruzzi hills outside Rome that turns out impeccable $4,000 suits. On the stand during one bankruptcy hearing, Brincko bewailed the fact that he was powerless to corral the Pressmans, but no one had really seen him try. Not that this endeared him any to the Pressmans. "They disliked him intensely and continually disparaged him behind his back," says a former executive.

Attempts to resolve the bankruptcy went nowhere and went there slowly. Most of the unsecured creditors—primarily the tradesmen who supplied Barneys—sold off their claims against Barneys early on to so-called vulture funds, which traffic in the debt of distressed companies. The vultures buy this debt for some fraction of its face value, betting that the company will pay its creditors a higher fraction when a new owner takes the company out of bankruptcy. Even in a notoriously risky business, the vultures considered Barneys tricky prey. They had no way of analyzing the value of the debt they were trading; they were flying blind. "We had no confidence in the numbers. The Pressmans never wanted to show us information," recalls a member of what is demurely called "the vulture community." "And when they did show us the information, they never wanted to show us the right information."

More than a few vultures lost their feathers. Barneys' debt generally traded below fifty cents on the dollar, but some of the bigger investors bought in during a spike in the debt price, when the debt was changing hands in the neighborhood of eighty cents on the dollar. It never approached those heights again, so the vultures who held the high-priced debt were in no hurry to endorse a bid for the company that left them with a huge loss.

Which meant the only real bid on the table—a $240 million offer from a debonair young Chinese named Dickson Poon, whose company, Dickson Concepts, had made a fortune selling luxury goods in Hong

Kong. Like Gene Pressman, Poon had grown up rich and he played like a rich kid, running through—and every so often marrying—a succession of starlets. But the similarity ended there. Poon grew into a tough-minded businessman to be reckoned with. He had already shown his mettle by buying and reviving London's Harvey Nichols, a once-grand retail name that had grown dowdy over the years. By the time Poon got done sprucing it up, Harvey Nicks, as it is fondly known, was worth roughly $225 million—around three times what Poon had paid for it in 1991.

Gene, of course, paid Poon no more respect than he paid anybody else, which meant none at all. At one of their early meetings, Gene insisted on telling Joseph Wan, Poon's top aide, exactly why Harvey Nichols wasn't fit to lace up Barneys' Blahniks. One of Barneys' advisers at Blackstone took Gene aside and pointed out gently that Wan was there to buy Gene's store, not the other way around.

Bob figured that Poon's low offer just opened the auction, and expected a lively bidding war to drive Barney's price higher. Valuing a company in bankruptcy is a highly inexact science, since the price is generally figured as a multiple of how much business the company could do were it in good health. That is unknowable, but the guesses for a reasonable selling price ranged from around $300 million up to as high as $500 million. Poon's revised bid left only $205 million in cash to divide among the creditors, plus half the equity in the new Barneys. The prepetition debt exceeded $550 million. The creditors would be hard-pressed to get 35 cents on the dollar. The bidding war Bob was expecting never materialized. Other companies looked Barneys over, drawn by the moonbeams its name still conjured, but they tended to vanish after scrutinizing it more closely.

There they all sat for two and a half years: glum vultures, stony Isetan, and Gene and Bob, who gradually scaled their fantasies down as time wore on. Still, Bob and Gene fought hard to hold on to whatever they could. Among their last proposals was a plan to spin off the Isetan royalties and licensing rights into a separate company, owned and managed by the Pressmans. "We said ha, ha, ha—thank you very much," says a member of the creditors committee. Barneys kept on bleeding: In the fiscal year ended August 3, 1996, Barneys lost $72 million; in the year ended August 2, 1997, it lost $95 million. This despite reduced rent payments to Isetan of $9 million a year. Much of these losses can be ascribed to reorganization costs as, one by one, the lamest of the old Barneys America stores were put to sleep. High on that list were the two stores that didn't show Texas a thing or two.

One store stands out among the casualties. On June 17, 1997, Barneys closed the doors to what remained of its original store on Seventh Avenue and Seventeenth Street. Barneys had already closed the old Barney Pressman part of the Seventeenth Street store when the lease expired in 1996. Ironically, the empty space was soon occupied by a store called Loehmann's, which started as a discounter of fancy women's fashions in Brooklyn two years before Barney Pressman opened his doors. Seventy-five years later, Loehmann's was still selling many of the chic designers Barneys carried, except it was selling them at half the price—and now in the same exact spot. The topiary hedge was plowed under, and the wild brambles reclaimed the garden. So goes the ecology of clothing.

The old Barneys stayed open in the adjacent quarters it owned and had spent so much money to beautify just ten years before, but its demise was by then a foregone conclusion. "From a traffic standpoint, it can only be positive," Gene told *Women's Wear Daily* just after Loehmann's moved in, mustering up his dent-proof bravado and denying any chance that the old Barneys would close altogether. "There's a great opportunity in this store." Of course, Gene didn't really believe that for a minute. He had been sucking inventory out of Seventeenth Street to keep the racks filled on Madison Avenue since Madison Avenue opened. As a result, the downtown store was always woefully understocked. Even if it had had enough customers, it didn't have enough clothing for them to buy.

Chris Ryan, who had joined Barneys in 1977 and looked on Fred as a father, had chosen to stay downtown after Madison Avenue opened. In career terms, it was obviously a foolish choice, and Fred remonstrated with his protégé. "I said, Fred, I can't go uptown. Who's going to take care of the customer that wants to stay behind? I said, Fred, these are the people that built your business. These are the people that founded this rock. The guy who only wears double-breasted, there's got to be someone here to say, Hi, this is Mr. Jones, don't show him single-breasted suits. The guy who only wants French-cuffs shirts. This guy should have someone to say, Hi, show him French cuffs—don't dare show him button cuffs. I said, You owe it to them. Fred came back to me two days later and said, Okay, you can do it. So I stayed behind, and I was thrilled to stay behind."

The night Seventeenth Street closed for good, Chris Ryan asked if he could turn the key in the lock for the last time, and he did. "I love Fred. I mean, he allowed me to have what I have, and I will forever be grateful to him. I'd also like to take him in the back room and beat the living shit out of him for letting his sons do this, because they ruined the most phenomenal organization that God put on this earth."

There but for the grace of God went Murray Pearlstein. Pearlstein may be the only person in the country with a claim to Fred's stature as a clothing man, and he heaved a sigh of relief as he looked down from Boston, knowing that his own family business might easily have gone the same way as Barneys. Pearlstein founded Louis Boston in 1950 and he still runs it. In its own much smaller way, Louis has the same exalted reputation for men's clothing that Barneys once had. Murray and Fred cultivated many of the same manufacturers as they crisscrossed the continent hunting down the finest menswear. From the woolen mills of Biella to the silk-printing plants around Lake Como, Murray is still treated like visiting royalty when he arrives on a buying trip, the same way Fred was. Like Fred, Murray can make any suit maker quake when he walks into a room.

"I know everything there is to know about the retail clothing business," says Murray, and few would contradict him. "You have to buy what you believe in." On a recent buying trip to New York, he rejects a lovely Lorenzini sport shirt with a light blue check. "Too easy," he growls. "Murray never buys easy," explains his younger daughter Deborah Greenberg, now forty-one years old. Deborah will carry on the business when Murray retires. It used to be Murray's elder daughter Nancy whom everyone expected to carry on the family business, but Nancy doesn't work for the company anymore.

In 1987, Murray opened a branch of Louis Boston on Fifty-seventh Street in Manhattan. Fred Pressman never sent Murray a note welcoming him to town. "We were a pimple compared to them, but I think Fred felt betrayed—this was *his* city." Murray's New York store got hammered almost immediately, and Murray was soon losing a great deal of money on it. Murray wanted to call it a day, but Nancy had her own ego to establish, the same way Gene did, and she fought back hard. "Everything I proposed she didn't like: I wanted to close New York; she didn't. I wanted to close our new store in Chestnut Hill; she didn't. She said to herself, He's not turning the business over to me. I begged her not to go—*begged* her," says Murray. "I told her, Whatever feelings you have now, stay with me—you're the only connection to the future. She said, No, Daddy.

"We just weren't that good at being a multistore company—maybe what made us so good in Boston is what contributed to our failure in New York. It's not our heart and soul. So I said, let's get out of here, and I went back to Boston with my tail between my legs. I'm a survivor. I think that by getting out, I saved the company."

Fred just couldn't bring himself to impose his will on his children the way Murray did—he didn't have the *kichas* for it, Murray might say, using a Yiddish expression for intestinal fortitude. In May 1998, Barneys' creditors finally agreed on a so-called "stand-alone" plan to bring Barneys out of bankruptcy themselves, taking a 93.5 percent stake in the company in exchange for their debts and the cash they will inject to fortify Barneys' weakened stores. Isetan will get a 5 percent stake and rent payments of $15 million a year. If someone was going to end up with Barneys for a lowball price, they figured, it might as well be them. Why give Dickson Poon all the upside potential many people believe its bedraggled glamour still holds?

The Pressmans? Gene and Bob got two-year employment contracts, along with other family members, but they're all hired help now. Bob made his last stand scrabbling for a 3 percent stake in the company his grandfather and father built, but the creditors knocked the Pressmans down to 1.5 percent. Kuniyasu Kosuge must have taken grim satisfaction from that.

"The Pressmans are gonzo," says a member of the creditors committee. The creditors have learned a few things about the Pressmans in the past two and a half years, and they structured the reorganization plan accordingly. "We put them in a place where they can't interfere with the running of the company. The fear is that they will proceed to do the old Pressman dirty tricks they've done each and every time they could, but they don't get their money unless they don't interfere. It's not payable up front, and can be terminated at the sole whim of the equity holders. If I could design a job for them, I would make them greeters at the store."

Gene always liked to say he was a member of the lucky sperm club, and that was certainly true enough. But to Gene, it seemed to mean something beyond the fortunate circumstances of his birth. It appeared to imply lifetime membership in a club that required no dues and couldn't expel you for peeing on the parquet. The store is in other hands now, and so is the steady income that supported a life built around the idea that all human values pale beside good taste. Gene's wife, Bonnie, left to work for Ralph Lauren, and, with no more appearances left to keep up, the loveless marriage was finally allowed to collapse. The house on Hommocks Road in Larchmont was put up for sale. The new owners won't have to lie about Bugsy Siegel; they can tell the truth about Gene.

Still, it's hard to extinguish hope, even at its flimsiest. One suspects Gene and Bob still have that. One summer day years ago, Gene and Glenn O'Brien went to visit Gene's old college buddy Ian Schrager at the beach. Schrager and Steve Rubell, another Syracuse pal of Gene's, had created Manhattan's Studio 54, the spangled heart of the nightclub universe during the 1970s. Schrager and Rubell went to jail in 1980 for tax fraud, but went on to start a wildly successful hotel empire from scratch after their release. Now Gene was driving up to Schrager's magnificent house in Southampton. "Gee, seven years ago, Ian was in jail," mused Gene. "America is a wonderful country." Barney Pressman could have told him that, but it would have meant something else altogether back then.

INDEX